The
Crafts
Business
Encyclopedia

Michael Scott is editor/publisher of *The Crafts Report,*
and president of the International Guild of Craft
Journalists, Authors and Photographers

Michael Scott

The Crafts Business Encyclopedia

Marketing, Management, and Money

Harcourt Brace Jovanovich
New York and London

Printed in the United States of America

Library of Congress Cataloging in Publication Data

Scott, Michael, 1924–
The crafts business encyclopedia.

1. Business—Dictionaries. 2. Handicraft.
3. Handicraft—Marketing. I. Title.
HF1001.S35   658'.91'7455   76–54209

ISBN 0–15–122752–7

First edition
B C D E

To
Sheila
Janie
and
Tim
for making the circle of
my life complete

Introduction

This book was written for anyone who makes craft objects for sale, whether as a part-time activity or a full-time profession. The key word is "selling," because once you sell, even on a very limited basis, you're "in business" and entitled to numerous tax advantages as well as certain legal obligations. Whether you succeed or fail, whether you make money or lose money, depends in great measure on how well you run your affairs, manage your money, find your markets, and understand your problems.

The word business often raises hackles when it is mentioned in the presence of artists and craftspeople. Many creative people are suspicious of anything associated with the impersonal business world. Indeed, a craftsperson's very work is the antithesis of mass production and mass marketing which have become synonymous with business today.

But let's face it: much of our life is ruled by laws which govern business activities. Taxes, banking, labor, accounting, copyright, licenses, even so simple a contract as renting space at a craft fair—all these are regulated by business laws. To ignore this fact is to invite economic and legal problems.

Similarly, the techniques of mass production brought forth numerous sales techniques which can, without violence to the conscience, be adapted to craft selling. Just because some of these techniques have, on occasion, been used by unscrupulous businessmen to fleece the public is no reason to throw out the baby with the bath water. Would anyone suggest that we abolish the use of electricity simply because electricity was invented to power the emerging industrial machine of the nineteenth century? No, we use that same electricity to turn our potter's wheels, fire our kilns, illuminate our work rooms, power our tools.

Let us explore what is useful, discard what is objectionable, and turn the techniques of marketing, merchandising, management, selling—yes, *business*—toward implementing and supporting our major purpose as craftspeople, namely to produce work which represents our best creative talents and allows us to survive and prosper.

This book is not designed primarily for the fine artist whose work finds its way into rich folks' collections, although many of the business principles discussed here apply as well. Our concern is the craftsperson who makes a living (or hopes to) by producing and selling quality craftwork.

What is the difference between fine art and craft? Aside from investment considerations, fine art normally has a purely esthetic value; craftwork usually has both an esthetic and functional value.

The boundaries between the two are often indistinct. Weaving, for example, is a craft which was born of the need to make things to keep people covered and warm. Weaving today has gone far beyond that elementary utilitarian purpose. An exquisite wall hanging uses the same craft technique, but its basic function is esthetic. However, even the magnificent rugs and tapestries in old castles served to keep the drafty place warm.

There was a time when no distinction was made between art and craft. Ancient languages had only one word to describe both functions; note the similarity between "artist" and "artisan." For many centuries, the limits of technology and resources required that everything made by human hands be useful. But the human spirit is such that everything also had to be made as beautiful as circumstances and talent would allow. It was simply unthinkable to produce a useful object without grace and beauty, or to produce an object whose only function was to be beautiful.

The industrial age brought the mass manufacture of goods whose utility and economy of production were the only important factors. If they also happened to look well, that was an accident.

When advertising became a major mover of goods, design again became a factor. But it was less a matter of beauty than an item's salability; it had to look different from similar products.

The esthetic emptiness of mass-produced merchandise, the void of the "plastic society," have sparked a remarkable increase in public awareness of crafts in recent years. The fact that an object was made by human hands, that its appearance expresses the human spirit, and that there is no other object precisely like it, fills a need at a time when individuality and personality are being drowned in a sea of impersonal mass marketing.

But craftspeople cannot be hermits. While no authority can dictate our creative integrity, all of our other activities are subject to the rules and regulations of the society in which we live. We must understand those rules and regulations if we want to survive economically without compromising our artistic and creative standards.

The pages that follow explain not only what happens on the business side of crafts, but why it happens; not only what you can do about it, but also why. Thinking people need to know the reasons behind events so that future events can be handled with greater understanding and competence.

This book does not intend to turn craftspeople into lawyers or accountants or even business specialists. But it will help steer you through the maze of rules and regulations which society has formulated (for better or worse); to serve as a ready reference whenever a problem arises in the area of marketing, management, and money; and to be a guide toward a more productive and more satisfying experience by taking the mystery out of the business aspect of crafts.

The entries are listed alphabetically, with cross references to related subjects indicated at the end of each entry. The Contents pages following this Introduction list entries under general categories such as selling, production, banking, pricing, taxes, legal, etc.

This is not a book designed to be read once, like a popular novel. Rather, it is hoped that this volume will find a permanent place in the workshops and studios of all craftspeople who love their craft and want to make it an important part of their life's work.

I owe a boundless debt of gratitude to so many wonderful people from whom I received indispensable help, advice, and cooperation.

I particularly want to acknowledge the many crafts marketing experts and others who have given so freely of their knowledge and experience whenever I had the need to call on them, including (alphabetically): Charles Counts, potter-designer-thinker of Georgia; Gerald Ely, Crafts Specialist of the U.S. Department of Agriculture; Robert W. Gray, Director of the Southern Highland Handicraft Guild; Lois Moran, Research Director of the American Crafts Council; Jean Hollander Rich, CPA; Terry Faith Anderson Weihs, Crafts Specialist of the State of Vermont.

I wish to express my appreciation to several organizations for their permission to use material from their publications: The American Crafts Council, the New York State Bar Association, The Crafts Report Publishing Co., Inc., and Van Nostrand-Reinhold Company for the use of quotes from *Selling Your Crafts* by Norbert Nelson, © 1967 by Litton Educational Publishing, Inc.

For their marvelous assistance in the various stages of preparing the manuscript I express my gratitude to Linda Konner, Hilda Menin, Meredith Rubel, and Marion and Archie Schacher.

A special note of appreciation for their support is due my associates at *The Crafts Report*: Madeline Busch, Frank Crohn, and Albert Landa; and to Connie Schrader, my editor at Harcourt Brace Jovanovich, whose cheerful advice all along the way made the project a joy.

Finally, a special word about my wife, Sheila, who was (as usual) a wise counselor and marvelous partner. Her understanding, encouragement, and love are as much a part of this book as any of the words that appear in it.

If any errors have found their way into these pages, they are my responsibility. If anything has been left out, readers are cordially invited to let me know so that future editions can be revised to reflect greater accuracy and be of greater service to the crafts profession.

MICHAEL SCOTT

Contents

The subjects which appear alphabetically in this Encyclopedia are grouped here under general categories for easy reference.

Management

(*Refer also to listings under Accounting, Financial Management, Insurance, Legal, Production, Selling, Taxes.*)

Contents

Insurance

Labor and Employees

Legal

Financial Management

(Refer also to listings under Accounting, Banking, Bookkeeping, Credit, Pricing, Taxes.)

Accounting

(Refer also to listings under Bookkeeping, Taxes.)

Contents

Credit

Pricing

Taxes

(Refer also to listings under Accounting.)

Contents

Selling and Marketing

Sales Promotion and Publicity

Contents

Organizations (*continued*)

Miscellaneous

The
Crafts
Business
Encyclopedia

Accounting

Accounting is a professional activity concerned with the financial records and activities of a business or individual. There is a significant difference between bookkeeping and accounting: bookkeepers maintain the records, accountants use and interpret them.

Proper financial records, properly kept, are required first of all for various legal reasons, such as calculating taxes. But equally important is the interpretation of those records to help a craft business analyze its strengths and build on them, or discover its weaknesses and correct them. This is called financial management.

Many small business enterprises which seem to have all the ingredients for potential success—a good product, a hardworking owner—nonetheless operate far below their potential or even fail because of inadequate financial records or the inability to interpret records properly. A set of books can be compared to a roll of exposed film. All the ingredients are there, but it must be developed before you can see the picture.

That's where the accountant comes in.

Even the most uncomplicated business activity should periodically utilize the services of an accountant—first to set up a system of financial record-keeping when the business is started, and thereafter, at least once a year, to prepare tax returns, furnish an annual statement, and analyze the financial condition of the business.

Each business has its own situations and problems, so each set of books has to be created to suit the particular need. Most systems include the following basic categories:

1) *Cash Receipts:* to record cash coming in.
2) *Cash Disbursements:* to record expenditures.
3) *Sales:* to record and summarize monthly income.
4) *Purchases:* to record the purchases of merchandise bought for processing, resale, or business operations.
5) *Payroll:* to record wages and deductions such as taxes and Social Security.
6) *Equipment:* to record capital assets, such as machinery, equipment, furniture, automobile.

7) *Inventory:* to record investment in stock (and arrive at a true profit picture).

8) *Accounts Receivable:* to record what is owed to the firm.

9) *Accounts Payable:* to record what the firm owes its creditors and suppliers.

The more extensive and involved the financial records and activities become, the more necessary it is to engage the services of an accountant on a regular basis. Many businesses use an accountant on a monthly or quarterly schedule to balance the books, check on the proper maintenance of the records, prepare periodic tax returns, and furnish other professional services. This is especially important for incorporated businesses.

An accountant's most important contribution to a business firm, large or small, may well be in the area of taxes; not only in preparing tax returns, but in providing advice, based on experience and continuing study of current tax laws, on how to organize financial activities for the best tax advantage.

Literally hundreds of decisions that involve money or management can benefit from an accountant's advice. For example: should you buy that new piece of equipment in November, or can you get a tax break if you wait six weeks and buy it in the next tax year? Will a move to bigger quarters at more rent be justified by the expected return? Which of your activities are profitable, which are not, which can be made profitable, and which should be abandoned?

Applications for business loans from a bank almost always require that the applicant furnish a financial statement prepared by a certified public accountant (CPA), who has passed rigid examinations to determine his or her qualifications.

A competent accountant is as important to a business activity as a competent lawyer, both to prevent problems from arising and to solve them if they arise. The proper use of an accountant's services requires a sense of trust and confidence, and also requires that you lay all your financial problems on the table. Your bank or business acquaintances can probably recommend a good accountant, especially one who is experienced in financial matters of a small business. Choose carefully and feel free to discuss fees in advance.

(*See also: Accural, Balance Sheet, Bookkeeping, Cash Basis, Cash Flow, Income Statement, Inventory, Pricing, Taxes*)

Accounts Payable

In four little words: what you owe others.

A current bill that is due to be paid—from a supplier, the phone company, rent, taxes—but not long-term obligations such as bank loans. Accounts payable are shown on your balance sheet as liabilities.

(*See also: Balance Sheet, Liabilities*)

Accounts Receivable

Four equally little words: what others owe you.

When you send out a bill and it hasn't been paid, it is carried on your books as an account receivable and is shown on the balance sheet as an asset. It is almost an axiom in the business world to keep accounts receivable as low and as current as possible. The older such an account gets (the longer it takes to get the money), the more difficult it becomes to collect. Meanwhile your creditor is working with your money without paying any interest. Accounts receivable should be followed up very carefully.

(*See also: Assets, Balance Sheet, Collections*)

Accrual Basis

An accounting method used for tax purposes in which items of income and expense are charged against the tax period in which they are incurred, regardless of whether the money was actually spent or received during that period.

For example: if you order a quantity of clay at the end of one year but do not receive the bill or pay for the clay until the next year, the accrual basis of accounting would list the expenditure for the year in which the clay was ordered. Similarly, an invoice you send to a customer for a dozen pots is credited as income on the date the invoice was sent, not the date you received the money. The accrual method is not generally used by small businesses such as crafts; the cash basis is much simpler for most craftspeople.

However, if you carry a large inventory of unsold work, the accrual basis may give you a better picture of your financial condition, and may also provide tax advantages, because the costs incurred in producing the unsold work can be charged against that work, regardless of when it is sold.

(*See also: Cash Basis*)

Advertising

Advertising is any form of mass communication for which you pay money. It differs from other forms of publicity which may be free, but over which you exercise relatively little control.

Advertising can take many forms: newspapers, magazines, radio, television, billboards, handbills, direct mail. Within certain limitations you are in complete control of what you want to say, how you want to say it, and to whom it is said.

One of the major limitations is money. Craftspeople who do no retail selling at all (except at craft shows) rarely have any occasion to advertise. But even if your retail operation is limited to a sale at your studio or workshop only twice a year, you have to bring customers in.

The simplest and least expensive method for that purpose may be a mailing piece you send to a list of former customers. It may not be the least expensive on a cost-per-customer basis, since printing and postage can add up to 25¢ or more per piece. But on the basis of the return you get it may be the most economical.

In selecting where and how you advertise, cost is not the only consideration. The returns are equally important. One hundred dollars worth of advertising space in the *Ladies Home Journal* may reach millions of readers at a fraction of a cent per reader. But those millions are totally wasted unless you have a hot item they can buy through the mail. You certainly don't expect them to travel thousands of miles to visit your studio to buy a $10 piece of pottery.

Your ego may feel great seeing your name in the *Ladies Home Journal*, but your wallet will feel a lot better to see your advertisement in the community weekly which reaches the audience you can reasonably expect at your studio or shop.

The first consideration, then, is to determine what medium can carry your message to the right audience at the right price. To do that, make a list of all the available publications that circulate among your potential customers. If you are in a resort area, the weeklies or the publications placed in hotel rooms may be ideal during the tourist season. In large cities which have their own city-oriented magazines, a classified ad in the proper section may bring good results.

Study the publications to see who else advertises, what type of audience they appeal to, whether your ad will be in the right company. You wouldn't advertise Beethoven in a rock magazine, no matter how inexpensive the space is, or how wide an audience the magazine reaches. The same principle applies to craftwork.

Testing Results

The second consideration is results. That can only be determined by experience and testing, and good record-keeping. Keep track of each advertisement, whether it's a display ad of ten inches on two columns, a classified ad, a handbill, or whatever. It is best, in the beginning, not to run more than one type of ad at a time. Using only one makes it easier to test results. See what each type of advertisement brings in. Does one newspaper produce better results than another? Dollar for dollar, does a mailing piece produce more sales than a magazine? Try them one at a time. This is not to suggest a specific sequence, but only an approach to testing various media. Since advertising is an expensive proposition, it pays to keep records of results so that you can concentrate on the more effective methods and eliminate the less effective.

Cost should be a factor only as it relates to results. A $100 ad that produces $1,000 worth of sales is often more productive than a $50 ad that produces $500 worth of sales, though the ratio is identical. Your overhead and the cost of preparing the ad remain fairly constant, no matter how much or little you sell. In the above situation, then, it is more profitable to produce $900 above the cost of the ad instead of $450. On the other hand, if the $50 ad produces $800 worth of sales, it is probably wasteful to spend another $50 simply to produce another $200 in sales. Each situation is specific, and each result must be judged by the advertiser's particular needs and objectives.

When noting results, take into consideration special conditions. If there was a severe snow storm the day after an ad ran, and customers couldn't make it to your shop or studio, that should be taken into account when measuring the advertisement's results. Similarly, an ad offering a half-price sale should not be compared with an ad for a gallery showing.

A good way to record the effectiveness of ads and other promotional materials is to paste them into a scrapbook and make notes of the results right next to them. Include not only the cost of the ad and what it produced, but also weather and other influences. Keep both the good and the bad so you can repeat your successes and avoid your failures.

Effectiveness depends in very large measure on the ad itself. Several ingredients contribute to results: 1) where the ad runs; 2) what the ad looks like (whether it will be read); and 3) the nature of the offer.

Simplicity is the mother of advertising success, all other things being equal. This is particularly true in small-space advertising. That small space has to stand out among all the other ads and articles appearing on the same page. Plenty of white space, a catchy headline that grabs the reader's attention, brief but explicit copy, and an uncomplicated illustration all contribute to readability.

The basic principle to observe is that your advertisement has to compete for attention. Everything in the ad should help toward that end, nothing should detract. Printing a headline upside down, for example, may strike the advertiser as being very clever, but it usually interferes with the readability of the ad.

Let's briefly examine some of these factors one by one.

White Space

When you buy advertising space, whether it's two inches in a newspaper, an 8½-x-11 sheet of paper, or a huge billboard on the highway, what you are really buying is empty space. You now have to fill it with your message. Don't fill it too full. If you cram ink from one border to the next, the eye won't know what to look at first. Keep a little white space—breathing space—in the ad. Properly used, white space is not wasted because it helps direct the eye to the written and illustrative material.

The Headline

A catchy headline need not be clever. "All Jewelry Half Off" is catchier to most readers than "A Jar of Jangling Jewelry" or "We Have Many Surprises." Put yourself in the reader's shoes. Does the headline include some benefit, some reason to read the rest of the ad? McDonald's "We Do It All for You" slogan is a perfect example of expressing a customer benefit. (If only their hamburgers were as good as their slogans.)

Body Copy

This is the text of your advertisement. The same principle of reader benefit applies. Describe what you are offering from the reader's point of view. Not: "I've made a roomful of mugs" but "You'll find mugs of every size, color, and description to fit every taste and every budget." The reader couldn't care less how many mugs you made; what he or she wants to know is whether there's likely to be one he or she likes and can afford.

Keep the copy brief. One advertising copywriter has this dictum posted over his desk: "Write it down, cut it in half, and it's still too long." If you're using very small space, don't try to tell the whole story. Strip it down to the bare essentials that will excite the reader.

In mail-order or catalog advertising, of course, you may have to be more specific and list all sizes and colors. But even here brevity is usually the better part of wisdom.

Illustrations

Simplicity applies here as well. Better to use a small, dramatic drawing that reproduces clearly than a cluttered photograph that can barely be deciphered and comes out a gray glob on the newspaper page. Photos may be necessary in catalogs, but they are generally inadvisable in small-space newspaper advertising.

Finally, every piece of printed material, every advertisement, must include your name, address, telephone number, and directions if you're located in some out-of-the-way place.

The Nature of the Offer

All advertising falls into two basic categories—immediate response or long-range impact.

Immediate response advertising is expected to produce quick results. Included in this category are announcements of sales, shop openings, gallery events, mail-order ads, offers of specific products, and the like.

Immediate-response advertising is relatively easy to measure. It either brings results at once or it doesn't. The more dramatic the offer, the greater the result is likely to be. A sale ad generally brings large crowds, though it may bring smaller profits. But when you do have a sale, the size of the crowd is an extremely important factor in its success. A mail order ad is the easiest of all to measure: you simply count the coupons. There's no confusion as to the source of the order, or what brought the customer in.

Long-range impact is created through advertising which expects to bring the craftsperson's or shop's name to the attention of the public and keep it there, so that potential buyers will remember it when they are ready to buy a craft item. This type of advertising would stress craftsmanship, artistry, exclusiveness, or whatever other attribute makes the shop or craftsperson distinctive and unusual.

Several other considerations enter into advertising planning. One concerns repetition. Should you repeat the same ad again and again? That question does not arise, of course, with ads for special sales or events. But advertising specialists generally agree that an "institutional" ad, one which sells your whole shop or your whole line on a long-range basis, works best when the same ad is repeated several times in the same publication. The cumulative effect often pays off better than running a different ad each time.

Even where ads are different, they should have a family resemblance. That's noted best in department store advertising. You could probably identify the ads of several local department stores even if the names were removed, simply because they have a similar appearance each day although the specific content of each ad is different. Stick to the same style of illustrative device, the same typeface for the headline and text, the same signature for your name and address. Familiarity, in this case, breeds recognition.

Your local newspaper is usually equipped to supply ready-made artwork and other advertising-preparation services for ads which run in their paper, often at no extra charge. Don't hesitate to ask them for help.

Everything mentioned so far is based on the concept that your advertising needs and budgets are very limited. If you have a retail store, or are engaged in extensive mail-order selling, the picture changes somewhat. You have a constant need for advertising to bring in the customers and the orders.

The same principles of effectiveness and measuring results apply, but now you are in a bigger league and probably need the services of an advertising agency.

Agencies come in all sizes and various specialties. Their services are concentrated in two important areas: selection of the media in which you advertise, and preparation of your advertisement.

Advertising agencies have two primary sources of income: 1) They are paid a 15-percent commission by the newspapers or magazines in which the advertisements appear, and 2) they are paid fees by the advertiser for such special services as preparing artwork, making engravings for printing purposes, and so forth.

The more complicated an advertising program is, and the larger the budget becomes, the more useful it is to engage the services of advertising specialists. On a very small budget, a one-man agency or a friend who works as an art director for a large agency may be enough to fill the need. But a retail store with an annual volume of $100,000 may spend as much as $10,000 on advertising. If you are in that category, take your business to professionals who are as experienced in creating effective advertising programs as you are in creating beautiful craftwork.

How to find an advertising agency? Pretty much the same way you look for any other professional service—legal, accounting, etc. Ask other business people who advertise extensively. Interview several agencies. Tell them what you hope to accomplish and what your budget estimates are. Ask them to make a brief outline of their approach to your advertising problems. Find out what they've done for others in similar situations.

The bigger the agency, the more likely it is that they have a variety of talent and expertise to serve you. But in choosing an agency it is sometimes better to be the big fish in a small pond than the small fish in a big pond. The more important you are to an agency's annual income, the better the service you get.

Don't look to advertising to solve any of your problems except one: to communicate quickly with large numbers of people. If your product is wrong, or your price too high, or your reputation for delivery poor, no amount of advertising will solve such problems for you.

(*See also: Catalogs, Press Release, Publicity, Public Relations*)

Agents

(*See: Sales Representatives*)

American Crafts Council

The American Crafts Council is a national nonprofit organization of 37,000 members which was founded in 1943 "to stimulate interest in contemporary crafts." It is the U.S. affiliate of the World Crafts Council.

ACC publishes the bimonthly magazine *Craft Horizons* as well as a variety of reference publications, books and exhibition catalogs, and operates the Museum of Contemporary Crafts in New York City. Its Research and Education Department serves as a resource center for twentieth-century American crafts. It operates a library open to members and the public, and is the producer/distributor of "Your Portable Museum," a rental program of craft slides.

ACC membership is open to anyone who has an interest in crafts, and includes four categories: subscribing ($18 a year), sustaining ($27.50), participating ($50), and sponsor ($100). Membership services include a subscription to *Craft Horizons*, free admission to the Museum of Contemporary Crafts, eligibility for group insurance, reduced prices on selected craft books, ACC events such as the Northeast Craft Fair and various conferences or seminars, and other benefits, depending on membership category.

The headquarters of the American Crafts Council is at 44 West 53rd Street, New York, NY 10019 (212) 977-8989.

(*See also: Organizations*)

Amortization

To amortize is to spread a particular cost over a long period of time. Financial obligations such as mortgages are amortized by making regular periodic payments. Capital investments such as equipment and tools are amortized through depreciation, which means they are carried on the books at a predictable annual reduction in value on the assumption that they will ultimately wear out. In simplest terms, a $500 loom with a life expectancy of ten years would be amortized at $50 a year. This is important both for tax purposes and for establishing the current value of your fixed assets at any given time.

(*See also: Assets, Depreciation, Loans*)

Apprentice

For most of human history, before there was a system of formal education, apprenticeship was the only way to learn a craft or trade. Boys from ten to fourteen would go to work for a journeyman, earning no more than subsistence-level room and board, doing all the unpleasant, dirty jobs around the shop at first, and learning the craftsman's trade bit by bit.

Apprenticeship is still the official term used for learners in some trades, for example, printing and skilled construction work. Such apprentices are now paid salaries and other benefits that increase according to specific formulas as they learn their trade.

The resurgence of handcrafts has led to a rebirth of apprenticeship in that field as well. While some basic techniques and principles can be learned in the classroom, most craftspeople find that their technical and artistic development depends to a great extent on working with an experienced craft artist. This helps them not only to refine their skills but also to understand the production methods, operational procedures, and business problems of earning a living in crafts.

The old method of room and board in exchange for learning the craft is no longer common, although it does still exist. Nor is the apprenticeship a lengthy process that extends over several years. Few apprentices today stay more than a year with the same craft artist, and in almost all cases, money changes hands: sometimes the craft artist pays the apprentice a small sum, often the apprentice pays the craft artist for the privilege of studying with him or her, and sometimes an outside source provides the funds. The National Endowment for the Arts, for example, provides about twenty annual grants of $3000 each to selected "master craftsmen" for the purpose of hiring apprentices for a nine-month period. The apprentice receives $2,700 of this sum, the craftsperson retains $300 for expenses.

A major problem encountered by some craft artists in hiring apprentices involves state and federal labor laws. It appears that the development of apprenticeships in handcrafts is so new that no national policy exists. Some craft artists have been required to pay their apprentices the minimum wage, withhold income taxes, and meet a variety of other requirements demanded by the labor laws. In other cases, especially where the apprentice pays a fee to the craft artist, the apprentice may be considered a student, and thus not subject to the labor laws, even though no formal curriculum exists. Still other craftspeople have proposed the term "intern" for someone whose work is both productive and a learning experience, to get away from the employee connotation of apprentice. It is advisable to consult with state and federal labor departments about the specific conditions that would apply in each case.

The relationship between the craftsperson and the apprentice is a very special one. Careful thought should be given to 1) whether the craft artist and the apprentice are personally compatible; 2) whether the craft artist is emotionally and psychologically equipped to teach his or her craft with patience and understanding; and 3) what the specific arrangements and working conditions will be.

Will the apprentice, for example, work on the craft artist's objects, will the apprentice have an opportunity to work on his or her own work, who pays for the materials for the apprentice's own work, is there a clear understanding about work hours and the operation of the shop, who is responsible for what particular chores?

The relationship between a craft artist and an apprentice is not a one-way street. The apprentice benefits from the learning experience; the craft artist benefits from the apprentice's contribution to the production process. But these benefits are available only if they select each other carefully and understand their arrangements completely before they begin.

(*See also: Education, Employees*)

Architects

Architectural and interior design commissions can become a lucrative part of a craft artist's income, especially in ceramics, metalwork, stained glass, woodwork, textiles, and similar media.

In the old days, handcrafted woodwork, stained-glass windows, elaborate chandeliers and intricately crafted metalwork or decorative accessories were basic elements of architectural design in castles, churches, even railway stations.

The incorporation of major craftwork has become important again in recent times with the advent of vast expanses of glass or marble or cement which require some eye-pleasing interruption.

Furthermore, the federal government and numerous state and municipal governments now require that from one-half to one percent of the construction costs of government buildings must be spent for art- or craftwork in those buildings.

Architectural commissions are available through a number of sources. Perhaps the most effective way is to let architectural firms in your area know of your availability.

Architects working on religious, university, or government buildings are particularly good prospects. Contact them with a brief resumé, some photos or slides of your work, and a request for an interview at which you can show your portfolio. The results will not be as immediate as an approach to sell a craft object to a retail store, but the ultimate results can bring very satisfactory returns. Design competitions provide occasional opportunities, especially for government buildings. In many cases the architect is responsible for interior design as well, or at least for selecting the interior designer.

Since construction of a new building is a lengthy process which requires the approval of numerous government agencies, buildings departments, zoning commissions, etc., it is not difficult to get in on the ground floor if you can find out where such information first becomes available in your locality (city clerk, county clerk, buildings department).

It is important to contact architects in the very early stages of the process. When you see the hard hats digging a hole in the ground, it is usually too late. The architectural work has been completed, budgets firmly established, and someone else may already have the commission you could have had.

Working with architects or interior designers usually requires a high degree of professional competence. Sketches, design proposals, color samples, even scale models are often required. There is usually a specific amount of money available, so it becomes necessary to calculate your costs and what you can do on the basis of the ultimate fee. The architect's requirements must be closely studied. If the craftwork becomes an integral part of the structure, as with a stained-glass window, it is necessary to work closely with the architect and the construction firm to coordinate the completion and installation of the craftwork with their schedules.

Architects do not normally take a percentage of the fee you are paid.

(*See also: Commissions, Customers, Interior Decorators/Designers*)

Arts Councils

(*See: State Art Agencies*)

Assets

A punster once observed that "assets make the heart grow fonder"—and for good reason. Assets are all the things you own, but accountants give them a slightly more restricted meaning, namely all the things you own that can be measured in terms of money.

Assets include real estate, property, machinery and equipment, cash in the bank, inventory, raw materials on hand, even the money others owe you.

You may think that your own good name is your biggest asset, but unless it's General Motors it is hardly likely that your good name, or character assets such as honesty, integrity, creative talent or a great sales personality, can be listed on your books as an asset.

For accounting purposes, there is a whole host of assets. For craftspeople the following are the most common:

Fixed Assets: Such items as real estate, property, tools, equipment.

Liquid Assets: Such items as bank accounts, inventory, accounts receivable; in a word, the kind of assets that can readily be turned into cash to pay bills if need be.

Tangible Assets: An asset which has physical properties, which exists in the real world. Equipment, bank accounts, tools, raw materials, inventory are all tangible assets.

Intangible Assets: Assets that have an obvious value far beyond their physical one. A list of customers, for example, a well-established trade name, or a unique craft process.

Assets and liabilities appear together on a balance sheet, which should be drawn up at least once a year and sometimes more often. This is necessary to calculate taxes, to get approval for bank loans, and numerous other purposes. It is also an essential procedure to reveal what (if any) profits you have made, and what your business is worth in dollars and cents.

(*See also: Balance Sheet, Liabilities*)

Audit

An audit is an examination of a set of books and financial records to determine whether they are kept properly, whether all financial transactions are entered according to accepted accounting and bookkeeping procedures, and to insure that all ingredients exist to evaluate accurately a company's financial condition.

Audits for small businesses are usually conducted by an accountant once a year. They may also be conducted by a government agency such as the Internal Revenue Service if tax problems arise. A financial statement or balance sheet is drawn up following an annual audit, and is required in almost all corporation bylaws and is usually necessary when applying for a major bank loan.

(*See also: Accounting, Balance Sheet, Income Statement*)

Back Order

When only partial shipment is made on an order, the balance is known as a back order, to be shipped at some future time. All the items on the original order should be listed on the invoice or packing slip, with the notation "back order" next to the items which are not included in the shipment. That indicates to the customer that it is not an error in shipment, and that it is not necessary to write a new order. Back order items are generally not billed until they are shipped.

(*See also: Billing, Orders*)

Balance

This word always represents the difference between two amounts, or what is left over after one amount is subtracted from the other. It has innumerable applications: balance of trade, balance of power, balance of payments, etc.

For craftspeople it has four basic applications:

1) Your bank balance represents the amount that remains after all the checks are subtracted from all the deposits. If you deposited $1,000 and wrote checks for $800, your balance is $200.

2) The balance on your account at a craft supply store is the amount you still owe after all your payments are subtracted from all your purchases. That shows up in your accounts payable. If you have overpaid, then all your purchases are subtracted from all your payments, and you have a credit balance.

3) If a customer leaves a $10 deposit on a $100 craft item, the balance due you is $90. This is noted in accounts receivable.

4) At the end of the year, after all your expenses are subtracted from all your income, the balance (hopefully) represents your profit.

The balance plus one amount must always equal the other amount. That's really what it's all about when you balance your checkbook or your accountant balances your ledger.

(See also: Balance Sheet, Bank Statement, Checking Account, Income Statement)

Balance Sheet

Unlike an income statement, which summarizes the income and expense activity over a given period, the balance sheet (often called a financial statement) reports the financial condition of a business at a given point, usually the last day of the year.

The balance sheet reports the assets (everything you own) and the liabilities (everything you owe) on the particular date. Subtracting the liabilities from the assets produces a figure which is the owner's equity, or the net worth of the business.

A balance sheet is prepared by an accountant and is used to inform the owners or stockholders of the condition of the business. It is also required with most applications for a bank loan. The bank generally wants to see a balance sheet that is less than three months old. Drawing up a new balance sheet involves an additional accountant's fee, so apply for a loan before March 31 if you can.

An imaginary balance sheet for an imaginary craft business is illustrated at right. In this example, the owner of the Pot Luck Pottery finds that the net worth of the business—in effect, the value of what he owns —is $15,629.84.

(See also: Assets, Equity, Financial Statements, Income Statement, Liabilities, Net Worth)

Bank Loans

(See: Loans)

POT LUCK POTTERY
BALANCE SHEET
December 31, 1976

ASSETS

Current Assets

Cash	$ 1,843.56	
Accounts Receivable	4,865.50	
Raw Material Inventory	1,116.46	
Finished Inventory	8,085.41	
Prepaid Expenses	340.80	$16,251.73
Less allowance for bad debts		97.30
Total Current Assets		$16,154.43

Fixed Assets

Building	$14,152.80		
Less Depreciation	2,100.00	$12,052.80	
Equipment	$ 2,629.44		
Less Depreciation	464.73	2,164.71	
	Total Fixed Assets		$14,217.51
	TOTAL ASSETS		$30,371.94

LIABILITIES AND CAPITAL

Liabilities

Accounts Payable	$ 1,389.63	
Mortgage	10,400.00	
Loans	2,666.78	
Payroll Taxes Payable	285.69	
Total Liabilities		$14,742.10
Capital (Equity)		$15,629.84

Bankruptcy

When you owe more than you can possibly pay, and when there's no other way to settle your debts, bankruptcy is a federal court procedure whereby the court, through a trustee, administers your assets to pay your creditors. This usually involves selling your assets, in which case the creditors receive only part of what is owed to them, but you are free from all further obligations. Your debts are wiped out and you can start all over again.

There are some situations in which the bankrupt is allowed to reorganize his business affairs under the court's watchful eye. This happens when creditors have reason to believe that there's a real chance that the financial difficulty can be solved under the conditions imposed by the court. They do this in the hope that they'll collect more of the debt, even though they may have to wait longer to do it.

Bankruptcy can be either voluntary (when you petition the court to declare you bankrupt), or involuntary (when your creditors petition the court to declare you bankrupt). Bankruptcy is certainly no crime, although for most people it is an embarrassment.

(See also: Collection Problems)

Banks

Banking used to be a very sedate affair, shrouded in an other-worldly mystique, but it's tough competition these days. Like any competitive enterprise, banks will do all sorts of things to get your business, and offer a wide range of services to attract customers.

Some old-fashioned bankers would still like you to think you're in court or in church when you talk to them. But business is business, so it pays to understand precisely what the different banks offer and what they charge, and it pays to shop around.

A bank is, essentially, a money store. Money is the product it buys and sells. The interest rate a bank charges on a loan is the price you pay for the use of the bank's product. Like renting a car, sooner or later you have to bring it back, and meanwhile you're paying rent for the use of it.

Conversely, the bank has to buy its product (money) somewhere. You are the supplier (depositor), and you get paid for the use of your money, just as a store pays you for your craftwork.

Like all successful enterprises, banks try to buy at the lowest price and sell at the highest. That's how profits are made, and that's why it always costs more to borrow money from a bank than you get paid for depositing money in a bank.

There are essentially two types of banks: commercial banks and savings banks or savings and loan institutions. As the name indicates, commercial banks deal primarily in business and commercial money transactions such as checks, credit cards, automobile loans, foreign remittances, and the like. Savings banks deal primarily in a variety of savings accounts and long-term loans such as mortgages. A number of banking services, such as safe-deposit boxes, traveler's checks, Christmas and vacation clubs, education and home improvement loans are offered by both types of banks.

Since banks are regulated by state and federal agencies, the specific services vary from state to state. In some states, for example, commercial banks can offer savings accounts and savings banks can offer checking accounts.

But different banks even within the same city often charge widely differing fees for the same service. A government study in 1976 found, for example, that home-mortgage interest rates in New York ranged from 8.5 percent at one bank to 9.25 percent at another. Three quarters of a percentage point may not seem like much of a difference, but look at the end result: a twenty-year $20,000 mortgage costs a whopping $2,306.40 more in interest at 9.25 percent than at 8.5 percent. Interest rates for home improvement loans showed an even wider spread in the study, from 9.05 percent to 13.58 percent.

Craftspeople who conduct extensive business activities through their checking accounts will find that it pays to shop around even here. Some banks charge a fixed monthly fee plus 10¢ or 15¢ per check. Others charge nothing for checks if a certain minimum is kept on deposit. Still others base their charges on an average monthly balance, and some banks even charge for the deposits that are made.

Minimum balance accounts are sometimes advertised as "free." While you do not pay directly for checking services, you do pay for them indirectly if you must maintain a minimum balance larger than the amount you would ordinarily keep in the checking account. If those excess funds were in a savings account they would earn interest.

For example: if you are required to maintain a minimum monthly balance of $400, but you need only $50 to cover your checks at any given time, you would lose the interest you could have earned on the other $350. At a rate of 5 percent a year, you would lose $17.50. If the alternative were to maintain no minimum balance but pay $1 a month for checking services, you would be $5.50 ahead at the end of the year.

That's not a huge sum, but it's an example of how carefully every aspect of a banking relationship must be examined in terms of the final dollar result.

The same principle applies to the extra services. The government study found that one New York bank charged $1.50 if a check bounces, while others charged nothing. One bank charged $4 for a stop-payment order, another only 50¢. One bank charged $2.50 to certify a check, another charged only 25¢.

As a savings account depositor, it is important to understand where the best returns are. Savings banks pay a wide variety of interests. The lowest rate is on accounts from which you can withdraw almost at will. Certificates of deposit, which last from one to seven years, pay different rates: the longer the term, the higher the rate. But you can't convert them into cash before their maturity without a penalty.

Even the same interest rate may provide different returns in actual dollars, depending on what basis the interest is calculated. The "low average monthly balance" method is less favorable to the depositor than the "day of deposit to day of withdrawal" method.

Like every trade or profession, banking has its own language. Don't be afraid to ask questions, and don't hesitate to ask your friendly neighborhood banker to explain what a particular transaction means in actual dollars and cents.

(See also: Bank Statement, Cancelled Check, Cashier's Check, Certified Check, Checking Account, Cleared Check, Commercial Bank, Deposit, Endorsement, Installment, Insufficient Funds, Interest, Letter of Credit, Loans, Money Order, Mortgage, Overdrawn, Savings Bank, Traveler's Checks)

Bank Statement

Every month you receive a statement from your bank which lists all the checks that cleared (were paid by the bank from your account), all the deposits that were collected, any bank charges, plus the opening and closing balance.

It makes good sense to check the bank statement against your own records. The bank usually provides a convenient form on the back of the statement to help you do this. Here's the procedure:

1) Note all the deposits that show up in your checkbook but are not shown on the bank statement because they were made after the statement was prepared. Add this amount to the final balance shown on the statement. This gives you a new figure which I call the credit balance. (Remember that it takes three to ten days between the time you make a noncash deposit and the bank collects it and credits it to your account.)

2) Total up the bank charges (if any) shown on the statement. Enter this figure in your checkbook and subtract it from the last balance shown.

3) Put all the cancelled (paid) checks the bank has returned with the statement in numerical order. Then go through your checkbook and mark all the stubs for checks that have cleared.

4) The stubs that are not marked indicate the checks that have not cleared. These are called outstanding checks. They are reflected in your checkbook balance, but not on the bank statement. Add up the amounts of all the outstanding checks. I call this total the debit balance.

5) Subtract the debit balance (outstanding checks) from the credit balance (bank balance plus recent deposits).

The final figure should agree with your final balance in your checkbook (after subtracting any bank charges). Often it doesn't; we all make an error occasionally. Sometimes it's simple arithmetic, sometimes we write a check and forget to enter it in the checkbook. Sometimes the bank makes a mistake. If you cannot reconcile your checkbook balance with the bank balance, go over all the entries and totals very carefully. If it still won't work out, go to the bank and have them help you.

The bank statement has another important value: it signals a problem if a check you wrote long ago hasn't cleared. If you send someone a check in April, and by July it still hasn't been paid by your bank, it's time to find out what happened. Perhaps it was lost in the mail.

Keep the bank statement and the cancelled checks together in a safe place and in proper numerical order. If ever a question comes up whether you've paid a particular bill, you can refer to the bill on which you've presumably indicated the number of the check you wrote when you paid it, and locate the cancelled check with the recipient's signature (endorsement) on the back, to prove that the payment was made and the check cashed.

(*See also: Checking Account*)

Better Business Bureau

A Better Business Bureau is a nonprofit organization of business establishments, set up to aid both business and the consumer. It is a way of self-regulation which utilizes the power of public opinion, if not of law, to keep businesses on the straight and narrow in their relations with their customers and with each other.

Over 150 local Better Business Bureaus throughout the country provide background information on local firms and merchants. Such information is free and available to anyone on request.

Ideally, the buyer makes use of the Better Business Bureau before making a purchase or signing a contract, in the hope of avoiding problems. However, the Better Business Bureau can also help the buyer if difficulties arise after the transaction is completed.

If a craft artist is scouting around to make a major purchase, such as a kiln or a loom, and finds a totally unknown source, it is wise to contact the Better Business Bureau in the area where the unknown manufacturer or advertiser is located. The Bureau's files should reveal how long the company has been in business, its record for reliability, how it deals with complaints, and any other relevant information which can help the craftsperson make an intelligent decision.

The Better Business Bureau will also handle complaints that are put in writing. While a Better Business Bureau has no legal clout, it often succeeds by exerting peer pressure on the offending merchant if investigation proves the customer's complaint to be valid. While that may not always succeed, the Bureau will at least have the complaint on file to discourage others from dealing with that firm in the future.

Most Better Business Bureaus also perform a great deal of work in the area of consumer education to help people make wise decisions before buying. But there are several things a Better Business Bureau will *not* do:

1) Handle matters that require a lawyer, such as contract violations;
2) Make collections;
3) Give recommendations or endorsements;
4) Furnish lists of companies or individuals in a particular line of business;
5) Pass judgment. The Better Business Bureau may indicate that a particular store has had complaints about its refund policy, for example, but will not say that the store is disreputable.

While many major cities and states have a Better Business Bureau, not all do. Where no BBB exists, the local Chamber of Commerce can often be helpful in solving problems that arise between buyers and merchants in their area.

Better Business Bureaus are supported by local businesspeople who pay annual dues, which vary from one BBB to the other. Craftspeople who conduct a mail-order business and advertise extensively may find membership in a Better Business Bureau particularly helpful. Mentioning such membership in an advertisement or catalogue adds to the advertiser's prestige and reputation for integrity, and thus helps attract new customers.

(*See also: Chamber of Commerce*)

Bill

(*See: Invoice*)

Bill of Lading

When you ship by freight, the trucker or carrier will give you a bill of lading which specifies what is being shipped, how it is to be shipped, and to whom it is to be delivered. The recipient of the shipped goods normally gets a copy of the bill of lading, which serves to notify him that the goods have been shipped, and also to identify himself as being authorized to receive the shipment.

Bills of lading come in various forms, including some that are negotiable. Such uses are rare for craftspeople. If you ship via freight you would normally get a straight bill of lading, which is not negotiable and authorizes delivery only to the person or company named on the document.

(*See also: Shipping*)

Bookkeeping

Aside from being the only word in the English language with three consecutive double letters, bookkeeping is an essential operation in the conduct of any craft business activity. It involves the recording of every financial transaction, every money item in the books of account, whether the craftsperson is an individual operating out of a downstairs workshop and serving as his or her own bookkeeper, or a large operation in which bookkeeping is a full-time activity for which a trained person is employed.

Bookkeeping is not a matter of choice, but of necessity. Your financial records are the basis on which your tax returns are prepared; they are used as supporting evidence in tax matters, whether income taxes, sales taxes, or other tax obligations.

When analyzed, properly maintained financial records can reveal where your activity is profitable and where it is unprofitable, where you may be able to save money, where the price of your work needs to be adjusted, how to plan your cash flow, and many other ingredients that spell the difference between economic survival and economic disaster.

Many craftspeople seem scared to death of bookkeeping. It seems like a deep, dark mystery, but it need not be. Many high schools and colleges offer adult evening courses in simple bookkeeping specifically for people who keep their own records. A few hours invested in such a course can reap big dividends. Simple standardized bookkeeping materials are available in most major office supply stores, or by mail from such firms as Dome Publishing Company (Providence, RI 02903), Ideal System Co., (P.O. Box 1568, Augusta, GA 30903), and others.

Unless you are involved in complicated credit transactions, elaborate accounts receivable operations, or other ultrasophisticated financial dealings, you'll find that the bookkeeping mystery really boils down to this simple principle: keep track of every penny that comes in and every penny that goes out. This can usually be done in a simple ledger which an acountant or even an experienced bookkeeper can help you set up.

Bookkeeping differs significantly from accounting. The bookkeeper maintains the records. The accountant interprets and analyzes the financial information recorded on the books, prepares the tax returns based on a thorough knowledge of the tax laws, and furnishes you with useful advice and information based on professional training and experience.

(*See also: Accounting, Double Entry, Single Entry, Systems*)

Books

It is doubtful that anyone has ever counted all the craft books ever written. There are literally thousands, covering every conceivable craft medium from every conceivable angle, from rank beginner to top-notch professional.

The library of books on the business side of crafts is extremely small, however. Many of the books specialize in one facet of the craft business or another, generally selling. In addition, there is a large number of books on business subjects in general which is too large to list here. Any good librarian can make some recommendations, depending on the reader's particular interest and background.

One particularly useful source of literature is the Small Business Administration, which has hundreds of marketing aids and management aids available, many free of charge. A list of these can be obtained from the nearest SBA field office (see telephone white pages under "U.S. Government, Small Business Administration") or write to the SBA at Washington, DC 20416.

Another splendid source is the Research Department of the American Crafts Council (44 West 53rd Street, New York, NY 10019), which has published extensively on management and marketing subjects of specific concern to craftspeople.

The Farmer's Cooperative Service of the U.S. Department of Agriculture has published a series of excellent outlines on organizing and operating craft cooperatives (500 12th St., S.W., Washington, DC 20250). One of the finest government publications is "Encouraging American Craftsmen" by Charles Counts, available from the Superintendent of Documents, U.S. Government Printing Office, Washington, DC 20402.

The two books which, in this writer's opinion, are of greatest all-around value to craftspeople in the conduct of their marketing and selling activities are:

> *Selling Your Crafts*
> by Norbert Nelson
> Van Nostrand-Reinhold Co.
> 450 W. 33 St., New York, NY 10001
> 1967; 126 pages; $3.95 (paperback)

> *How to Earn More Money from Your Crafts*
> by Merle E. Dowd
> Doubleday & Co.
> Garden City, NY
> 1976; 223 pages; $7.95 (hardcover)

Other useful books include:

> *The Craftsman's Survival Manual*
> by George & Nancy Wettlaufer
> Prentice-Hall
> Englewood Cliffs, NJ
> 1974; 94 pages; $2.95 (paperback)

Craftsmen in Business:
A Guide to Financial Management and Taxes
by Howard Connaughton, CPA
American Crafts Council
44 West 53rd St., New York, NY 10019
1975; 73 pages; $6.50, $4.95 members (softcover)

Crafts Are Your Business
by Gerald Tooke
Canadian Crafts Council
46 Elgin St., Ottawa K1P 5K6
1976; 83 pages; $3.50 (paperback)

How to Make Money with Your Crafts
by Leta W. Clark
William Morrow & Co.
105 Madison Ave., New York, NY 10016
1974; 240 pages; $6.95 (hardcover)

How to Start Your Own Craft Business
by Herb Genfan and Lyn Taetzsch
Watson-Guptill Publications
One Astor Plaza, New York, NY 10036
1974; 203 pages; $7.95 (hardcover)

Marketing Art
by Calvin J. Goodman
Gee Tee Bee
11901 Sunset Blvd., Los Angeles, CA 90049
1972; 318 pages; $15.95 (hardcover)

Special publishing projects of interest to craftspeople include:

"The Handcraft Business"
Small Business Reporter
Bank of America
Dept. 3120, PO Box 37000
San Francisco, CA 94137
1972; 16 pages; $1

"Tax Guide for Small Business," Publication 334,
Internal Revenue Service
U.S. Government Printing Office
Washington, DC 20402

"Craftspirit '76"
Artisan Crafts
PO Box 398, Libertyville, IL 60048
3 issues in 1976; $6.00

Several useful directories include:

Artist's Market
edited by Kirk Poling and Liz Prince
Writer's Digest
9933 Alliance Rd., Cincinnati, OH 45242
1976 edition; 624 pages; $9.95 (hardcover)

Contemporary Crafts Marketplace
compiled by American Crafts Council
R. R. Bowker Co.
1180 Ave. of the Americas, New York, NY 10036
1975–76 edition; 502 pages; $13.95 (paperback)

Craft Sources
by Paul Colin and Deborah Lippman
M. Evans & Co.
216 E. 49 St., New York, NY 10017
1975; 240 pages; $12.50 (hardcover), $5.95 (paperback)

Craft Supplies Supermarket
by Joseph Rosenbloom
Oliver Press
Willits, CA
1974; 210 pages; $3.95 (paperback)

Marietta College Craft Directory USA
compiled by Arthur Howard Winer
Marietta College
Marietta, OH 45750
1976 edition; 264 pages; $11.50 (hardcover)

National Guide to Craft Supplies
by Judith Glassman
Van Nostrand Reinhold
450 W. 33rd St., New York, NY 10001
1976; 224 pages; $6.95 (paperback)

Several books on craft photography are listed further on in this book under "Photographs."

(*See also: Periodicals*)

Borrowing

(*See: Loans*)

Break-even Point

The point at which income and expenses match exactly is called the break-even point. You neither make money nor lose money at this point. It's a standoff. The name of the game, of course, is to move beyond the break-even point because that's where the profits are. The losses are below the break-even point.

Knowing your break-even point is not an academic exercise. It can be an important tool in proper pricing, controlling costs, and scheduling production.

Finding the break-even point is not complicated, once the principle is clear. Two things must be known; the price at which you plan to sell an item, and your costs.

Let us assume that you want to make copper bowls this week to sell for $10 each. You have two cost factors to consider: the *fixed* cost (rent, overhead, etc.) which remains pretty much the same whether you make one bowl or a 100, and the *variable* costs (copper, polishing supplies, labor, etc.) which change in direct proportion to the number of bowls you make.

In this example we'll set the fixed costs at $100 and the variable costs at $3 per bowl. Each $10 bowl now contributes $3 toward its own cost of production, which leaves $7 for fixed costs. Without drawing any charts or graphs it is clear that you have to make more than fourteen bowls just to cover the fixed costs (14 x $7 equals $98). No profit yet. This is the break-even point.

If you can make only twenty bowls a week you'll spend the bulk of your time working for the landlord and the telephone company. In other words, fourteen bowls is not a good break-even point. Of course, if you can make and sell fifty bowls, you're way ahead—$7 on each of thirty-six bowls, or $252.

The thing to do now is to make up a chart which shows the break-even point at various price ranges, with the same fixed and variable costs:

Price per bowl	Variable cost per bowl	Part of fixed cost per bowl	Total fixed cost	Break-even number of bowls
$10	$3	$7	$100	14.3
$12	$3	$9	$100	11.1
$15	$3	$12	$100	8.3

According to this chart, you could do quite well if you make twenty bowls at $15. But suppose you can't increase the price. Perhaps you can cut costs. If the total fixed costs, for example, could be reduced to $90, you would reach the break-even point (at the $10 price) with the thirteenth bowl (13 x $7 equals $91). Now, if you could reduce the variable expense to $2.50, which would leave $7.50 toward the fixed cost of $90, you would reach the break-even point at twelve bowls (12 x $7.50 equals $90).

To save all this arithmetic, a graph comes in handy.

GRAPH A

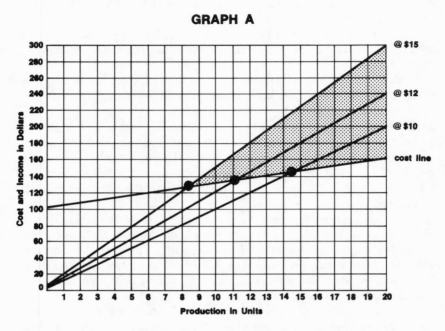

The shaded area above the break-even points is profit. Note the greater profit area at $15 each than at $12 or $10.

In Graph A you find one line to indicate costs, and three lines to indicate production of twenty pieces at different prices: $10, $12, and $15 each. The cost curve starts at a fixed cost of $100, and adds $3 in variable costs for each bowl, up to $60 for twenty bowls, a total of $160. Note where the curves intersect, and note how much bigger the cone-shaped profit area above the break-even points gets as the price per bowl goes up.

In Graph B we've kept the production curve constant at the $10 price level, but we've cut costs. The cost curve now indicates total costs of $120, $140, and $160. Note how the break-even point changes, even though the cost per bowl on all twenty bowls has been reduced by only one dollar each time.

GRAPH B

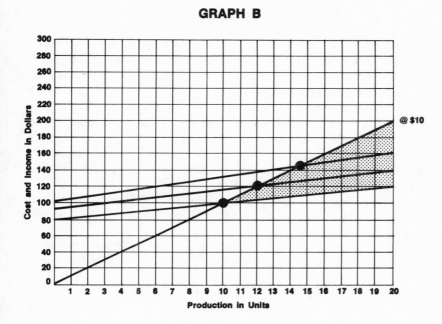

Fixed price ($10 each), variable cost lines. Profit is greatest when total costs are lowest, here $120.

If you find that the break-even point is satisfactory, all well and good. If it is unsatisfactory, you have five options: 1) lose money; 2) raise prices; 3) cut costs; 4) increase production; 5) cease production.

But be careful of points 2 and 4. If you can't sell your work at the increased price, or if you can't sell the greater quantity, you are left with only two options: 1) cut costs; or 2) stop production. The break-even point is based on the assumption that you'll sell everything you make.

Brochures

(*See: Advertising, Printed Materials*)

Budget

A budget is simply a plan—a realistic plan, or it won't work—which outlines expected income and expenditures during a given period in the future. It helps to anticipate future needs and to decide how to meet them. A wide variety of budgets exist in the business world, but two are of interest to a small enterprise such as a crafts business.

The *capital budget* concerns itself with the purchase of equipment and major outlays that are not immediately used up in the production of craftwork. Preparing such a plan for the coming year, for example, indicates not only what you expect to buy and when, but also how you expect to pay for it, whether through loans, saving up in advance, out of income, or taking in a partner.

Much more important to the success of a small business is the *cash budget*. This should indicate, on a monthly basis for six or twelve months ahead, what you expect to take in as a result of sales, and what you expect to pay out in order to operate. The number of entries can be as brief or as elaborate as you feel you may need in order to forecast properly and check up on yourself later.

Under "Income," for example, it might be sufficient to have three lines: Wholesale, Shows and Fairs, Other. If you operate your own store, Retail would be a fourth line.

Under "Expenses," it may be sufficient to enter just a few categories: Raw Materials, Rent & Utilities, Selling Expenses, Payroll, Taxes, and Miscellaneous.

At the beginning, when some of this may be no more than guesswork, it is useful to create two columns next to each line. In the first column you enter the budget figure, how much you estimate the income or expense for that item will total. Leave the second column blank. When your accountant has worked up the actual figures, enter them in the second column. You will see at a glance where your budget has been accurate, where it needs amending for the future, where the weak spots and the strong points are. That makes your next budget more realistic.

By pinpointing the periods of high expense versus low income which happen in almost every business, the cash budget can also help to reduce the need for borrowing money, or predict more accurately how much needs to be borrowed or how much should be held in reserve.

Budgeting, in other words, is not simply a bookkeeping exercise. It is an indispensable tool in avoiding costly mistakes and correcting errors of judgment.

(*See also: Cash Flow*)

Bulk Buying

Despite the penchant for independence that is almost inbred in craft producers, more and more craftspeople have found that joining hands to buy materials and supplies together can save substantial sums of money because the price goes down the more you buy. That's known as bulk buying. It may not always be possible to buy specific craft materials such as clay or yarn if the craft media of the participating craftspeople are different, but there is always the possibility of bulk buying packaging materials, office supplies, and other items.

(*See also: Suppliers*)

Bulk Sale
(*See: Collection Problems*)

Business Expenses
(*See: Accounting, Expenses, Overhead, Sales Cost, Shows and Fairs, Wages*)

Business Forms

Once upon a time there was a theory that the more paperwork you did, the more efficient you were. That may have been a great boon to printers, but some doubt has been cast on that notion elsewhere, although it still enjoys considerable prestige in the bureaucracies of government and industry.

However, a minimum of paperwork does seem to be required, no matter how much we may loathe it, and no matter how large or small our operations may be.

It is necessary, occasionally, to write to a customer or supplier, to send out invoices, fill out a bill of lading, have an order form available, mail a past due notice, furnish expense accounts for tax purposes, and so forth.

If your need for a particular business form is sufficiently large, you will want to have that form printed to your specification. Letterheads, envelopes, invoices and order forms may be among these. But considerable sums of money can be saved if you can use a preprinted form (stock form) and either have it imprinted with your name, or rubber stamp your name and address at the top.

Such stock forms are available through local printers, stationery supply stores, or by mail from a manufacturer and include virtually every type of form you might use.

Even the formality of a letter on a letterhead is being replaced on many occasions by forms known variously as speed letters, speed memos, or read-and-reply speed messages. These are preprinted forms which come in sets of two to four parts with the carbon already in. You write your message on one half of the form, send two copies to the person with whom you're communicating, and that person writes his answer on the other half and sends one copy back to you. That not only speeds up the letter writing at both ends, but you have your original question at hand when you receive the answer and need not dig around for it in the files or wherever you keep such things.

Letterheads, envelopes, and business cards, as well as a variety of forms, are generally less expensive when they are ordered by mail (it eliminates a middleman's profit) but they may not always be as personalized as something you can order from your own printer. Among firms which have descriptive catalogs and price lists available, and will fill mail orders, are the following:

Apex Business Systems
131–01 Sanford Avenue
Flushing, NY 11355

The Drawing Board
256 Regal Row
P.O. Box 505
Dallas, TX 75221

Grayarc
882 Third Avenue
Brooklyn, NY 11232

Revere Business Graphics, Inc.
1123 Broadway
New York, NY 10010

Vermont Business Forms Co.
118 Summer Street
Barre, VT 05641

Williamhouse Inc.
P.O. Box 1393
Hagerstown, MD 21740

Business Name

(See: Trade Name)

Business Tax

(See: Income Tax—Business)

Business Trips

When you go out of town to a craft fair at which you've rented a booth, or when you take to the road to visit stores to sell your work, it's a business trip and therefore tax deductible. The important thing isn't how much you sold at the show or how successful the trip was, but only that it was for business reasons.

If the trip is primarily for business, all reasonable and necessary expenses are deductible. If the trip is primarily for pleasure or personal reasons, then expenses are not deductible, although expenses incurred at the destination for incidental business activities may be deducted.

Extending a business trip for pleasure, or making a nonbusiness side trip, do not qualify for business deductions. There are many combinations, of course. If you take a trip to Vermont for a craft show, and then spend another week skiing, your travel expenses are covered, as well as the expenses during the craft show. Only the ski week is not deductible.

Expenses for your spouse and family have to be treated very carefully. If your spouse is an active participant in your craft business, helps you sell at the show, etc., the expenses are deductible. But even if your kids run a few little errands for you, you'll have a hard time proving to the tax collector that they are essential to your business. Car expenses, of course, are usually totally deductible. They don't change whether you're driving alone or moving the whole family.

You can take several precautions to be able to prove to the Internal Revenue Service that your trip was for business purposes. First, set up an itinerary which spreads your business contacts along the whole route of the trip. This is not necessary when you travel to a craft show because your booth at the show is in itself sufficient reason to go that distance.

Next, write to all the business contacts you plan to see. Tell them when you want to see them and what you want to discuss. Keep carbon copies of the letters on file. They prove what your intentions were.

Make a note of all the business calls you make during the trip, whom you saw, when and where, what the results were.

Finally, keep an accurate record of all expenses.

(*See also: Expense Accounts, Sales, Shows and Fairs*)

Buyers

Although any customer is a buyer in the dictionary sense of the term, in retail commerce a buyer is the person who does the buying for a retail store. In small stores that is generally the owner. Large establishments like department stores have numerous buyers who specialize in particular merchandise lines, e.g., gift buyer, home furnishings buyer, boutique buyer. The largest department stores often have several buyers in major departments, some of whom are assistant buyers.

To sell craftwork to a department store, it is necessary to contact the right buyer for the particular type of product. For ceramics that might be the gift buyer, for leather belts the men's wear buyer, for jewelry the jewelry buyer, and so on. Most department store buyers have specific days or hours in which they see vendors (that's you). Their time is usually limited, so it is best to be prepared for a brief presentation with a few samples. Be prepared also to leave a sample so that the buyer can think about it, discuss it with other store executives, and determine whether an order should be written and for what quantity.

Store buyers are under considerable pressure to perform, so they may be very demanding in terms of price, quality standards, delivery schedules, and sales conditions. They must be sure, for example, that the order you deliver will match the sample, and that you will make delivery when specified.

The better buyers attend wholesale days at craft fairs to find new sources of supply. Remember that they need you as much as you need them, except that there are more craftspeople than store buyers, so they can pick and choose what they think will sell best in their stores.

That decision involves a whole bagful of ingredients: design, price, competition, what will appeal to the store's customers, what is already in the store, and sometimes pure intuition. What will sell in a fashionable Fifth Avenue store may not appeal to customers in a popular-price small town store, and vice versa. That doesn't make one better than the other, just different. Similarly, if a store doesn't have a jewelry department, it is pointless to approach that store with jewelry.

Most buyers will look for items that are not sold in another store around the corner, especially for such unique merchandise as craftwork. But they will often be impressed with the fact that other stores in other cities already stock your work and have reordered a number of times. It helps them to make a decision based on someone else's experience, and thus reduce the risk of making a mistake.

Some stores find that staging events in connection with a particular line of merchandise helps bring customers in and make sales. The public enjoys watching a craft artist at work. If you have a craft that can be easily demonstrated and explained, and you have the stage presence to do it, a store buyer may react positively to a suggestion that you demonstrate your craft for an hour or two every afternoon for several days. That gives them a peg for advertising you and your merchandise. Try it out on a major store in your area. Your costs are almost nothing, except for time, and the results, both in sales and publicity, may be excellent.

(*See also: Retail Outlets, Samples, Wholesaling*)

Buying Habits

(*See: Buyers, Customers, Mail Order, Marketability, Salesmanship*)

Cancelled Check

A check which you have issued and which your bank has paid from your account is called a cancelled check because its function is over and it cannot be used again. There was a time when littles holes were punched into such checks, but other forms of cancellation today accomplish the same purpose. A check that has gone through this procedure is often referred to as a check that has cleared.

Cancelled checks are returned to you with your monthly bank statement. They serve two important purposes: 1) to enable you to double-check the bank statement, and 2) as proof that you have made payment. Since checks have to be endorsed by the person or firm to whom they are issued before they can be cashed or deposited, it's the best evidence to have in your files. Cancelled checks should be kept in numerical sequence. If you mark the bills you pay with the check number and date of payment, it is easy to locate the check as proof if a question comes up later.

The other side of the coin is a situation in which your records don't show that you have been paid, but your customer says he has the cancelled check. In that case, ask to see the check or a Xerox copy (of both sides, so you can see whether you endorsed it). Perhaps it's a simple bookkeeping error. Then again, perhaps the check was lost or stolen and someone forged the endorsement.

(*See also: Bank Statement, Checking, Endorsement*)

Capital

This word has two meanings in business.

One definition refers to the total worth of the business in terms of all its assets.

The accountant's definition, which is of more immediate interest, refers to the investment expressed in terms of money. This includes not only the cash put up by the owner(s) of the business, but such sources as loans, trade credit, equipment, or real estate which are brought in.

Capitalizing a new business often draws on a combination of resources. Suppose you and a partner want to open the Pot Luck Pottery. You calculate that you'll need $5,000 to get started. Where do you get that capital? Partner A invests a kiln, a wheel, and other equipment worth $1,200, plus $300 in cash. Partner B puts up $1,500 in cash. You're still $2,000 short, so you go to the bank or your mother-in-law to borrow the balance. And you're in business.

The initial investment is not the only source of capital. The income earned by your business increases the company's capital if some of it is invested in new equipment. Similarly, if you borrow money in order to expand several years after you've started, that also counts as capital.

(*See also: Equity, Loans*)

Capital Gain Tax

Suppose you own a woodworking shop: building, tools, equipment. You decide you want to move to some other part of the country so you put the shop up for sale, and you sell it at a profit. That profit is known as a capital gain—your capital investment has increased in value and you realized the increase in dollars and cents.

The capital gain becomes part of your income for tax purposes, but is taxed at only *half* your regular tax rate, provided you've owned the assets for more than nine months (twelve months as of 1978). The regular tax rate applies to capital gain on assets held less than the required period. The capital gain tax applies to the profit on the sale of any capital asset, including corporate stocks, buildings, equipment, and similar capital investments.

Cash Basis

An accounting method used for tax purposes in which items of income and expense are charged against the tax year in which the money actually changed hands, regardless of when you received the bill or sent the invoice. This is the most common method used by small businesses such as crafts, unless you carry large inventories of unsold work. Accrual basis is the other type of accounting procedure; you need permission from the Internal Revenue Service to switch from one method to the other.

(*See also: Accrual Basis*)

Cash Discounts

The term "2/10–net 30," which you often see on a bill, means that 2 percent can be deducted from the stated amount if the bill is paid within ten days, and that the entire amount is due within 30 days.

That 2-percent amount is known as a cash discount. It is used as an inducement for prompt payment of bills.

When you take 2 percent off a bill sent by a supplier, you are reducing the cost of the merchandise you bought by 2 percent. If you buy $2000 worth of supplies in a year, you've saved $40. You'd probably have to sell more than $200 worth of craftwork to clear $40.

If you allow a 2 percent cash discount to your customers, you are reducing your income by 2 percent on all amounts which are paid within ten days. If your cash flow depends on prompt receipt of bill payments, that may be worthwhile, particularly if the alternative is to borrow money at 8 or 12 percent.

(*See also: Sales Conditions*)

Cash Flow

It has been said that "cash is the fuel which runs your business."

We're not speaking here of the original investment which gets you started, but the cash that's needed day in and day out to keep you going; to pay for materials, rent, telephone bills, and the hundred other expense items.

It's much like owning an automobile. Buying the car is the original investment, but you have to keep it supplied with gas or it won't take you anywhere.

Some craftspeople may protest that they are "too small" to worry about cash flow. But there's no such thing as too big or too small, unless you're independently wealthy.

Controlling your cash flow has two important functions: 1) to make sure you have cash on hand to pay current bills when they are due, and 2) to plan ahead for expansions, promotions, craft-show costs, and similar expenses you may want or need to incur in the future.

Knowing your cash flow situation is also essential if you experience soft spots in your craft activity—certain times of the year when money is slow in coming in but regular expenses keep on going. Knowing ahead of time what your cash needs will be helps you to put some money away to pay the bills during the slow periods.

Cash flow, then, is simply the manner in which cash comes in and goes out. Handling the cash flow so that you keep out of financial trouble involves two basic operations:

1) Knowing what you need to spend and when you need to spend it
2) Controlling how the money comes in

Current Cash Flow

Even the simplest set of records will tell you what your regular obligations are: rent, utilities, telephone, wages, loan payments, taxes, cost of materials. The most accurate reflection is a balance sheet, which an accountant can prepare periodically; but for a business that involves only one or two people, even this isn't essential. You can pretty well add them up yourself.

You need to know not only what you must spend each month, but also when you must spend it. Your cash flow chart, therefore, should indicate how much rent is due on the first of the month, how much you have to pay on a bank loan on the tenth, and so forth.

Now you have some idea how much money you must have available at various times of the month to pay those bills. You may not be able to do much about timing your expenses, but you can exert considerable control over your income.

For example, if you know you must have cash in the bank to meet a sizable bill on the fifteenth of every month, send out your invoices to customers sufficiently far in advance so that you can reasonably expect the money to reach you by then. Sending a bill on the first may be too late, unless you offer a cash discount for paying within ten days and your experience tells you that customers take advantage of a cash discount for promptness.

Some expenses are also within your control. Your own wages, for example. If your cash receipts are fairly steady throughout the month, but your expense peaks come on the first and the fifteenth, then time your own paycheck to the tenth and the twenty-fifth.

Ideally, you should have an expense plan and an income plan for twelve months ahead. You may find that the income plan reveals several very strong sales periods: a couple of specific craft shows during the summer, or perhaps a heavy volume just before Christmas. Compare this with your expense plan. Are there any heavy expense items which you could shift to these periods?

Almost everyone has had the unhappy experience of being short of cash. There are $200 worth of bills in the drawer, but only $100 in the bank. Proper handling of your cash flow is designed to reduce those embarrassing situations.

There are, of course, unforeseen circumstances when you either have to delay payment of bills or accelerate income. Knowing your cash flow situation enables you to discuss with a supplier why you need a little extra time, and when you can pay the bill. The telephone company won't usually wait, but your landlord might, especially if you've always paid the rent on time.

By the same token, you can ask a customer who owes you money to send the check a little ahead of the normal payment schedule. It may be worth your while to offer a cash discount of 4 or 5 percent instead of 2 percent for immediate payment. It's certainly cheaper than borrowing from the bank.

Long-Range Cash Flow

On the assumption that nobody stands still, a craftsperson needs to plan ahead. There will come a day when you want to buy a new kiln, or another loom, or a certain set of tools. You may want to print and mail a brochure, go on an extensive sales trip, buy your own workshop building. None of these expenses can reasonably be paid out of current income. Some will have to be financed with long-term loans, such as a real estate mortgage. Remodeling a shop may require a short-term bank loan.

But others can be financed by setting aside a specific portion of your income for those purposes. A sales trip or a brochure, for example, can be expected to produce specific sales results, even though the actual income may not appear until six months later.

Anticipating cash flow needs for growth expenses is an integral part of cash flow planning. At the same time, that very same growth may well require some new planning for income cash flow.

Having moved into a larger shop and installed another wheel and a bigger kiln, it is safe to assume that you hope to produce more pots. Producing more pots means that you'll have to buy more clay, pay a bigger electric bill, perhaps hire a helper. Is your cash flow projection sufficiently detailed to indicate whether there will be enough income to make such commitments?

No blueprint is available for this sort of thing. Every crafts producer has his or her own needs, work methods, resources, collection techniques, supplier relations. The only guideline here is that you maintain an adequate cash supply to meet your obligations, and that you plan ahead so that the cash supply remains adequate.

Cashier's Check

Most checks are written by depositors against their bank checking accounts. A cashier's check is written by the bank against its own funds. This is done mainly for the convenience of savings-account customers who wish to withdraw their money in the form of a check rather than cash. Most crafts professionals have a regular checking account at a commercial bank. However, the occasion may arise when you need to transfer a sizable sum from your savings account to your checking account to pay for a major equipment purchase. Rather than withdrawing the money and carrying cash around town from the savings bank to the commercial bank, it is safer to carry the money in the form of a cashier's check. A cashier's check can also be made out to someone else and used like any other check in payment of a bill. The only drawback is that you don't have a cancelled check as proof of payment. You do have a carbon copy of the cashier's check, but you would need to go to the bank to determine how, when, and by whom the cashier's check was cashed if that question should ever arise.

While a cashier's check and a certified check are similar in that the bank is responsible for payment in both cases, they differ in that the certified check is drawn against the depositor's own account, while the cashier's check is drawn against the bank's account. A cashier's check is often considered as reliable as a certified check.

(*See also: Banks, Certified Check, Money Order*)

39

Catalogue

A catalogue is a fairly expensive promotional device which few crafts-people can afford to produce, though groups of craftspeople have joined together successfully in a common catalogue.

Since the initial costs of preparing a catalogue, especially the photography and printing, are very high, they can be justified only if the catalogue is produced in a sizable quantity. This requires a considerable cash outlay, as well as the availability of a good list of names to whom to send the catalogue, which in turn requires quite an expense in postage. The crafts producer should be sure that the potential demand can be satisfied. The craft objects shown in the catalogue, in other words, must be capable of being produced in quantity, and the crafts producer must be willing to produce, pack, and ship in small quantities to large numbers of customers.

Some retail stores which produce their own catalogues often ask manufacturers whose work they show to share in the cost. That can be legitimate if the price is right. However, if the crafts producer has already sold the craftwork to the store at 50 percent off the retail price, then he should not also be expected to pay part of the promotion cost. If a cooperative arrangement is sought by a retailer, then a different price structure should be agreed on so that the crafts producer does not take his share of the cost out of his wholesale profit.

Catalogue sheets are another matter. These are single sheets, usually letter size (8½ x 11), three-hole punched to fit into a looseleaf book. They can be used by a sales representative or a retail store which may not be able to carry your whole line, but can sell to prospective customers by showing some samples of your work and then referring to the catalogue sheet for details on other sizes, colors, styles, or similar types of products. These would then be individually ordered from the crafts producer.

Where a retailer sells from a catalogue sheet, sends the order and the wholesale price to the crafts producer, and expects shipment to be made directly to the retailer's customer, a special price arrangement should also be made to cover the shipping and packing costs. Either the wholesale price should be somewhat higher, or there should be a basic packing/shipping charge of a dollar or two, depending on the particular type of craftwork. There should also be a minimum charge so that all the profits are not eaten up in filling orders.

This margin is covered, of course, when a crafts producer fills orders at the retail price from his own catalogues or catalogue sheets, although even here a minimum order or a packing/shipping charge is often required.

Selling through a catalogue requires three basic ingredients: 1) very explicit illustrations; 2) very explicit descriptions of the items, including colors and sizes; and 3) very explicit ordering instructions. Study some of the catalogues which you get in the mail. See how they handle the illustrations and descriptions. Note that every item generally has an identifying number to avoid misunderstandings on the order form. Note particularly how the order forms are designed to make it as easy as possible for the customer to write the order, and as easy as possible for you to understand it.

(*See also: Advertising, Direct Mail, Mail Order, Minimum Orders, Printed Materials*)

Certified Check

A certified check is as good as cash. When a check is certified it means that the bank has confirmed that the person who writes it is a depositor, and that the money has been set aside to pay that particular check. The bank is now responsible and liable for payment. The depositor has no further access to that money. There is no such thing as a bad certified check. They never bounce and cannot be stopped.

To have a check certified, you present it to the bank on which it is drawn (where the depositor's account is kept). An officer rubber stamps the certification across the face (front) of the check and adds his or her signature.

A check is normally presented for certification by the person who writes it, but it can also be done by the person who receives it, as in the case of a check which will not be cashed until some future time when the service for which it is presented has been performed.

Certified checks are often required in substantial or irrevocable transactions, such as the transfer of real estate.

(*See also: Cashier's Check, Checking Account*)

Chamber of Commerce

A chamber of commerce is a group of businesspeople and companies whose purpose it is to reflect the views of the business community.

Chambers of commerce are organized on local, state, and national levels, and occasionally even within certain industries. They are supported by dues payments from members, and engage in a variety of activities. Since they represent a diversity of business interests, one of their major functions is to bring various businesspeople together to exchange ideas and help support each other.

Some chambers of commerce have given support to artists and craftspeople by sponsoring local craft fairs. Others are involved in attracting tourists to their areas, and occasionally include listings of local craft outlets and craft activities in their literature. More would probably do so if approached by local craft artists.

Craftspeople who intend to relocate to another area of the country often find that information about business conditions, taxes, facilities, and other details from the local chamber of commerce can be very helpful in reaching a decision. In this connection it should be remembered that a chamber of commerce rarely, if ever, mentions any negative aspect of its community.

(*See also: Better Business Bureau*)

Chattel Mortgage
(*See: Mortgage*)

Checking Account

The very first thing to do after you have established your craft business is to open a checking account. Unless your operation is on an extremely small and part-time basis, a business checking account is the only safe method for keeping your business income and expenses separate from your personal income and expenses.

A check, essentially, is simply a piece of paper by which you transfer money to someone else. It represents money in your account at the bank whose check you are using. When the recipient receives it, he presents it to his bank. His bank then presents it, through channels, to your bank. Your bank withdraws the money from your account and transfers it to the recipient's account at his bank, again through channels. When all that is done your balance is adjusted, and the cancelled check is returned to you with your monthly bank statement as proof that the transaction has been completed. The check has made a full circle, starting and ending with you.

Bankers call a check a negotiable instrument, but its negotiability is very limited. Only the person or firm to whom you wrote the check is entitled to cash it or pay it over to someone else. To cash a lost or stolen check requires forgery, and that's a crime.

It is easiest to open a checking account at a bank where you are already known; perhaps where you have your personal checking account. If your account is to be opened in the name of a company rather than in your own name, you will have to furnish the bank with a *d/b/a/* (doing business as) document, which you receive from your county clerk when you register a business that is conducted under an assumed name, or with a corporate resolution if your business is incorporated.

Bank accounts cannot be opened under fictitious names unless those names are properly registered with the authorities.

Checks are valid only if they are signed by the person or persons whose signatures are on file at the bank. In a joint account, for example, both a husband and wife can have their signatures on file, and either signature can make the check valid. Business accounts for enterprises in which a number of participants are involved often make it a practice to require that each check be signed by two people to be valid. Such businesses can even place three or four signatures on file, and specify that any two of those signatures are required.

The bank will furnish deposit slips and checks, usually with the account's name imprinted. Charges vary. Some banks make no charge at all on business accounts as long as a specified minimum balance is maintained. Others charge a fee based on the average balance in the account during the month.

On so-called special checking accounts, which many people use for their personal banking affairs, a minimum balance is not required, but there is a fixed monthly fee to maintain the account, and many banks also charge 10¢ or 15¢ for each check that is written.

Shop around if you can, and find the bank that has the best arrangement based on the balance you intend to keep in your account and the number of checks you expect to write each month.

Checks come in a wide variety of sizes, shapes, designs, and colors. None of these frills affect the balance in your account when it comes time to write a check. For business checks, the only important consideration is that there be a section on the face (front) of the check in which you can indicate the invoice number or item for which the check is written. Even that isn't essential, but it helps the recipient identify the purpose of the check.

Two general precautions should be observed when writing a check:

1) Never (except in the most unusual circumstances) sign a blank check which does not yet have the recipient's name or the amount written on it. If such a check is lost or stolen, anyone can fill in the empty spaces with their own name and amount and cash it.

2) Write the check carefully so that it cannot be altered to increase the amount. Where you indicate the amount in figures, write the first figure as close to the dollar sign as possible. Where you indicate the amount in words, place a line in front of the first word so no other word can be added. On the next page is an illustration of three checks, all for the same amount. The first one (A) was written improperly, making it possible to raise the amounts (B). The last one (C) illustrates how a check should be written, leaving no blank spaces in front of the dollar figures or words, so that it cannot be altered.

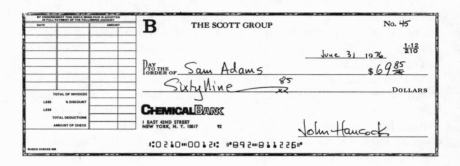

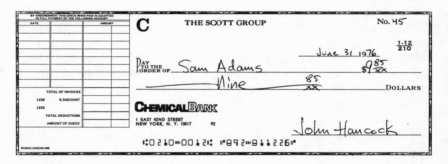

If you make an error in writing a check, tear the check up into little pieces, mark the stub "void," and start again with the next check.

Keep a running balance on your check stubs. Subtract from the balance whenever you write a check, and add to the balance whenever you make a deposit. That way you'll always know how much money you have in the bank. It takes between three and ten days for a check deposit to clear. That means that a check you receive from someone else and deposit in your bank will not actually show up on your cash balance at the bank for several days. That doesn't necessarily mean you can't write a check against it, as long as you're certain that your deposit will have cleared before the check you wrote arrives at your bank for payment. Since the recipient of the check you wrote is a few days behind you in sending his check through for clearance, it will likely arrive at your bank when your cash balance is up to expectations. But be careful if you're playing it tight. A bad check which you deposit, and which cannot be collected by the bank, can throw a monkey wrench into your calculations.

A bad check, also known as a rubber check (because it bounces), is one for which there isn't enough money in the bank account. To write such a check intentionally in order to buy something for which there's no money in the bank to pay for it can expose the writer to lawsuits.

If you write such a check by accident or because your arithmetic was off when you figured your bank balance, you will probably receive an angry telephone call from the recipient. He or she deposited the check, but it was returned marked "insufficient funds." That's embarrassing to you, but as long as your conscience is clear and you're sure that you now have enough money to cover the check, tell the recipient to redeposit it.

The only way to interrupt the payment of a check once you've sent it off is by giving your bank a stop payment order. However, this should be done only for very good reason, such as a lost or stolen check. Stopping payment for frivolous reasons or to break a contract is illegal in most states.

(*See also: Bank Statement, Cancelled Check, Cashier's Check, Cleared Check, Collection Problems, Commercial Banks, Deposit, Endorsement, Insufficient Funds, Outstanding Check, Overdrawn, Savings Banks, Stop Payment, Travelers Checks*)

Cleared Check

The procedure used by banks to transfer money among themselves based on the checks that are written by depositors is known as clearing. The term cleared check has come to mean that the process has been completed: the person to whom you wrote the check deposited it in his bank, that bank presented the check to your bank, your bank paid it from your account, and you received the cancelled check with your bank statement.

(*See also: Banks, Cancelled Check, Checking Account*)

Collateral

In financial terms, collateral is something of value that is pledged as security against the repayment of a loan. If the payments are not made, the bank (or other lender) can claim the collateral and sell it to satisfy the outstanding balance of the mortgage. In a real estate mortgage, for example, the real estate itself is the collateral.

(*See also: Loan, Mortgage*)

Collection Agencies

(*See: Collection Problems*)

Collection Problems

Making a sale is only half the problem; collecting for it can often be the other half. Don't be so anxious for the sale that you don't take proper precautions. A sale for which you don't get paid is no sale at all.

Collection problems fall into three major categories:
1) Cash sales when payment is made by check;
2) When a store changes hands or goes out of business;
3) Slow payers

Cash Sales Where Payment Is Made by Check

There's not much of a problem when you're face to face with a cash customer, as in a store or at a craft show. The only thing to be concerned with is the matter of payment by check. It would be nice if everyone in this world were honest. Unfortunately a good many checks have been known to bounce. Protect yourself by following a few simple rules:

1) Before you accept a check as payment, ask for identification that includes the person's signature. Driver's licenses and major credit cards are best. Double-check the signature. On the back of the check, mark the driver's license or credit card number, and the customer's address and telephone number. Do not accept as proof of identity such items as business cards, bankbooks, library cards, social security cards, and the like. Anyone can get these under any name and address.

2) Never cash a check for someone you don't know.

3) Accept a check for payment only if it is made out to you and in the exact amount of the sale. Don't accept a check for $20 if the sale is $15 and you have to give $5 in change.

4) Don't accept third-party checks, i.e., checks made out to someone else and endorsed to you. That only adds another element of potential trouble. You don't even know the person who wrote the check originally; it could be a stolen check.

5) Mark all checks "for deposit only" the moment you receive them. That makes it impossible for a thief to cash them. Don't wait until later. The extra few seconds you spend now to take this precaution can save a lot of grief.

None of this guarantees that a check won't bounce, but you'll at least be able to find the maker of the bad check. You'll also protect yourself from being known as an easy mark for bad checks. An ounce of prevention, in this case, is definitely worth the pound of cure which is involved in trying to collect a bad check or prosecuting the passer of such a check. And if you get stuck with a bad check, it comes out of your profit.

It can happen, even with the best of intentions, that a check is returned to you because there were insufficient funds in the maker's bank to cover it. Sometimes a deposit hasn't cleared in time to make money available to cash a check. In that event it is best to make polite contact with the customer, who will usually tell you to redeposit the check. In almost all cases the check clears the second time. If it bounces again, take legal action. Your bank won't accept a redeposit more than once.

A stop payment order is another matter. If you haven't delivered the merchandise, it may not be worth the trouble to pursue the matter. Just forget about the sale. But if the customer has the merchandise, and doesn't have a darn good reason for stopping payment, you may have to take legal action to prosecute for theft or breach of contract.

When a Store Changes Hands or Goes Out of Business
This can create situations where your original customer may no longer consider himself liable for what he owes you, or may not have the money to pay you. There are four common ways this can happen, and in times of economic distress, problems such as bankruptcy become more common.

1) *Bulk sale.* When a business with inventory is sold, the creditors (that's you) of the selling business have a continuing claim on the sold assets, even after the buyer of the business has paid for it. Very often the sales contract stipulates that the buyer takes over all assets and liabilities of the business. When that doesn't happen (and often even when it does), the creditors have to be notified.

Laws vary from state to state, but the basic requirement generally is that a ten-day notice of sale must be given to all creditors before the sale closes. This is to allow creditors to make their claims, find out when and how they will be paid, and take legal action if they are not satisfied with the terms. Prompt action is necessary.

2) *Common law composition.* This is the most flexible and least formal way for a business which owes more than it can pay to liquidate in an equitable manner, or arrange to continue in business. The debtor offers a certain proportion of the amount owed to all creditors who agree to take that amount in full payment. Since the legal costs are low, there is usually no point in rejecting such an offer if you are satisfied

that the debtor is acting honestly and no other creditors are being treated better than you are. If a check for the proposed settlement is enclosed with the notice, remember that depositing, cashing, or even just keeping the check may be considered acceptance of the plan.

3) *Assignment for benefit of creditors*. This is a more formal way of liquidating a business, but it is less formal and less expensive than bankruptcy. It is a state court proceeding in which all the assets of a business are turned over to a court-appointed assignee, who sells off the assets, usually at auction. The proceeds are distributed to the creditors in proportion to their claim after such items as taxes, the assignee's fee and other expenses have been paid. It is important to file a claim on the proper form when you receive a notice of assignment.

4) *Bankruptcy*. This is more or less like an assignment, except that the proceeding is in federal court and costs are usually higher. In a bankruptcy proceeding, if the debtor has given preferential treatment to some creditors, they can be made to return what they got so it can be divided among all the creditors. The court clerk notifies creditors of a bankruptcy; prompt filing of your claim is very important.

If you have a meaningful amount of money at stake, legal advice for your particular circumstances is a worthwhile investment.

Slow Payers

This is probably the most common collection problem. It's not serious in times of prosperity, but when the economic going gets rough, bills are often left unpaid for sixty, ninety, or more days, even by reputable firms.

The reasons are simple. If a firm is temporarily short of cash, it can go to the bank and borrow money to pay its bills. But the bank charges interest at the rates of 8 to 12 percent. When a firm leaves bills unpaid, the net effect is that it uses your money—borrows it, if you like —without paying interest.

A basic principle in money management is "the older a bill gets, the harder it is to collect." A good follow-up procedure for collecting unpaid bills is absolutely essential.

Let us assume that you have checked the customer's credit rating and found it satisfactory. (If the credit rating is poor, you can expect serious collection problems. Indeed, a poor credit rating reflects collection problems experienced by others with the same account.) Most orders specify when payment is due. To encourage customers to pay their bills quickly, it is a common practice to allow a 2 percent discount if the bill is paid within ten days. The entire amount is due within thirty days. In recent years, some firms have added a 1 or 2 percent penalty if the bill is paid later than thirty days.

Some customers, especially large stores, pay their bills once a month, regardless of when they receive them during the previous month. You will also have to allow for slow mail delivery. But if you haven't been paid thirty-five to forty-five days after you send the bill, mail a courteous reminder. Ten or fifteen days later, if you still don't have your money, another reminder should be sent, this one more insistent. In most cases, sixty days should be the outside limit for the final reminder. That one should alert (not threaten) the customer that you plan to take further action if the bill is not paid immediately. If that doesn't bring results, turn the bill over to a collection agency (see below), especially if the customer has not even had the courtesy to contact you and explain what the difficulty is.

There are always exceptions. If a customer with whom you have had good payment experience suddenly falls behind and explains that he's had a fire in his store and needs a few extra weeks to get back on his feet, it is usually wise to cooperate. But just because past experience has been good does not necessarily mean that a store can't get into trouble. Judge each situation on its own merits. If you have any real reason to worry, activate your collection effort promptly.

Follow-up. Several systems can be used for collection follow-up. First of all, every bill you write should have at least one duplicate copy. If you don't do much billing, keep the duplicate in a follow-up file and check that file every week to see who's late. Mark your copy of the bill to indicate the date you sent a follow-up. That helps you to determine when the next follow-up needs to be sent.

If you do an extensive amount of billing, it is often most economical to have bills made up in sets of four or five copies, with carbons already interleaved. Such invoice sets can be obtained, with your name, address and other information imprinted, from most good business-form suppliers, whose names you find under "Business Forms" in the telephone yellow pages. These forms also allow you to preprint the follow-up messages on the appropriate copies: "A friendly reminder that this invoice is past due" on the first reminder; "Please remit promptly on this past-due invoice" on the second reminder; and on the last one: "This invoice is more than sixty days old. We will have to turn this over for collection if we do not receive payment by return mail."

The initial cost of such forms may seem expensive, but they save untold hours of writing and typing and can be very effective in a business-like way to collect the money that is owed you.

With the preprinted bills, you simply send the appropriate follow-up on the appropriate date, without the necessity of writing individual letters. Most businesspeople also find that enclosing a reply envelope (even without a stamp) helps speed up bill payments.

Collection agencies. If all else fails, the services of a collection agency may be necessary. Collection agencies generally charge a percentage of the amount they collect; the smaller the bill, the larger the percentage. But it's worth the money if there's no way you can collect the bill on your own. Customers know that collection agencies turn their experience with bad debts over to credit bureaus, and you'd be surprised how quickly a Dun & Bradstreet sticker, for example, brings results.

Dun & Bradstreet is one of the better known collection services, with seventy offices throughout the country. As of early 1976, their annual service charge was $75. For that you receive forms and/or invoice stickers for two reminders, plus a ten-day "free demand" period. If you turn a bill over to them for collection they charge nothing extra if the bill is paid within ten days after they send a notice to the customer.

Thereafter they perform various services, such as locating the debtor, sending further demand notices and lawyers' letters if need be, for which they get a fee ranging from 15 percent of the collected amount if the bill is over $6500, to 24 percent if it is under $1000. On any bill less than $66 they charge 50 percent.

It is important to select a collection agency whose reputation is sound. Heavy-handed tactics can backfire on your own reputation. Check with other businesspeople in your area to learn what their experience has been with particular collection agencies, or if they have recommendations to make.

Collection problems that need a lawyer's service are another matter entirely, and the size of the bill has to be balanced against the size of the lawyer's fee to determine whether a court case is worth the expense.

Collectors

Collectors are a particular breed of customers, usually with money in their pockets, who specialize in acquiring certain types of objects (e.g., glass, pottery, etc.), or work by certain artists. They are most prevalent in the field of fine art (painting and sculpture), but have begun to appear in craftwork as well. They are generally reached through gallery shows and exhibitions, and almost always seek one-of-a-kind work of considerable artistic accomplishment.

(*See also: Fine Art*)

Commercial Bank

This is a bank whose main function it is to handle checking accounts, although it also performs numerous other banking functions such as lending money and renting safe-deposit boxes. While many commercial banks also offer savings account services, the interest paid on those accounts is generally lower than that offered by savings banks.

(*See also: Banks, Savings Banks*)

Commission

This word has many dictionary meanings, two of which are of interest to craftspeople:

1) The amount of money paid to a salesperson or agent, usually a percentage of the dollar value of the sale. The percentage a gallery retains on consignment sales is also called a commission. The specific percentage should be agreed on before the selling activity begins.

2) Commission is also a fancy word for order. The term does not usually apply to work that is resold, but is generally used in connection with a large work made to certain specifications, e.g., a large tapestry incorporating a company theme for display in a corporate headquarters.

Such a commission should always spell out the details in writing: how and when the customer approves the work; payment schedules (advances, etc.); completion date; installation responsibility, if any; what happens if the artist or the client dies before the work is completed; does the craft artist retain rights to the work if the customer finds it unacceptable? Most important, detailed specifications of the work itself (size, materials, design style, subject matter, etc.) should be clearly defined to avoid later controversy or, worse yet, rejection.

(*See also: Architects, Customers, Orders, Industrial Design, Selling*)

Common Carrier

Most of the craftwork you ship will move by common carrier; some orders even specify that. A common carrier is anyone, individual or company, who publicly offers to transport goods for a fee. Truck companies, bus lines, railroads, airlines are typical examples. They are usually regulated by some government agency, operate on a franchise, and are required to charge the same fee for the same service to all customers.

Common carriers have the responsibility for transporting the goods safely, speedily, and correctly, and are legally liable for most cases of loss or damage.

Local truckers with whom you make your own arrangements are called private carriers. They can charge anything the market will bear, pick and choose their customers, and their liability and responsibility is much less clearly defined.

(*See also: Freight Allowance, Shipping*)

Consignment

One of the common selling techniques in crafts—rare in most other areas of merchandising—is consignment selling. It is frowned upon, even denounced, by many craft marketing experts, yet practiced by many craftspeople.

The difference between wholesaling and consignment is essentially this: when you sell a craft object to a store, the store pays for it and it becomes the store's property. When a store takes your work on consignment, it remains your property, and you don't get paid for it until after it has been sold (if it is sold).

Among the questions raised about consignment selling are these:

1) Why should you, the craftsperson, make an investment in the store's inventory?

2) If the store doesn't have enough capital to stock its shelves, can it be a sound business operation?

3) If the store doesn't have enough confidence in your work to buy it outright, how effective or enthusiastic will be its efforts in selling your work on consignment?

4) Are you ready for a mountain of paperwork?

5) The store takes no risk. Who, for example, pays for insurance while your work is on the store's premises? What happens if your craftwork is returned to you six months later and is no longer in salable condition? This occurs frequently, and represents a total loss to you in time, labor, and material, as well as profit.

6) What happens if a store goes bankrupt? What legal hassles do you have to undergo to establish your property right to the consigned merchandise?

Although it is generally thought that retail stores prefer consignment selling because they don't have to invest their money in merchandise, many enlightened shop and gallery owners have come to consider consignment an archaic way of selling.

"It's not a feasible way of doing business for the craftsman or the shop," said David Brooks, owner of the Appalachian Spring Gallery of Washington, DC, as reported in *Craft Horizons* (February 1976; published by the American Crafts Council). "It is a fantastic bookkeeping problem to keep track of items piece by piece, and to pay on a regular basis."

Mr. Brooks deflated the notion that consignment selling saves the shop money. "The only thing you're saving," he explained, "is the cost of capital, the interest on the loan, which is nowhere the 10 to 15 percent difference in the cost of the piece that results between consignment and outright purchase." He added that retailers are more likely to push harder if their own money is invested in the craft objects they're selling.

Norbert Nelson says in *Selling Your Crafts* that "there should be almost no exceptions to the 'no consignment' dictum."

Craftspeople are tempted to participate in consignment selling because their share of the retail price is larger than it is in normal wholesaling—approximately 60 to 70 percent on consignment versus 50 percent on wholesale. That is, *if* the work is sold, and *if* you can afford to wait for the money.

Consignment may be rational for unknown young craftspeople just getting started, but even then it should be with the understanding that as soon as the worth of their work has been established, the store will buy the items on a regular wholesale basis.

However, as long as consignment is with us, take steps to protect yourself. Before entering into a consignment arrangement, it is imperative that an agreement be signed to avoid several pitfalls and misunderstandings. The following are five major points that should be included in every written consignment agreement:

1) *Description of Products.* Every time you ship goods on consignment, describe the items in detail. Don't simply sign a blanket consignment agreement which does not specify the merchandise being consigned.

2) *Term of Consignment.* Specify how long the items can remain unsold in the store's or gallery's inventory before you have a right to demand their return.

3) *Pricing.* The most common method is to establish the retail price for your work, and to spell out the percentage of that retail price which you will receive if the work is sold.

You can also agree to a specific dollar amount and let the shop set its own retail price, but that's not recommended except in unusual circumstances.

Under no circumstances should the store be allowed to reduce the price on your craftwork without your permission.

On very high priced one-of-a-kind gallery items it is sometimes useful to establish a minimum price and allow the gallery to negotiate a sales price at or above the minimum. In all instances you should get the stated percentage on the ultimate sales price, not the minimum. This kind of relationship requires a high degree of confidence in the integrity of the shop or gallery.

4) *Method of Payment.* This depends on the nature of the items. Where a relatively large number of low-priced items is involved, monthly payment for sales is logical. Immediate accounting and payment when the item is sold makes more sense for high-priced items which sell in small numbers. There are many variations on this theme. The important thing is to spell it all out in writing.

5) *Risk of Loss.* What happens if consignment items are damaged, stolen, or destroyed by fire? The consignment agreement can place this risk on the shop, but damage by fire or theft to property the shop does not own (e.g., craftwork on consignment) may not be covered by the shop's insurance policies. One of two solutions is possible:

a) Craftspeople can carry their own inventory insurance, including items out on consignment;

b) Stores and galleries can carry special insurance to cover consignment items

These are just a few of the major considerations that must be included in every consignment agreement. Two things are clear: if substantial amounts of money are involved, consult an attorney; and the integrity and solvency of the shop with which you do business is one of the most important elements of consignment selling.

(See also: Memo, Retailing, Salesmanship, Wholesaling)

CONSIGNMENT MEMORANDUM

Date _____

1) <u>Consignor</u>: John Craftsperson
      address

2) <u>Consignee</u>: Jane Merchant
      address

3) <u>Goods Consigned</u>: The articles listed below and additional articles to be listed on consignor's invoices from time to time:

Quantity	Item	Retail Price on % to Consignee	Price to Consignee

4) <u>Accountings</u>: Consignee will furnish a listing of items sold and price each month, together with a check for the purchase price. Consignor may check inventory at any time during normal business hours.

5) <u>Risk of Loss</u>: Goods lost, stolen or damaged will be treated as if sold.

6) <u>Returns</u>: Unsold goods in good condition may be returned at any time by consignee, and will be returned at consignor's request.

7) <u>Other Provisions</u>: (Insert provisions as to insurance, compliance with Uniform Commercial Code, or other special provisions which may be required).

8) <u>Signatories</u>:

_____
John Craftsperson

_____
Jane Merchant

Consumer

The consumer is the ultimate customer, the person who buys the craftwork for his or her own use and enjoyment, not for resale.

(*See also: Buyers, Commission, Customers*)

Contracts

A contract is an agreement between two or more people, enforceable by law.

Simple? Not quite! Contracts involve all kinds of ramifications, a few of which we'll discuss here. The more complicated ones we'll leave to the lawyers.

Whether you know it or not, you enter into contracts every day of the week. Every time you offer craftwork for sale and someone accepts the offer a contract exists. Every time you buy supplies, you are entering into a contract that requires one party to deliver and the other party to pay.

Your mortgage, your lease, your relations with the telephone and electric companies, employees you hire, consignment agreements, the booth you rent at a craft fair—all of these are contractual situations, and they are all enforceable in the courts.

It is important to understand that a contract, to be enforceable, must meet *all* of the following four conditions:

1) *Competence.* The parties to the contract must be competent to enter into an agreement. Children, the insane, convicted prisoners, and certain other people are not considered competent to make contracts in the legal definition of the term.

2) *Mutual agreement.* Both parties must agree on the terms of the contract. That's why there is often a great deal of negotiation before a contract is signed.

3) *Consideration.* The parties have to do something for each other. This is usually expressed in terms of money, although that's not necessary. It can be the performance of some kind of service. But there has to be some balance. A contract which is very obviously lopsided in favor of one party or the other may not meet the requirements of the law.

4) *Lawful purpose.* An agreement to do something illegal is no agreement at all. The courts won't enforce it.

Now let's look at a few cases and check them out against those four conditions:

a) You promise your cousin that you'll make a pair of cufflinks for him. Somehow you're always too busy. What can your cousin do?

b) A twelve-year-old girl admires a $25 necklace at your booth at a craft show. "Here's a $5 deposit," she says. "I'll get the rest from my mother and be back in a little while." She comes back and says her mother won't let her buy the necklace and she wants her $5 deposit back. Can you insist that she buy the necklace?

c) You want a booth at a craft show and you are offered space at $50. You send the check, but when you appear at the show there's no booth for you. Can you sue?

d) You pay the building inspector $50 to overlook the kiln you installed in violation of the zoning laws. But he's an even bigger bandit than you are. He takes the money and reports you anyway. Can you sue?

Let's examine the answers:

a) Your cousin may be sore, but he has no legal leg to stand on. There was no consideration involved, no agreement that he would pay for the cufflinks or do something for you in return. All he can do is never speak to you again.

b) A twelve-year-old has no legal standing to enter into an agreement. Better give her back the $5 and sell the necklace to someone else.

c) Here's a perfectly good contract. Both you and the show management are competent to enter into an agreement, you both agreed on the terms, it's a perfectly legal activity, and you upheld your end of the bargain. You can sue.

d) A contract to commit a crime is not enforceable. Better keep quiet about the whole deal.

A contract does not have to be in written form. Oral contracts, even contracts which are created through the actions of people, are legally enforceable. It is always better to put an agreement in writing to avoid misunderstanding. The law does require certain contracts to be made in writing: all real estate transactions, and most contracts which extend over a long period of time (more than a year) or involve large sums of money.

It is also wise to specify a starting date and a termination date under certain conditions, as in employment or consignment agreements. They can always be renewed if both parties agree.

Most ordinary, everyday contracts require no legal advice; you'd need a full-time lawyer to handle them all. But it is important that you read all the fine print conditions. When you receive an order, read it carefully, front and back, so that you understand not only what was ordered, but all the conditions that attach to the order. When you apply for a bank loan, read every clause and ask the bank officer to explain anything you don't understand. After all, their lawyer drew up the form. You have a right to read and understand what you're signing.

When you come to more complicated contracts, a lawyer's advice is absolutely essential. A real estate sale or purchase, for example, should never be undertaken without a lawyer present to protect your interests. A partnership agreement or incorporation also requires legal advice. In fact, any long-term or out-of-the-ordinary contractual relationship should be signed only after consultation with a lawyer. Expensive as legal advice is, it is a lot more economical to hire a lawyer before you sign a difficult contract than it is to hire one to sue the other party or defend you if trouble develops later.

Remember: a contract does not obligate the other party alone. It also requires you to make certain commitments. Be sure you know what those commitments are in every detail.

(*See also: Consignment, Corporation, Employees, Labor, Lawyers, Lease, Loans, Partnership, Shows and Fairs*)

Cooperatives

"A cooperative is a business formed by a group of people to obtain certain services for themselves more effectively or more economically than they can obtain them individually."

That is the nutshell definition in a booklet prepared by the Farmer Cooperative Service of the U.S. Department of Agriculture. The service has been deeply involved in helping crafts cooperatives get started, particularly in rural areas.

Most cooperatives are organized because its members have a need for centralized marketing services. But many have gone beyond that to buy supplies at quantity discounts for their members, or to develop technical assistance programs, group insurance, and other services.

While cooperatives generally are incorporated and follow established business procedures, they differ from the usual corporation in several significant ways. First of all, they are not organized for profit. Getting a return on their investment is not the major reason why people join a cooperative; providing service at cost is its basic purpose. If there is a profit at the end of the year, it is usually distributed among members according to a formula based on patronage, resource or labor participation, or some other basis.

The other major difference is that a cooperative is democratically controlled by its members. Unlike the normal corporation, in which stockholders vote according to the number of shares they own, most cooperatives operate on a basis of one vote per member. The members elect a board of directors, and employ specialists in business administration or marketing to conduct the business affairs of the cooperative.

Since most crafts cooperatives have marketing of craftwork as their primary purpose, the activity of the members is usually in the production of the craftwork. The staff specialist takes care of the marketing, purchasing, and so forth. Knowing the market conditions and what will sell, the marketing specialists often make useful design suggestions to the members of the cooperative.

Some craft retail stores are also organized on a cooperative basis. In those cases, members obligate themselves to spend a specific amount of time in the store.

The membership-fee structure of cooperatives, especially those in depressed rural areas, is very modest. Many such co-ops are launched with long-term loans and even with federal assistance under various economic development programs.

Several excellent booklets on the principle of cooperatives and how to organize them have been published by the Farmer Cooperative Service of the U.S. Department of Agriculture (500 12th Street S.W., Washington, DC 20250). Included among these are "The Cooperative Approach to Crafts" (Program Aid No. 1001); "How to Start a Co-operative" (Educational Circular #18), "Economic Development Through Cooperatives" (Program Aid No. 1088).

Copyright

A copyright is the registration of an exclusive right to make and sell copies and otherwise control literary, musical, and artistic work. Only authors and artists who created the work, or those to whom they assign their rights, can claim copyright to it.

Owning a copyright does not mean that no one else can use your work. It means that such use can be made only with your permission and whatever financial arrangements you agree on for its use.

It has been a common misconception that copyright applies only to printed material. This may trace back to the original protection written into the U.S. Constitution (Article 8, Section 1) which gave Congress the power to "promote the progress of science and useful arts by securing for limited times to authors and inventors the exclusive right to their writings and discoveries."

To this day, the language of the Copyright Office uses words like "published" and "author" to refer to all types of work and its creators, including artists and craftspeople.

A special application (Form G) is used to copyright "a work of art, or design for a work of art." These forms are available without charge from the Copyright Office, Washington, DC 20559. Each registration costs $6 and is valid for twenty-eight years, renewable once for another twenty-eight years. In 1978, the new copyright law increases the fee to $10 but replaces the two twenty-eight-year terms with a single term that runs for the artist's lifetime plus fifty years.

What is a "work of art?" Form G describes it thus: "Works of the fine arts and works of artistic craftsmanship insofar as their form but not their mechanical or utilitarian aspects are concerned. Common examples of works of art are paintings, drawings, sculpture, ceramics, artistic jewelry, original designs applied to textile and the like." This category also includes glass, embroidery, tapestries, enamels, and many other forms. The essential factor is the presence of artistic craftsmanship. The work's dollar value has nothing to do with its eligibility for copyright protection.

Such "common property" subjects as geometric designs, lettering, or coloring are generally not copyrightable. Nor are ideas, no matter how original. It is the manner in which the idea is expressed or executed, not the idea itself, which can be protected.

A copyright ultimately is only as good as your determination to take legal steps if your rights are violated. There are occasions when such action may cost you more than the damages you might collect. In almost all cases, however, it serves as a strong deterrent to theft of your creative work.

To copyright a work of art that is almost impossible to duplicate by mass production, such as a piece of fiber sculpture, for example, may not be necessary. On the other hand, an original jewelry design that could easily be turned into a machine-made pendant may very well benefit from copyright protection.

Changing the use to which your original art work is put does not change its protection if it is copyrighted. If you create a piece of art work for a pendant, and someone steals the design to make belt buckles, you are still covered. It is the artwork, not how it's used, that is protected.

The Copyright Office does not act as an attorney in any problems you may have. Nor does it research your copyright claim to determine whether someone else registered a similar copyright previously, as is done by the Patent Office for inventions. The function of the Copyright Office is to register copyright claims and to verify such registration when the need arises.

Very specific procedures have to be observed for indicating copyright ownership on the work itself, and for registering the claim with the Copyright Office. (*Note: The new copyright law enacted in late 1976 changes some of the following requirements. See last paragraph in this section.*)

Normally, copyright protection goes into effect upon "publication," i.e., when the work is placed on sale or otherwise offered for public distribution. In the case of works of art which are registered on Form G, there are two methods for claiming copyright.

For "unpublished works of art," i.e. the original and perhaps a few sample copies, a photograph or other identifying reproduction of the work must be submitted with Form G and $6. If the work is later "published" (copies are reproduced in quantity), it is necessary to make a second registration, again with $6.

To secure copyright in a "published work of art" you must:

1) Produce copies with copyright notice as explained below;
2) Publish (make copies) of the work;
3) Register the copyright claim

In order to secure and maintain copyright protection, it is essential that all copies contain the statutory copyright notice. This ordinarily consists of the word "copyright," the abbreviation "copr.," or the symbol ©, accompanied by the name of the copyright owner. The year date of publication may be included, but it is not usually required.

Normally, then, the copyright notice would appear as follows: © John Doe 1977.

A special form of notice is permissible for works of art. This special notice may consist of the symbol ©, accompanied by the initials, monogram, mark, or symbol of the copyright owner, if the owner's name appears on some accessible portion of the copies. Detachable tags bearing copyright notice are not acceptable as substitutes for a notice permanently affixed to the copies.

The copyright notice is not required on unpublished works, but it is advisable to affix such notice to any registered work that leaves your control, to avoid inadvertent publication.

There is no provision for securing blanket copyright on all your work. Each work must be copyrighted separately.

Copyright Form G ordinarily requires that two copies of the work accompany the application. Exceptions are made when it is impractical to deposit actual copies because of size, weight, fragility, or monetary value. In such cases, photographs or other reproductions may be acceptable. Consult the Copyright Office before submitting registrations in this manner.

If you print a catalog or advertisement in which the copyrighted piece is illustrated, but in which the copyright notice is not clearly visible, it is advisable to print a small notice to readers that the work is registered with the U.S. Copyright Office on Form G, Work of Art.

If you want to retain copyright in your name when you sell a major one-of-a-kind work, it is advisable to specify in the sales contract that copyright transfer is *not* included. That will avoid any misunderstanding regarding the purchaser's right to have the work reproduced without your agreement.

As this book went to the printer, the U.S. Congress enacted a new copyright law, the first substantial change in copyright legislation since 1909. The law's effective date is January 1, 1978. One provision raises the fee from $6 to $10, but replaces the two twenty-eight-year terms with a single term that runs for the artist's lifetime plus fifty years. Another provision changes the manner in which the copyright notice must be indicated on the work. After enactment of the new law in late 1976, the Copyright Office began formulating explanations of its various requirements in non-legal language. Readers are advised to write the Copyright Office, Washington, DC 20559 for information about requirements that apply to work being copyrighted after January 1, 1978.

(See also: Patent, Trademark)

Corporation

Incorporation provides the only sound protection against personal liability for business debts. In the eyes of the law, a corporation is a person, and its shareholders are not individually liable for the corporation's debts.

A corporation can have any number of shareholders. If there is more than one shareholder, there should be a shareholder's agreement which defines what each gives to the business and what each gets from the business. If some of the shareholders are employees of the business and others are not, the agreement should also spell out the specific employment arrangements, compensation, etc.

A certificate of incorporation (called a charter in some states) must be filed with the secretary of state in the state where the business is located. Costs for such filings range from $14 in Oklahoma (the cheapest) to $60 minimum in New York (moderate) and $288 in California (one of the highest). In addition there are annual fees, taxes, and reports to be filed. All this involves legal and accounting expenses.

(See also: Joint Venture, Partnership, Sole Proprietorship)

Cost Accounting

While simple accounting concerns itself with the accurate recording and interpretation of the financial activities of a business or individual, cost accounting analyzes those records in terms of the various costs involved in the production and distribution of goods and services.

Most craftspeople engage in some form of elementary cost accounting every time they determine the price to be charged for a particular craft item. You may not call it that, but whenever you take pencil in hand to break down the cost of raw materials, time, and overhead invested in an item you are, in effect, engaged in cost accounting. When an accountant does that for you, it becomes much more sophisticated and serves to pinpoint problems of which you may hardly be aware.

Cost accounting won't tell you how to solve problems, but what problems need solving. Why, for example, did it cost 10 percent more in September to produce a dozen pots than it did in May? Are you in a rut with your present supplier, who keeps raising prices? Perhaps you should go shopping. Or do you spend more time on sweeping and packing than on productive work? Maybe you should hire a part-time helper.

Cost accounting is also helpful in avoiding errors in pricing and in determining your real costs. For example, suppose you have determined that your annual sales costs are $1,000. The simplest way to apply that cost is to break it down by the week ($20) or even by the hour (50¢) and apply that figure to the work you produce that hour or that week. Let us further assume that you have a regular customer for whom you produce $200 worth of items a month all year long. You made that sale once, you spent $100 to do it, and have hardly any further sales costs for the $2,400 you're going to produce this year. On the other hand, you go to a craft show, spend $100 on booth space, transportation, meals, etc., and sell $600 worth of craftwork. Proper cost accounting would obviously apportion a larger sales cost to the show than to the one good customer. Averaging the sales cost would not be a true reflection of your real costs in this example, even though the totals come out the same at the end of the year.

While raw materials and labor are usually simple to apportion to a specific item, expenses for supplies, equipment, selling, and overhead are not. And that's where your profit can disappear down the drain. A good cost accounting system helps you to determine what steps must be taken to improve performance and reduce expenses.

Your profitability, in the final analysis, depends on only two factors: increasing production and sales, and controlling costs. And the only way to control costs is to know precisely what the costs are and how they are incurred.

Having a professional do the cost accounting may be a luxury in a small crafts business where the owner does all the work. But the greater and more varied the activities of the business, the more necessary it becomes to analyze the specific cost ingredients of everything that is produced.

(*See also: Accounting, Balance Sheet, Pricing, Profit and Loss Statement*)

Costing

(*See: Pricing*)

Cottage Industry

The cottage industry system of craft production, which is fairly prevalent in depressed rural communities of the United States such as the Appalachian region, is based on a central marketing and management operation, with production of craftwork at home. Some cottage industries are organized as cooperatives or associations in which the members have a voice and share in the profits; others are private enterprises.

The central office generally specifies what is to be produced, sets the quality standards and furnishes the models or samples as well as the material. The finished work is paid for on a piece basis and sold by the central management.

A number of cottage industries have recently come under the scrutiny of the U.S. Labor Department to determine whether the craftworkers are employees, independent contractors, or truly members of a cooperative association.

(*See also: Cooperatives, Employees*)

Credit

This word, in all its meanings, traces back to the Latin root *credito*,
m

ibility to borrow money based on the lender's belief that
t⎮ repaid.
ibility to purchase goods without cash on the seller's be-
l⎮ will be paid.
⎮re issued to people considered reliable enough to pay
t⎮ ⎮nd of the month.
⎮ as good credit. It means that the lender or seller be-
l⎮ ⎮wer or customer to be honest, trustworthy, reputable.
⎮ns that the lender or seller doesn't think much of the
⎮⎮ or reliability to repay.
⎮r credit line means that money can be withdrawn from
⎮⎮rchases can be made, up to a certain amount. An adap-
⎮nciple is revolving credit, very common in department
⎮unts and with credit cards, where a maximum credit line
⎮d the balance of available credit changes as purchases
⎮e made.
⎮ considered a valuable asset in business as well as per-

⎮ an accountant's definition: it means that an asset or a
⎮ists somewhere else in your name. For example, if you
⎮ur supplier's bill, you have a credit (the amount of the
⎮th that supplier. Accounts receivable can be considered

a credit. In fact, any asset which has not been collected is in reality a credit.

Similarly, some of your liabilities, such as bills that have not been paid, represent someone else's credit on your books.

(*See also: Credit Card, Credit Reference, Revolving Credit, Trade Credit*)

Credit Card

A credit card, or charge card, has been called "plastic money" because it allows the user to buy goods and services without paying cash. Almost anything, from a pair of slippers to a world cruise, can be charged on a credit card. For millions of credit card holders it is an easy and convenient way to shop. It is not, however, without its problems.

The most widely used credit cards are those issued by banks, such as BankAmericard and Master Charge, which are honored at thousands of stores and other business enterprises. Other cards, such as American Express, Diners' Club, and Carte Blanche, cover primarily travel, hotel, restaurant, and entertainment expenses. Still others, such as gasoline and department store credit cards, are even more limited, being honored at only the issuing stores or gas stations selling a particular brand of gasoline.

A bank credit card is relatively easy to obtain through a local bank, usually the one at which you do your other banking business. The bank will make a quick credit check and place a top limit on the credit available on purchases with the card. There is rarely a fee for a bank credit card. The bank makes its money in two ways: 1) by charging the merchant a percentage of each credit card sales slip, and 2) by charging the credit card holder interest on the unpaid balance.

Department store and gasoline credit cards also do not charge customers for having the card, but benefit from it by bringing repeat business to their establishments, as well as earning high interest on unpaid balances.

A few cards, such as the American Express card, charge cardholders an annual fee and expect full payment of the outstanding balance each month, unless specific arrangements for three-, six-, or twelve-month credit is arranged on major purchases such as airline tickets.

The procedure for buying with a credit card is simple. The cardholder presents the card to the store when the purchase is made. The card is then run through a machine which imprints the card's name, number, and expiration date on the charge slip. Your signature on the charge slip is your commitment to pay the bill.

The charge slip comes in three parts: one goes to the customer, one is kept by the merchant, and one is submitted to the bank or credit card company, which pays the merchant and collects from the cardholder on a monthly bill.

When the cardholder gets the bill, it will show all the purchases made during the preceding month, plus any outstanding balance from the previous month. Some companies enclose copies of the original charge slip which the cardholder has signed; if not, it is especially important that the cardholder keep his or her copies of all charge slips.

On many credit card bills a minimum payment amount will appear next to the total amount due. This is generally in the neighborhood of 10 percent of the total. The cardholder has a choice—to pay the total amount and clear the decks, or pay the minimum amount or any amount higher than that, and pay interest on the unpaid balance.

The unpaid balance is, in effect, borrowed money, and the interest rates are very high, ranging from 1 to 1½ percent per month, an annual rate of 12 to 18 percent. The interest rates vary according to state law and the amount of the unpaid balance. A common practice, for example, is to charge an effective annual rate of 18 percent on the first $500 of unpaid balance, and 12 percent on anything above that.

This annual interest should be taken into account when paying a credit card bill. Unless the credit card is used only when necessary and bills are paid promptly, the final cost may outweigh the card's convenience. It is certainly more economical to borrow the money at a lower interest rate, or take it out of the bank account to pay a credit card bill in full, than to run up high interest payments.

But even these percentages do not tell the whole story. The amount of money on which you pay interest is computed in various ways by different banks. Remember that cards such as Master Charge and Bank-Americard are issued by individual banks, each of which set their own policies. Thus you should read the fine print to see how the interest is computed. There are four basic methods: adjusted balance, previous balance, average daily balance excluding current transactions, and average daily balance including current transactions. Without going into extensive arithmetic, it is not at all uncommon for the actual interest charges (in dollars and cents) to be twice as high under the average daily balance including current transactions method than under the adjusted balance method, even though the *rate* of interest is the same.

Since you are not required to have a credit card at the same bank where you do your other business, it pays to look for a bank card which bills under the adjusted balance method. This is particularly important if you pay off your total monthly balance each month. Under the adjusted balance method, you are, in effect, getting an interest-free loan for the entire period from the time the purchase is made until the payment is due, which can be more than sixty days.

Credit card purchases need not be made in person. The cardholder can furnish the number and expiration date, and the merchant fills out the form and signs it with his name plus the initials MO (mail order) or TO (telephone order). One copy is sent to the customer, one to the credit card company, and the merchant's copy is attached to the original order which serves as authorization in place of the customer's signature on the charge slip.

Credit cards can also be used for actual cash borrowing. Some banks will make cash advances on presentation of a credit card, and others will, in addition, automatically cover any overdraw on a checking account (up to a set limit) by charging it to the credit card. Cash advances begin to accrue interest from the moment they are made; there is no interest-free grace period as with purchases.

The American Express card entitles holders to go to any American Express office, write their own check for up to $500, of which $100 can be for cash and $400 for traveler's checks. Credit cards are also often accepted as identification if you want to write a check for a purchase at a store which is not a credit card merchant.

Now let's look at it from the other side of the fence. The following is the procedure if you have been authorized by a bank or credit card company to accept credit card payments for craftwork you sell. You deposit your copy of the charge slip exactly as you would deposit your checks, except that a special deposit slip is provided. The bank immediately credits your account, even though it has not yet collected from the charge customer. That's why you often have to maintain a minimum balance, so the bank can charge your account in case it cannot collect from the customer.

The fee the credit card company, bank or otherwise, charges merchants ranges generally between 5 and 10 percent of the charge slips. The amount depends on the size of each credit card sale and the total volume of credit card sales you make. Once a month your account will be debited with the service charge.

The procedures vary among different credit card companies, but the basic principle is the same. The credit card merchant is also provided with the card imprinting machine, as well as decals to put on his front door.

The most important concern for a craftsperson who makes credit card sales is to be sure the card is valid. The customer's signature on the back of the card should be compared with the signature on the charge slip. The expiration date should also be noted. If the effective date has expired, the cardholder is no longer entitled to use the card, and if a sale is made under those circumstances the credit card company cannot collect and will charge the merchant's account.

Some credit card companies require that sales in excess of a certain amount, $50 for example, must be checked by phone with the credit card's central office before the sale is made. It is always advisable, even where this is not required, to check the card number against the list of lost or stolen credit card numbers which the card companies furnish periodically. Some even give an award for picking up such cards. Of course, a sale should never be made on a credit card if the number shows up on that list.

For the same reason, lost or stolen cards should be reported immediately by the cardholder. If the loss or theft of a card is not reported promptly, the cardholder may be held responsible for purchases made by others.

(*See also: Credit, Loans, Revolving Credit*)

Creditor

A creditor is anyone to whom you owe money and who has a legal claim to payment. It may be a bank which has made a loan, a supplier who has shipped raw material, an employee who has worked in expectation of being paid, or the government which wants to collect taxes.

If someone owes you money, you are that person's creditor.

Creditors come in all shapes and sizes, which is important only when the debtor (the one who owes the money) runs into trouble. That's why banks occasionally require collateral or a cosigner. The bank then becomes a "secured creditor" because its interests are secured by something more than your promise to pay. If you've borrowed to buy a car, for example, it can repossess your car and sell it to satisfy the rest of your loan.

In cases of failure to pay, the law provides for several types of creditors. A first mortgage, for instance, has prior claim over a second mortgage. That's why the interest on a second mortgage is generally higher; the lender takes more of a risk.

In bankruptcy proceedings, the government's claim on unpaid taxes normally take precedence over all other claims. Employee claims on wages usually come next.

(*See also: Credit*)

Credit Reference

Most of us like to get paid when we send a bill. But when we have a new customer we don't know, how can we be sure we'll get paid? Conducting a credit check is a very important precaution when a new customer such as a store or gallery wants to buy your work without paying cash. Getting credit information up front can avoid a lot of collection problems later on. This isn't considered offensive by stores. After all, they conduct their own credit checks when their customers apply for credit.

If you know the customer well, either personally or by reputation, it isn't generally necessary to run a credit check. Sears Roebuck or Macy's, for example, have been around a long time. In other cases, however, there are many ways to find out how reliably the prospective customer pays his bills, especially if the order is large.

There are numerous local credit bureaus and national credit rating organizations such as Dun & Bradstreet, but they require you to be a member, and that can be expensive for a small crafts business with only occasional need for credit checks.

Your bank can be helpful. It has access to numerous sources of credit references. But don't abuse the privilege. Use it only if you have a prospective account on which you need a very detailed and careful credit check.

The most direct way to get some idea of a prospective customer's credit rating is to ask him for references; generally one bank reference and three trade references (other firms from whom he's bought). While none of these will give you specific financial information, just as you wouldn't want them to give information like that to others about you, they will usually cooperate by telling you what their experience has been, how reliable the customer is, how long they've had business relations, and whether he is considered a good credit risk. Suppliers are willing to cooperate because they expect such cooperation in return when they run a credit check on a new customer.

To get such information just write a simple and courteous letter to the references, tell them the name of the customer who has referred you to them, and request that they advise what their credit experience with him has been. Enclose a self-addressed stamped envelope for their convenience in responding to your request.

If you have doubts about the credit risk after having made these inquiries, it is a perfectly acceptable business practice to ask for payment on the first order, with future orders to be billed. If it's any easier for you, tell them your accountant insists on it. Anyone who refuses such a request may well turn out to be a deadbeat anyway.

True, you may be taking a chance on losing a customer, but the other way you're taking a much bigger chance. A customer who doesn't pay his bills is a customer you could do without.

(*See also: Collection Problems, Credit*)

Customer

Anyone who buys something from someone else is a customer. For craftspeople there are basically two types of customers: the retail customer, who is the ultimate consumer or owner, and the wholesale customer, the store buyer or gallery who buys in order to resell to the ultimate consumer.

Most craftspeople sell to both types of customers. While the retail customer may bring a high profit per unit, the wholesale customer orders more merchandise and thereby can increase the craftperson's total profit even though the profit per unit is smaller.

A mix of the two approaches is the most common. Even craftspeople who do the bulk of their selling on a wholesale basis to retail stores attend a number of craft shows and fairs where they sell at retail prices to the ultimate consumer.

Another group of customers, less common in terms of total sales but very important to some craftspeople, are architects, interior designers, corporations, and the like, who buy craftwork created to particular specifications.

The prices and discounts vary according to the nature of the sale. Wholesale customers almost always buy at 50 percent off the retail price; interior decorators normally buy at 10 to 30 percent off the retail price. Architects buy at the full price since the work they order is one-of-a-kind and the price is negotiated after all the specifications have been examined. Consignment sales are usually paid for at 60 to 66 percent of the retail price, after the work has been sold. These are the most prevalent conditions; there are always exceptions.

(*See also: Architects, Buyers, Commission, Consignment, Orders, Retailing, Selling, Shows and Fairs, Wholesaling*)

Customs

All the suggestions, hints, and regulations outlined in "Packing" and "Shipping" sections apply to export shipments as well—and then some. That's especially true of ocean shipments, where rough seas and salty air may perform their special magic on tender craftwork.

In addition, there are all the import regulations of all the various countries.

The simplest way to ship small packages worth less than $50 out of the United States is via mail. No export declaration is needed. The Post Office supplies the customs declaration (form 2966), the international parcel post sticker (form 2933), and a dispatch note (form 2972), all of which you fill out and attach to the outside of the package.

For other shipments, the paperwork gets more complicated. There is, of course, the bill of lading and a packing list, which the recipient at the other end needs to claim the shipment and sometimes for customs inspection. A consular invoice and certificates of origin are also needed. These differ from country to country.

An export declaration has to be filed with the collector of customs at the point where the shipment leaves the United States. If the object being shipped will ultimately be returned to the United States—a craftwork on loan to a museum, for example—the details should be noted carefully on the export declaration so that no trouble develops in getting the item back into the country duty free.

Customs works in two directions, import as well as export. If you are the recipient of a shipment from another country, you will have to clear it through customs. It is necessary to have the bill of lading, invoices, and other documents to bring the shipment into the United States.

This is all a very specialized kind of activity, and most people who only occasionally do this sort of thing find that the services of a specialist are worth his fee in the time and aggravation you save. Freight forwarders who specialize in overseas shipments can handle the whole export operation. To clear an incoming shipment through customs, a custom house broker is often the most knowledgeable expert to call. These specialists are listed in the telephone yellow pages. Freight forwarders can be found in most major cities. Custom house brokers are most likely to be found in cities which have major ports and international air terminals.

For specific information about specific problems, the U.S. Customs Service can be consulted. The service maintains offices at every point of entry into the United States: border crossings, international air terminals, ports, and other locations. Their telephone number can be found in the white pages under U.S. Government, Treasury Department, Customs Service. Or you can write to the U.S. Customs Service at 1301 Constitution Avenue, N.W., Washington DC 20229.

(*See also: Shipping*)

Damage Insurance

(*See: Property Insurance*)

Debts, Bad

There comes a time in every business when a customer simply doesn't pay a bill. No matter how many reminders you send, how many phone calls you make, the bill remains unpaid. When economic times are difficult, the problem increases. Customers go bankrupt. Stores go out of business. The trouble and expense of having a collection agency go after the account is rarely worth the effort in the crafts field if the uncollected amount is fairly small. But even if you use a collection agency, the day arrives—at least six months but not more than a year later—when you have to decide that it's a lost cause. At that point it becomes a "bad debt."

Accountants make provision for bad debts on your books because they're tax deductible. The provision is based on estimates of prior experience in your business. Bad debts should not exceed 1 percent of your accounts receivable (the bills your customers haven't paid). If they are higher than that, it's time to examine how you extend credit and how carefully you investigate credit references before you bill a customer.

(*See also: Collection Problems, Credit, Credit Reference*)

Deductions

(*See: Accounting, Expenses, Income Tax, Overhead, Sales Cost, Shows and Fairs*)

Deficit

When liabilities exceed assets, or expenses exceed income, the difference is known as a deficit. A deficit, in effect, is a shortage of money, as opposed to a profit, a surplus of money. A brand-new craft business often runs at a deficit in the beginning. In the long run this is something to be dearly avoided.

The word deficit is also used to describe any other shortage. If your books show fifty pieces of an item in inventory, but there are only forty-eight, your inventory shows a deficit.

(*See also: Profit, Surplus*)

Delivery Charges

(*See: Post Office, Shipping, United Parcel Service*)

Delivery Methods

(*See: Shipping*)

Deposit

This word has two meanings in the business world:

1) Making a partial payment in order to reserve the merchandise for purchase at a future time.

2) Putting money in the bank, either by cash or check.

There are two major types of bank deposits: demand and time. A demand deposit is one where you can get your money out any time you want it, as in a checking account. A time deposit is one where the bank reserves the right to require notice that you want to withdraw the money. Savings accounts, for example, are time deposits because most savings banks reserve the right, though they rarely use it, to be given thirty days' notice of withdrawal.

(*See also: Banks*)

Depreciation

When you make a major capital investment, such as buying a building or a piece of equipment, the assumption is that it will last a number of years. These costs are, obviously, part of doing business and must be reflected in your costs. However, it is not realistic (nor do the tax laws permit it) to apply the total cost of such investments in one year. After all, you'll be working in that building and on that equipment next year too, and the year after that.

Depreciation is the method that is used to determine how much you can deduct from your taxes as a business expense each year. Every fixed asset is given an estimated life expectancy by which time it is likely to be worn out and obsolete. A building, for example, might reasonably be expected to last forty years. A car might last four, and a particular piece of equipment ten. The total cost of the investment is spread out for tax purposes over its estimated life expectancy.

Two methods of calculating depreciation are most commonly used:

1) *Straight Line.* The total cost is divided into equal parts over the expected number of years the item will last. If a kiln costs $600 and is expected to last ten years, it will be depreciated by $60 every year. After one year, then, the kiln has a book value of $540, after two years $480, until at last, ten years later, it theoretically has no further value at all.

2) *Declining Balance.* The value of the item is redced by a specified percentage each year. If the amount is, for example, 10 percent of the balance each year, then the $600 kiln would be depreciated $60 the first year (to $540), $54 the second year (to $486), $48.60 the third year, and so on.

When a fixed asset has both a business use and a personal use—a building which houses both your home and your shop, or a car which is used for family as well as business purposes—only that portion of the depreciation which applies to the business purpose can be deducted as a business expense.

Depreciation not only helps you calculate your cost of doing business more accurately, but also establishes the value of your fixed assets at any given time.

(*See also: Accounting, Equipment, Taxes*)

Design

Everyone knows that design is an integral part of the creative process. But to ignore design as an integral part of the marketing process as well is to proceed into troubled waters at one's own peril.

Design for the sake of design, no matter how imaginative or innovative, may be fine for artists who are already so well established that they can sell whatever they produce, or for artists who are independently wealthy (or don't care much about eating regularly). The rest of us have to consider design not only from the creative viewpoint, but also from the viewpoint of whether it will sell.

This does not mean we have to lower our standards or compromise our good taste. But the marketing process always involves at least two parties, buyers and sellers. While we can influence our customers, we cannot dictate to them. Furthermore, taste and fashion change constantly. What a craft artist designs must be in tune with the times and the mood of the marketplace, or else it won't sell.

This is most evident in fashion design, but applies in one degree or another to craftwork as well. Fashion designers influence customers, but the disaster of the maxi-skirt proves that customers will not take dictation if it contradicts their own sense of fashion.

The esthetics of good design won't be argued here; it's a subject which has occupied eminent artists and thinkers for centuries, and will probably continue to occupy them until the last moment of eternity. Good design, after all, like good books or good music, is in the eye of the beholder. The concern of craft producers is to design work which will be viewed with appreciation by the customer. Complaining about the customer's taste may give our ego some satisfaction, but it won't put bread on the table. Craft artists can lead customers into an appreciation of their design, but they can't drag them.

The sources for design ideas exist everywhere at all times. The inspiration can come from popular magazines or scholarly journals. It can come from the daily newspaper (both the fashion pages and the front pages), or the current rage on television. Ecology and peace both inspired craft objects that combined excellence of design with popularity of appeal. If the fashion pages indicate that elegance is back in style, the successful craft artist in jewelry will design earrings and necklaces that complement the current fashion.

Again, none of this requires a compromise in creative standards, only a recognition that design talent must be effectively translated into salable craftwork. The truly great designers are those who discern the mood of the marketplace and have the talent to interpret this mood into innovative and tastefully designed craftwork.

(See also: Marketability)

Design Patents
(See: Patents)

Direct Mail

This is a method of advertising which uses the mails to reach the public, rather than using such media as newspapers, magazines, radio, or television.

The advantage of direct mail is that prospective customers can be identified with much greater certainty by using selective mailing lists. The disadvantage is its relatively high cost. Catalogues, mail order promotions, invitations to shows and sales are all forms of direct mail.

(*See also: Advertising, Catalogs, Mailing Lists, Mail Order, Post Office, Printed Materials*)

Disability Income Insurance

In the event of a serious illness or accident, a major economic disaster can befall an individual craftsperson who is not eligible for unemployment benefits and has no source of income other than his or her labor. While medical and hospital insurance may cover the cost of treatment, the loss of income is not covered.

A craftsperson who has partners or employees in a successful enterprise may continue to receive income even while disabled, but lacking that, disability income insurance can be a wise investment.

It allows you to choose a specific weekly or monthly income for the duration of the disability or for a specified period of time. Premiums are based on the type and amount of coverage requested. Savings in premiums can be effected with a deductible clause, which provides that no benefits are paid during the first week or month of a disability. Most people can make it through a short disability, and the savings are worth the deductible.

Disability income insurance generally cannot be bought in excess of normal income, or it would become more profitable to be sick than to work.

(*See also: Insurance*)

Discounts

A discount is a legitimate reduction in price, based on some stated reason, and deducted before payment is made.

A common discount encountered by craftspeople is the 2 percent discount allowed when the invoice is paid within ten days. That's known as a cash discount and is usually stated as 2/10 on the invoice. It means that an invoice for $100, for example, is paid in full if you send a check for $98 within ten days.

When the shoe is on the other foot, and the craftsperson is the supplier, it is often necessary to extend similar terms, especially to wholesale buyers such as department stores. But be careful. Some customers try to take the 2 percent discount even when they don't pay the invoice within ten days. Bill them for the difference. The whole purpose of the cash discount is to bring in the money quickly. It's cheaper to allow a customer a 2 percent discount than to borrow from a bank at 10 percent (or more) when you need the cash because your money is tied up in goods that have been sold but not paid for.

Another common practice is the quantity discount. That applies to the price if the purchase exceeds a certain minimum, e.g., 100 pounds of clay may be 10 percent less per pound than ten pounds of clay.

A trade discount is a reduction from the normal retail price when the merchandise is sold to someone in the trade, e.g., a crafts professional can often buy materials at a craft supply store at a lower price than a hobbyist can.

The word discount has taken on another, somewhat unsavory, meaning in recent years, namely any reduction in price, as in discount stores. But those are not discounts in the true sense of the word, since they are not based on some stated reason or qualification. That version of the word is simply a substitute for price-cutting.

(See also: Sales Conditions)

Display

"All the world's a stage," Shakespeare said, and we can easily apply this observation to craft displays. The display, after all, is the stage upon which your craftwork acts its part, either to delight or to bore its audience (your customers).

The first rule of thumb is to keep the stage as uncluttered as possible so that you can see the actors. It is not necessary to put everything you brought to a craft fair, or everything you have in a store, out on the table or in the window at the same time. A good display will show enough to demonstrate the range of work available and allow the customer to browse, but not so much that the customer gets confused and can focus on nothing.

The second rule of thumb is to create displays that are consistent with the type of product being shown. Fine filigree silver earrings show up better on black velvet than on raw pine. Rough-hewn pots, on the other hand, can do very well on unpainted shelving but would look foolish on black velvet.

Lighting and color are important ingredients of good display. Neutral colors for table coverings and backdrops are normally most effective to show craftwork, especially when the object itself is colorful. Wild, colorful patterns generally conflict with the colors of the craftwork. But like all the other rules, this one is not inflexible. Macramé, for example, can be displayed very effectively against a brilliant green or red background.

As for lights, there's little to be done about this at an outdoor show. The sun will do the job, and there's rarely electricity available anyway. Indoors, it is not always safe to rely on overhead lighting. How much light you need is dictated by the type of work you show. A display case of fine jewelry, for example, should be very well lighted so that the objects sparkle. The light can be built right into the case, or provided through an overhead spotlight.

While an 8-foot folding table is probably the craftperson's most commonly used display unit, more and more exhibitors have developed display units which are easily assembled and disassembled, with pieces small enough to fit into a car or van. Such units not only help to display the craftwork properly under a variety of circumstances, but also make the display stand out from among all the rest of the craftspeople sitting behind their tables.

These units need not be elaborate or expensive productions. A dozen pieces of lightly stained two-by-fours with predrilled holes can easily be assembled with nuts and bolts into a striking three-dimensional display for hanging ceramic planters. Or several wooden boxes of predetermined size and shape can be stacked upside down in various arrangements to display craftwork on several levels. The same boxes can be used to transport the craftwork to the show, thus serving a double purpose.

An excellent illustrated section on designing such display units is included in George and Nancy Wettlaufer's *The Craftsman's Survival Manual* (see entry *Books*). They describe, for example, how they adapted a child's swing set to create a dramatic display unit for their pottery.

Although many craft-show managers provide signs for their exhibitors, more and more craftspeople find that their own signs, using distinctive approaches, color schemes, or logotypes, provide much better identification and recognition value. Often such signs become an integral part of a display unit, or are fashioned in the medium of the exhibitor's craft, e.g., a woven or wooden sign.

As designers, many craftspeople can undoubtedly find numerous good ideas by studying the display methods and devices used in department stores, museums, and at craft shows they visit.

It may seem elementary, but neatness and cleanliness count wherever craftwork is shown. The work into which you have poured so much of your time and talent deserves better than a flea market atmosphere. A craft artist who shows so little respect for his own work as to display it in a messy or shopworn setting can hardly expect a prospective customer to respect its quality or value. The very nature of craftwork demands that it be displayed in an attractive setting. As designers of beautiful things, we deny our own talents when we offer our work to the public in less-than-beautiful surroundings.

(*See also: Shows and Fairs*)

Distributors

(*See: Sales Representatives*)

Dividend

In the literal sense, the dividing of profits. The most common dividends are those paid on the basis of stock ownership, insurance policies, and other investments. A dividend is the investor's share of the profits in proportion to the size of his investment. Dividends are generally paid on a regular basis: annually on insurance policies, quarterly on many stocks, though the size of the dividends may vary from period to period according to the profits of the company. Dividends must be declared as income for tax purposes.

Double Entry

A bookkeeping and accounting method by which every transaction is recorded twice. This is based on the premise that every coin has two sides —a sale, for example, is both a delivery of goods and a receipt of payment. The delivery of goods would be recorded as a debit (it reduces your inventory), while the payment would be counted as a credit (it increases your bank balance). The two halves of double entry always have to be equal. This procedure is rarely used in small enterprises such as most craft businesses.

(*See also: Bookkeeping, Single Entry*)

Education

Since it is generally agreed that talent cannot be created, only developed or refined, the education of a craft artist is a lifelong process.

Most practicing craftspeople get their first taste of making beautiful things by hand when they are very young. Almost all children draw and paint and work with clay or yarn. That's part of the fun of growing up. Most turn to other interests as they get older. Many continue to find enjoyment and develop their skills as hobbyists. And some turn their skills into earning a livelihood, or at least a part-time vocation.

The traditional method of learning a craft through apprenticeship to a master craftsman dates back hundreds of years, and is still very much in use, even in highly industrialized countries of Europe. It is not common in the United States or Canada.

Formal education in craft art is a fairly recent development. Many colleges and universities today offer craft courses, sometimes leading up to master of fine arts degrees, particularly in ceramics. A formal education, however, does not automatically create a fine craft artist. It may help in developing an understanding of design and an appreciation of the history of the medium. And a degree is usually required for school or college teaching.

More and more craftspeople, students and educators are coming to the conclusion that some combination of formal education and apprenticeship is a desirable goal.

An extensive list of educational institutions and the craft courses in their curriculum is included in *Contemporary Crafts Marketplace*, compiled by the American Crafts Council and available for $13.95 (plus 40¢ postage) from Bowker Publishing Co., PO Box 1807, Ann Arbor, MI 49481. This book is also available in many libraries.

Travel is another excellent educational experience at any level of a craft artist's development, especially for those whose work has its roots in some specific geographic or ethnic environment. This is particularly true of the traditional crafts such as weaving, pottery, and silversmithing; these can be seen within comparatively easy travel distance in the Western Hemisphere in such places as New Mexico, Appalachia, Guatemala, or Mexico, as well as Europe, Asia, and Africa.

An immense body of literature is available to craftspeople who want to continue their education, both in the form of books and professional craft publications. These provide technical knowledge, new methods and processes, and design inspiration.

The plethora of workshops which are conducted all over the country provide an important means of continuing education. Most of these are one- or two-day affairs, some run for several weeks during the summer. They offer a face-to-face opportunity for craftspeople to meet and study with outstanding artists in their particular medium, and to exchange opinions and experiences with other craftspeople. Workshops are generally conducted by craft guilds or associations, and by established educational institutions. A careful reading of publications like *Craft Horizons* or *The Crafts Report* provides a fairly thorough listing of upcoming workshops and seminars.

A major lack in the education of working craftspeople, which is currently in the early stages of solution, is the scarcity of business education. Several universities, notably the Boston University Program in Artisanry, have recently begun to incorporate classes on business subjects of special concern to craftspeople into their curriculum. Workshops have begun to appear here and there at which experts discuss such subjects as taxes, bookkeeping, legal affairs, and other problems which confront crafts-people who sell their work and are therefore in business.

Educational expenses that are necessary for *improvement* in your field are normally tax deductible. This can include the purchase of craft books, attendance at seminars and workshops (travel included), as well as formal education. The key to tax deductibility of educational expenses is whether you are already working in crafts as a livelihood. Education expenses to *become* a working craft artist, for example, are not deductible; education expenses to upgrade your position as a working craft artist usually are.

(*See also: Apprentice*)

Employees

When you hire someone to help around the shop, you've signed up for a whole new ball game. The moment you become an employer, you assume responsibility for meeting a payroll, for considerable paper-work, for payment of Social Security, Workmen's Compensation and un-employment insurance, for collecting withholding taxes and paying them to the government, for the payment of nonproductive time such as holidays and vacations, and a variety of other managerial functions.

All this is worth the effort, of course, if what the employees produce is worth more than what you pay them in wages and fringe benefits. In other words, if it helps you make a better profit.

The labor laws, both national and state, make no distinction between permanent or temporary employees, whether payment is in wages or commissions, whether the employees are paid by the hour or by the piece, or even necessarily where the work is done.

This is how the U.S. Department of Labor defines the term employee as it relates to the enforcement of labor laws: "Generally the relation-ship of employer and employee exists when the person for whom services are performed has the right to control and direct the individual who per-forms the services, not only as to the result to be accomplished by the work, but also as to the details and means by which the result is accom-plished. That is, an employee is subject to the will and control of the employer not only as to what shall be done but how it shall be done. In this connection, it is not necessary that the employer actually direct or control the manner in which the services are performed; it is sufficient if he has the right to do so.

"The right to discharge is also an important factor indicating that the person possessing that right is an employer. Other factors characteristic of an employer, but not necessarily present in every case, are the furnish-ing of tools and a place to work to the individual who performs the services.

"In general, if an individual is subject to the control of direction of another merely as to the result to be accomplished and not as to the means and methods for accomplishing the result, he is not an employee."

The Labor Department also explains that it doesn't matter what you call the employee: partner, salesman, agent, independent contractor, or whatever. If the relationship meets the definition given above, then it is an employer-employee relationship, and all the obligations and responsibilities imposed by the labor laws, tax laws, etc. apply.

Two examples: If you hire a plumber to fix the pipes, you direct him to do the repair work. How he does it, what tools he uses, where he buys the supplies and so forth are his decision, not yours. Therefore he is not an employee.

On the other hand, if you engage a helper to make leather belts, and you buy the leather, you tell him where to punch the holes, what tools to use, when to come to work and go to lunch, then you have an employee.

In the case of a corporation, the corporation is the employer, and everyone who works for it under the terms outlined above is an employee. That even includes you, the president, if you work for the corporation and draw a salary. The size of a paycheck does not determine whether an employer-employee relationship exists.

Some ticklish situations have arisen in the case of apprentices, cottage industries and cooperatives, in which some Labor Department officials have determined that an employer-employee relationship exists, and others have found no such relationship. In questionable situations each case is judged on the particular set of circumstances and can be appealed to higher authorities.

The only exceptions which generally apply concern the spouse and children (under 21) of an individual owner.

As an employer, it is important to keep abreast of the constantly changing labor laws. Aside from minimum wage and overtime provisions, which are discussed elsewhere, some of the key provisions of both federal and most state legislation prohibit the employment of children under 14, the regulation of employment of children to age 18 in certain types of occupations, and the prohibition against any form of discrimination in hiring, training, upgrading, or wages based on race, nationality, sex, age, or other conditions not related specifically to the objective requirements of the job.

When you first become an employer, it is necessary to obtain a federal employer identification number from the Internal Revenue Service, and in some states a separate state identification number. This number will then appear on all forms, tax payments, and other documents you file as an employer. For most such documents it is advisable to obtain the regular services of an accountant so that tax payments are made properly and on time, and payroll records and other books are kept in proper order for possible inspection. Be sure to consult your state labor department for applicable rules and regulations which go into effect the minute you put the first employee on the payroll.

Aside from all the rules and regulations, there is the intangible problem of selecting the right employees. The first hurdle is where to look. This depends to a great extent on what you're looking for. If you want a young, inexperienced potter whom you can train, a local craft school may be the first place. If you're looking for a handyman-driver-packer, a classified ad in the local newspaper may be best.

It is surprising, however, how many employers rush headlong into hiring someone without the necessary preliminaries. W. F. Rabe of San Fernando State College, writing in a "Management Aid" for the Small Business Administration, puts the problem in this perspective:

"The owner-managers of most small companies would not think of buying a piece of equipment until they had evaluated it systematically. They want to be sure that the machine meets specifications, can help pay for itself, and last for a reasonable length of time. However, when selecting personnel to operate the equipment, some owner-managers use no system. Little, if any, time and energy are spent trying to match the applicant to the job. The result is waste. In the long run, mistakes in selecting employees may cost far more than the loss caused by selecting the wrong equipment."

It is prudent, therefore, to take these four steps:

1) define in your own mind exactly what the job is and what qualifications, experience, and attitudes you are seeking in a prospective employee;

2) interview a number of applicants to determine how they meet those standards;

3) check their references, if any, especially if they're going to handle money or if you have to leave them alone in your shop or studio;

4) tell them they're being employed for a probationary period, perhaps four weeks, and evaluate your decision during that time.

The first few weeks are critical. Any new employee, no matter how experienced, will need a little time to function effectively in a new situation, working with unfamiliar people and under differing circumstances. As an employer it pays to keep a watchful eye on new employees to see how they fit in and how they perform. You won't get your money's worth the first few weeks because the new employee is still being broken in. But if you think you've made a mistake, don't compound it by wasting more time and money. Find someone else.

For most of us, the only thing more difficult than hiring is firing. After all, you're holding someone else's livelihood in your hands. Try to make it gentle. Don't fire someone in the presence of others. During the probationary period, dismissal notice or severance pay is not necessary. But if someone has been on your payroll for some time, two weeks notice is generally expected, just as you would want two weeks notice if someone quits. Many employers prefer to give a discharged employee two weeks pay instead of two weeks notice to avoid ill-feeling or a demoralizing situation if there are other employees in the shop.

Finally, be certain that all employees understand the rules and regulations, and that you uphold them equitably. It is not fair to allow one employee to get away with lateness every morning when you require others to be prompt. Nor is it right to penalize or even discharge employees for not observing rules you never told them about. Changing the rules in midstream without giving employees an opportunity to reorient themselves is also poor practice. If you're going to change the working hours, for example, give sufficient notice; don't just tell everyone to show up half an hour earlier starting tomorrow. If at all possible, notify employees of expected overtime somewhat in advance, as they may have made other plans.

How you treat your employees has a significant effect on how effectively and enthusiastically they work for you, and that in turn has an effect on your profits.

Ask yourself this question occasionally: would *you* want to work for a boss like you?

(*See also: Apprentice, Cooperatives, Cottage Industry, Minimum Wage, Unemployment Insurance, Unions, Workmen's Compensation, Withholding Tax*)

Employer Identification Number

(*See: Employees, Withholding Tax*)

Endorsement

When you want to cash or deposit a check made out to you, your signature has to appear on the back of the check. It has to be signed exactly as it appears on the face of the check. If that is different from the name you use on your bank account, sign it twice: first as it appears on the face of the check, then as it appears on your account. For example, if you receive a check made out to Mrs. Tom Jones, but your account is under the name of Susan Jones, endorse the check first as Mrs. Tom Jones, then as Susan Jones.

If you cash a check made out to someone else, the same principle applies. First have the other person endorse the check, then add your endorsement. If you don't know the person for whom you are cashing such a check, be sure you see satisfactory identification, preferably a driver's license, credit card, or other document bearing a signature for comparison. Note the document number on the back of the check, as well as the person's address so you can find him or her if something goes wrong.

It is poor practice to endorse a check and then leave it lying around. If it is lost or stolen, it can easily be cashed by a second signature. Any check which is to be deposited, and any check on which you are the second endorsement, should have the words "for deposit only" and your bank account number written right under your endorsement. That way it cannot be cashed by anyone else.

The endorsement (reverse) side of the check can also specify other restrictions, such as making the check payable upon delivery of the goods or when a certain service has been performed. When the recipient of the check endorses it, he accepts those restrictions.

(*See also: Checking Account, Collection Problems*)

Equipment

The most important pieces of equipment are your hands and your head. Without those, even the most elaborate and sophisticated tool or machine will stand idle or turn out junk.

But equipment and tools are natural extensions of your hands and your head. In the process of learning a craft, you become familiar with the basic equipment with which you work: a loom, a potter's wheel, a kiln, hammers, saws, vises, and all the rest.

But when you go into business, when you start your own shop or studio, equipment and tools suddenly take on an entirely new dimension. What kind of production capacity do you foresee? What kind of investment are you able to make?

A kiln is a good example of the various problems and solutions. If the kiln is too small, you will not be able to fire enough pieces to keep you in bread and butter. If it is too large, you will waste not only the original investment, but the cost of energy to fuel it.

If you're working alone and just beginning to produce for sale, a small, used kiln might make sense, knowing full well that in another year or two you hope to build or buy a larger, more efficient one. Then again, if you can share the cost with another potter and work out a schedule you both can live with, a large kiln may be a wise investment.

Occasionally you might even be able to rent or lease equipment from a craft supply shop if a temporary need arises.

Maintaining equipment and tools in good working order is as essential to the production of fine craftwork as using good raw materials. Without a good violin, even the finest musician cannot do justice to the music. While the care with which you've bought your raw materials and used your tools and equipment cannot be seen as separate qualities in your craftwork, the end result reflects both.

Since equipment is often a major expense, financing its purchase can become a problem. The best way, of course, is to plan ahead and save the money. That way you not only avoid paying interest on a loan, but the savings themselves earn interest while they're sitting in the bank. Don't save in a checking account; it pays no interest. Even if the plan is to put away only $100 a month for six months in a 5 percent savings account, you'll earn almost $8 in interest.

If you must finance the purchase out of future earnings, the best source is a bank loan. Shop around; interest rates and other conditions are not always the same among different banks.

Before you invest in a new piece of equipment or a tool that represents a considerable expense, sleep on it. Two nights are better than one. Two heads are also better than one, so discuss it with some friends, some other craft artists. And avoid an instant love affair with a sensational invention that promises the sky. If you can afford it, by all means take a chance. Perhaps it will do all that it promises. But if you're going into hock for it, look it over twice as carefully as you would any other piece of equipment with which you're more familiar. Consider all the possibilities, both positive and negative, of how this particular equipment will solve your specific problems in your particular operation.

Actually, that's a good rule of thumb for any major equipment purchase. Just because it worked well for someone else does not necessarily mean it will work well for you. Every situation and every need must be judged on its own merits.

(*See also: Credit, Loans, Tools*)

Equity

The value of the investment an owner has in a business is called equity. This value is determined by subtracting the total liabilities of the business from its total assets. Equity is not necessarily the amount of money the owner has invested. In a prospering business, the equity would most likely be higher than the original investment; in a failing business it may be zero, regardless of how much was originally invested.

In the case of a mortgage, the term equity is used to describe the owner's (borrower's) share of the total value of the property. As the mortgage loan is paid off month by month, the owner's equity increases. Thus, if you buy a $20,000 house with $5,000 in cash and a $15,000 mortgage, your equity is $5,000. After you've paid off $4,000 of the mortgage, your equity has grown to $9,000, and so forth, until finally your equity is 100 percent and you throw a big party to burn the mortgage.

(*See also: Capital, Mortgage, Net Worth*)

Escrow

In financial terms, escrow is an account into which money is placed for a specific purpose, to be held by a third party until the purpose is accomplished. An escrow account, for example, may be established to put funds into a bank for payment of a large order if credit references are not satisfactory. The money can not be withdrawn by the depositor or touched by the person for whom it is intended until the order is delivered.

An escrow account is also used by a bank to collect money for taxes, water bills, and other obligations of people to whom it has made mortgage loans. The bank then pays those obligations for the mortgagee, although it does not usually pay interest on this type of escrow account.

(*See also: Mortgage*)

Estimated Tax

All income from which no payroll taxes are withheld is subject to estimated tax payments. For craftspeople, such income generally results from the sale of craft objects. Estimated tax payments on such self-employed income are due April 15, June 15, September 15 and January 15.

A Declaration of Estimated Tax (Form 1040 ES) must be filed on or before April 15 of each year for the current year. Estimated taxes must be paid even if some of your income is subject to withholding taxes. Such a combination situation is quite common among craftspeople who earn part of their income as teachers or at some other job (on a payroll), and another part in their own studio or shop (self-employed).

The penalty for underpayment of estimated taxes is 7 percent. There are two ways to avoid paying penalties:

1) Pay the same quarterly estimated tax this year as last, less any payroll taxes that may have been deducted from wages or salary if you held a job this year but not last year.

2) If you pay lower estimated taxes because you expect your income to be less this year than last, your total estimated tax payments must be at least 80 percent of your final tax obligation, paid on an even quarterly basis. The balance of 20 percent or less is payable without penalty when you file the next tax return on April 15.

Suppose things change in midstream? Suppose you suddenly run into a big selling streak after you filed your estimated tax return last April, and you are therefore likely to have more income than at first expected. In that case you amend your return when the next estimated payment is due, and increase those payments.

The reverse is also true if your self-employed income falls below what you had expected. This can happen if you switch from self-employed to a salaried job in the middle of the year, or if an illness puts you out of commission for an extended period. In that case you reduce your quarterly payments by amending your return.

Be careful, though, to avoid estimating too low. If your payments drop below 80 percent of what is due in any quarter, you'll owe the 7 percent penalty on the shortage. If they fall very far below you may be subject to extra penalties for willful failure to pay the proper estimated tax.

If you have had any income subject to withholding, the amount withheld is figured into the 80 percent determination. Here's what that means in practical terms. If, for example, your self-employed income owed $1,000 in estimated taxes, and your salary was subject to $1,000 in withholding taxes, your total tax obligation would be $2,000. Let's assume you paid only $700 (70 percent) of the $1,000 estimated taxes. That would seem to fall below the 80 percent requirement. However, 80 percent of the $2,000 total is $1,600. The withholding tax payment ($1,000) and the estimated tax payment ($700) total $1,700, which is above the $1600 requirement. In this example you're safe.

The Internal Revenue Service also assumes that withholding taxes, even if only earned in part of the year, are spread over the entire year to meet the even quarterly payment rule.

Social Security taxes, at the rate of 7.9 percent on self-employed income, have to be included in the estimated tax declaration and quarterly payments.

(See also: Income Tax—Personal, Social Security, Withholding Tax)

Excise Tax

When the federal government imposes a sales tax it goes by a different name: excise tax. Such taxes are imposed on certain products such as gasoline, cigarettes, alcoholic beverages, and the like, and are collected from the consumer at the point of purchase just as other sales taxes are. However, they are not calculated separately but are part of the posted price. Craftspeople rarely, if ever, get involved in selling products subject to an excise tax.

(See also: Taxes)

Exclusive Rights

The more artistic, unusual, or salable a craft object is, the more likely it is that the craftsperson will be asked to grant exclusive rights to a store. That means the store wants to be the only one in a specified geographic area to sell your work. The assumption is that it will therefore exert more effort to sell your craftwork.

This is a double-edged sword. The store's desire for exclusive rights is understandable. A certain prestige attaches to offering exclusive craft objects, and competition or even price-cutting is eliminated. But the craftsperson is entitled to something in return.

Garry Barker, Executive Director of the Kentucky Guild of Artists and Craftsmen, has written that "exclusive arrangements in smaller towns are great, but putting all your eggs in one basket can hamper your sales in a large metropolitan area."

A few precautions are advisable:

1) Put the exclusive arrangement in writing. Include a termination date, no more than six months or a year at first.

2) Specify the exact geographic area that is covered.

3) Specify the exact nature of the craft objects which are covered. If you make a line of dishes and a line of hanging pots, is all your pottery included in the exclusive arrangement?

4) Require a certain minimum volume from the store.

5) Spell out what advertising and other promotion activities the store will engage in to promote sales of your work.

6) Be sure you have the right of approval on prices and promotions.

The store, in return, may want certain commitments from you: can you produce an adequate supply, will you maintain quality and price, will you participate in an exhibit they may want to run?

Exclusivity may work very well for you, especially in opening up new markets. But examine each situation carefully, evaluate each store's reputation and track record, and be prepared to observe every clause in your agreement.

(*See also: Consignment, Retail Outlets*)

Exhibitions

As the status of crafts as an art form grows, so do the opportunities to participate in exhibitions sponsored by museums, galleries, organizations, universities, and other institutions. Most notable among recent exhibitions is the Craft Multiples exhibit by the Renwick Gallery of the Smithsonian Institution, which went on a national tour after its debut in Washington, DC.

Some exhibitions restrict participation to certain geographic areas, such as the Seven State Art Exhibition at Eastern Illinois University, which is open only to craftspeople in seven midwestern states. Others concentrate on a particular medium, such as the Contemporary Glass Exhibition staged by Peters Valley Craftsmen of New Jersey.

Some last for a few weeks, such as the Cooperstown (NY) event each summer; others go on a year-long tour, such as the American Embroiderers biennial stitchery exhibition.

Most exhibitions offer cash prizes or purchase awards, and many also provide opportunities for the purchase of works which are delivered to buyers after the exhibition is over.

Many exhibition sponsors take a commission, rarely more than 20 percent of the purchase price, when a work on exhibit is sold.

The immediate rewards of winning a prize or making a sale, however, are not the only reasons for participating in an exhibition. Equally important to craft artists is the recognition and prestige which result from acceptance in an important exhibition.

Being part of the Smithsonian's Crafts Multiples show and being included in the show's handsome catalogue, for example, is likely to bring rewards to the participating craftsperson far beyond the immediate sale of his or her work. Recognition as an outstanding craft artist enhances the value and price of the craft artist's future work.

Almost all exhibitions are juried by slides, and many also require viewing of actual work after the slides pass the jury. A reputable exhibition sponsor will outline the conditions and responsibilities of handling the work in great detail. Under most circumstances, entrants are responsible for shipping the work to the exhibition and for insurance in transit. Thereafter the exhibition sponsor should be responsible for proper care, insurance, and ultimate return of the work. Slides and craft objects which are not accepted should be returned to the entrant promptly after jurying. If this is not spelled out in the exhibition prospectus, ask questions.

A modest entry fee, usually $10 or less, is required by many exhibition sponsors to help defray the cost of the judging process, but craftspeople should not be expected to help defray the cost of the exhibition itself, or to provide the kitty from which the prizes are awarded.

All entries, whether by slide or actual work, should be properly identified. Many exhibition sponsors provide forms for this purpose. Where special hanging or display instructions are necessary, the craftsperson should describe those clearly and send them along with the entry. Also accompanying the entry must be the price at which it may be sold. If the work is not to be sold, that too should be indicated.

An important ingredient of any exhibition from a craft artist's point of view is the printed exhibition catalogue. This enables prospective buyers to contact the artist to see other examples of his or her craftwork. If no catalogue is planned, then the exhibition sponsor should at least provide all visitors with a list of names and addresses of participating craft artists.

Unlike craft shows and fairs, exhibitions do not require the presence of the craftsperson, only his or her work. A reputable exhibition can bring long-lasting rewards, and often even immediate sales.

(*See also: Shows and Fairs*)

Expense Accounts

These two words mean precisely what they say: to account for expenses. Since every business-connected expense is tax deductible, it makes good sense to record all such expenses completely.

The term "expense account" does not refer to items of expense that are billed and paid for by check, and thus appear accurately on the books of the business anyway. The term applies more to the incidental, out-of-pocket expenses. They may seem small at the time, but they add up.

If you go to an out-of-town craft fair, for example, the cost of the booth does not show up on the expense account since you've already paid for it by check. But the car mileage, tolls, meals, lodging, laundry, and similar expenses should be accounted for.

Keep a notebook handy and jot down every last little item, including the quarter tolls and the dime telephone calls, as soon as the expense is incurred. Memory plays strange tricks, and ten forgotten dimes make a forgotten dollar. Get as many receipts as possible to confirm the expenditure. Toll booths on turnpikes give receipts. The more receipts you have, the easier it is to prove to the government that you spent the money you say you spent, and that it was spent for a business purpose.

The Internal Revenue Service requires that all lodging expenses be supported by a receipt, as well as any meal expense that exceeds $25, and all business entertainment expenses. If you use a credit card, the sales slip will serve as a receipt. Details of the business nature of the expense (with whom you had lunch, for example) can be recorded on the back of the credit card slip.

A special situation exists with regard to automobile expenses. You can, of course, keep a record of all the gasoline you bought, plus the repairs and depreciation of the car over a year's time, and so on. However, the government allows a standard expense of 15¢ per mile (as of 1976) which includes all car expenses except parking and tolls. That way you simply keep track of the mileage and show it on your expense account, multiplied by 15¢. This is the procedure applied to car expenses by most business travelers.

For purposes of record-keeping, it is best to keep an expense account on the basis of a specific time period (perhaps weekly), or according to a specific business trip. Mark the top of each list with the time period or the activity is covers. Be sure every entry is dated. Attach all receipts to the list of expenses, indicate by date and check number how you were reimbursed, enter the transaction in your bookkeeping ledger, and file the whole thing away where you or your accountant can find it.

(*See also: Accounting, Business Trips*)

Expenses

Anything you spend in order to make craftwork for sale is a business expense. That includes rent, raw materials, supplies, wages, utilities, sales costs, traveling expenses, shipping, and a great many other items.

Business expenses are generally tax deductible. In the case of craftspeople who devote their full time to producing craftwork for sale, all such expenses are deductible, even if they exceed the year's craft income.

In the case of people who have other jobs, but who work at their craft regularly in their spare time with the intent to sell, business expenses are deductible up to the amount of income realized from the sale of craft objects in any given year.

In the latter category it is very important to observe the Internal Revenue Service code which specifies that a profit must be shown in at least two out of five consecutive years in order for an activity to be considered a business rather than simply a hobby. People who pursue crafts purely as a hobby cannot deduct their expenses.

A critical factor, if the IRS questions your business deductions, is your intent. In other words, did you really intend to make a profit? Did you really intend to run a business, even if only part-time? Your business intentions will be much easier to substantiate if you have kept a good set of financial records, if you can show that you have invested in equipment, have a separate business bank account, have stationery with your business name, and similar evidence.

Under the two-out-of-five-year rule, life is much easier if you show a profit early during the five-year period. Profit is what shows up on your tax return. There's no law that says you must take deductions. There may come a time, especially in a year when income and expenses are very close together, when you find it worthwhile to omit some expense items in order to show a profit that year. That will, in turn, allow you to take all the deductions in a year when expenses may be considerably higher than income.

But no matter what taxpayer category you're in, the most essential point to remember is that a sound and consistent method of recording every expense item is required if you are ever called upon to prove your expenses to the tax collector.

(*See also: Accounting, Income, Overhead, Profit, Wages*)

Export

(*See: Customs*)

Fees

Payments for such professional services as lawyers, accountants, doctors, are known as fees, as distinguished from wages and salaries. If a craftsperson serves as a consultant or speaker, payment for that service is also known as a fee. Other payments called fees include admissions to entertainment or sports events, craft shows, some educational activities (such as seminars), official documents, licenses, registrations, and charges established by law for the services of a public official.

Time and again, craftspeople are asked to contribute their time and talent for free to commercial ventures. You may be asked, for example, to perform for an educational film made for a commercial sponsor. "There's no money," you are told, "but you'll get credit"—as though credit can be deposited in a bank.

The people who produce a film are paid. The teachers who use the film in a classroom are paid. The commercial sponsor obviously has a profit motive. Why should craftspeople be expected to donate their time and talent?

Perhaps this reflects the popular misconception that weaving and pottery and such is only fun, and who ever heard of paying people to have fun. Unlike the people who do the asking, craft artists are rarely on salary. Their time is literally their money. Asking for that time without payment is asking too much.

Unless a free appearance can be tied directly into sales, it should be turned down. Craftspeople also have bills to pay. They have a right to be proud of their skills, their talents, their artistry and creativity. That is not something to give away lightly for someone else's profit.

Craft artists, like all good citizens, give generously of their time, talent and money to worthy causes of their choice. But when commercial interests try to use craftspeople for commercial purposes without payment, the time has come to say no.

Better yet, negotiate a fee.

(*See also: Income*)

Financial Management

(*See: Accounting, Balance Sheet, Banks, Bookkeeping, Budgets, Capital, Gross, Income Statement, Investment, Loans, Taxes*)

Financial Statement

Although very small, individually owned enterprises do not usually get involved in this, a larger business and every partnership or corporation has its accountant draw up two types of financial statements at least once a year.

The income statement reports the income and expenses of the business over the year's period. The balance sheet reports the assets, liabilities and equity at year's end. They complement each other because the income statement helps to indicate how you got to where the balance sheet says you are.

(*See also: Accounting, Balance Sheet, Income Statement*)

Fine Art

This term is applied to such media as painting and sculpture which are almost always sold through galleries. Several craft media (woven wall hangings, some glass, clay, and metalwork) have recently begun to cross over from craft art to fine art, especially where the object has purely esthetic value and bears no resemblance to any functional object.

The word "fine" need not be interpreted as a definition of the artistic quality of the work, but only of its nonfunctional purpose. Fine art is generally purchased by collectors, some of whom view it as an investment which will grow in value or which can provide certain tax advantages. Under the tax laws, for example, a collector can donate his collection to a museum, take the contribution as a charitable tax deduction, but still retain the work in his possession for the remainder of his lifetime.

(*See also: Collectors*)

Fine Arts Floater

Craftspeople often suffer losses due to breakage or theft while transporting or exhibiting their work at shows and fairs. Such losses are not always covered by the show management (certainly not transportation). Nor are they covered by the usual property insurance which you may already have on your home or shop and its contents.

Proper protection for what insurance companies describe as periods of "storage, transporting, and exhibiting" requires the addition of a fine arts floater to your property insurance policy.

To protect against theft from your car, the policy must be endorsed to include off-premises theft coverage. To protect work that is transported by other means (parcel post, UPS, freight, someone else's car), specific transit coverage must be added to the fine arts floater. Rates for floater coverage depend on such variables as the type of storage area (home, shop, warehouse, garage), whether the vehicle has a burglar alarm, security conditions in the exhibition building, packing of items, etc. Some work is more fragile or more tempting to thieves, and that can also affect the rates.

The only way to write this fine arts floater is by adding it to an existing homeowner or tenant/homeowner policy. Floater premiums ordinarily are about $5 per $100 of coverage, with a $25 minimum. If the risk is large enough ($10,000 or more) it may warrant being underwritten separately. A $50 deductible per occurence is usually made part of the policy.

This coverage is offered by all casualty and property insurance brokers. To determine whether you need such coverage, how much to buy and what it will cost, craftspeople should consult their insurance agents.

(*See also: Insurance, Property Insurance*)

Fire Insurance

(*See: Insurance, Property Insurance*)

Fire Prevention

Few disasters are as drastic or as costly as a fire, and most such disasters can be prevented with some proper attention to safety precautions. Consider not only that a fire can pose a serious threat to your life and the lives of those who live or work with you, but that it can also destroy your life's work, your prized possessions, your business records, your means to earn a living.

The following recommendations for safety in five major areas of fire danger are based on information from the National Fire Protection Association.

Smoking Hazards

This is one of the most common causes of fires, especially around vapors and/or dusty areas. Post No Smoking signs in potential danger areas, and be sure the signs are observed.

If you must smoke, be sure to use an ash tray. Do not rest cigarettes on window sills, edges of your work bench, or other surfaces. Do not throw matches or cigarettes into waste baskets, even if you think they're out.

Of all the fire hazards, those caused by smoking are the easiest to prevent if proper precautions are taken.

Electrical Hazards

Never hang electrical wiring over nails, around metal pipes, near heat or oil, across passageways, or running across the floor. Frayed insulation, broken plugs, loose connections, defective switches or outlets must be repaired promptly. Keep hot bulbs away from liquids.

Overloading electrical equipment, or bypassing the safe amperage of the fuse box, creates a real fire danger. If a motor emits sparks or gets wet it needs attention. A spark can cause a fire. The pennies saved on delay or skimping can easily become dollars of fire loss.

If you must use electrical equipment near flammable liquids, gas, or dust, be sure it is designed for that purpose and is explosion proof.

Cutting and Welding Hazards

All such work should be done in a safe place, away from flammable materials or explosives. Walls, ceilings, and floors can also catch fire from flying sparks. It is always best to have a fire watcher on hand to distinguish flying sparks that land in cracks or crevices. Don't walk away when you're through; stand watch for a while to be certain no sparks are smoldering anywhere. Use covers and shields to reduce sparks and protect yourself.

Flammable Liquid Hazards

Don't ever allow flammable liquids to accumulate. Use them only outdoors or in a well-ventilated area. Always clean up spilled liquids immediately, and keep only a small amount in a clearly marked metal safety container (never glass) near your work area.

Using gasoline as a cleaning fluid is one of the most dangerous things you can do. Don't take the chance. Gasoline is a fuel, not a cleaner.

Keep flammable liquids away from all sources of flame or sparks (kilns, torches, heaters, electric tools). Oil-soaked rags should be kept only in tightly covered metal containers. Get rid of them as soon as you can. And if you have a cigarette dangling from your mouth while working with flammable liquids, watch yourself go up in smoke.

Housekeeping Hazards

Neatness counts! If your work area is littered with cartons and scraps and leftover materials, you're inviting a fire. Ditto with accumulations of chips, cuttings, oil drippings, dust, and other trash. Keep such stuff in covered metal containers.

Be sure that exit doors, stairways, and fire escapes are not blocked, and that your sprinkler system, if any, is in good working order at all times. Have a fire drill once in a while, even if it's only for your family.

Fire Extinguishers

Every workplace and every home should have one or more fire extinguishers, depending on the size of the premises and the potential nature of a fire.

Different types of fire require different types of fire extinguishers:

TYPE A (water type) is used for ordinary combustible fires such as paper, cloth, wood, trash;

TYPE B (dry chemical or foam type) is used for flammable-liquid fires such as gasoline, paint, oil;

TYPE C (carbon dioxide type) is used for electrical-equipment fires such as motors and wiring;

TYPE D (dry powder type) is used for combustible metal fires, such as certain chips, shavings, etc.;

TYPE A-B-C (multipurpose chemical type) can be used for any of the various types of fire created by combustible materials, flammable liquid, or electrical equipment.

Never use a fire extinguisher on a fire for which it is not intended. Using TYPE A (water) on an electrical fire can cause an electric shock.

Read the instructions on the fire extinguisher carefully. Be sure you know how to use it before you need it. Getting acquainted with the fire extinguisher after a fire starts may be too late.

Place the fire extinguishers in strategic locations so they are easily accessible.

What To Do if a Fire Starts

The whole point is to stop a fire from starting, and if one does start, to keep it from spreading.

If you see smoke or fire, the *first* thing to do is to turn in a fire alarm.

If the fire is small fight it while you wait for the firemen, but stay low and be sure you have an escape route available. Those first few minutes are vital, but remember that your own life is more vital.

If the fire grows and gets out of hand, get out fast! Close doors behind you to retard the spread of the fire.

(*See also:* Work Area)

F.O.B.

These three little initials, meaning free on board, indicate to which point the seller of a product will deliver it, and at which point the buyer takes over. F.O.B. is most commonly followed by the word "factory," which means the seller will get the goods all packed up and ready to go for pick-up by the customer or his/her agent (such as a freight carrier) at the seller's factory. In practice this means the customer pays the shipping charges and makes the shipping arrangements.

Sometimes the initials F.O.B. are followed by the name of a location other than the factory. This means the seller is responsible for delivering the goods to that pick-up point, whereupon the buyer takes over. If you are located in Los Angeles, and buy a heavy piece of equipment from a manufacturer who has a factory in Philadelphia and a warehouse in San Francisco, then the difference between "F.O.B. factory" and "F.O.B. San Francisco" can become a significant factor in shipping costs. "F.O.B. factory" means you pay the shipping costs from Philadelphia to Los Angeles. "F.O.B. San Francisco" means the manufacturer pays for shipping from Philadelphia to the West Coast, and you pay the shipping costs only from San Francisco to Los Angeles.

The term F.O.B. involves another important consideration, especially when claims for damage in transit are involved. Title to the goods changes hands the moment the goods are picked up at the F.O.B. point. From that moment on the buyer owns them, even if they have not yet been delivered.

Foreclosure

(See: Mortgage)

Franchise Tax

(See: Income Tax—Business)

Freight Allowance

With shipping costs going through the roof, most producers of merchandise add the cost of shipping to the cost of the items themselves. In certain cases they make a freight allowance; that is, the freight charges will be paid by the shipper. This is usually based on two considerations: 1) the size of the order and 2) the distance it has to travel.

For example, all orders over $500 may have the freight paid by the shipper. That is important to craftspeople both as purchasers of equipment and supplies, and as suppliers themselves. In both cases the question is: do you pay the freight charges, or does the other party?

Some shippers make a freight allowance for deliveries within a certain limited area, e.g., 100 miles if they have their own truck delivering to that area anyway. In other instances, a freight allowance may be made to very distant points if the supplier wants to build customers in that area but can't compete if the freight charges are added.

A freight allowance need not be 100 percent. It can be graduated, say 10 percent if the order is under $200, 20 percent if it is $200 to $500, and so forth.

As a supplier, a craft producer should not offer freight allowances unless they are necessary to make the sale. As a buyer of equipment and supplies, on the other hand, craftspeople should try to get whatever freight allowance is possible.

Any freight you pay for—coming in or going out—is an expense item that eats into profits.

(See also: FOB, Shipping)

Freight Collect

This means the recipient of the shipment pays the freight costs when the shipment is received. The delivering carrier will not leave the shipment unless those costs are paid.

If this situation applies, it should be stated in all price lists, order forms, etc.

(*See also: FOB, Freight Allowance, Freight Prepaid, Shipping*).

Freight Forwarders

(*See: Shipping*)

Freight Prepaid

This means the shipper pays the costs of shipment, even if those costs are ultimately added to the bill.

If this situation applies, it should be stated in all price lists, order forms, etc.

(*See also: FOB, Freight Allowance, Freight Collect, Shipping*)

Gallery

A gallery is a retail sales outlet for craftwork, painting or sculpture, with some important features which distinguish it from other outlets we call stores or shops. Those distinctions are traceable to the original meaning of the word, whose definitions included: a walkway, a promenade, a place where the audience sits at a performance. In other words, a room with a view. The upper balcony of an opera house, the spectator section at a golf match, and exhibition halls at museums are still known as galleries.

A gallery which sells craftwork is still a room with a view, since its selling activity is based on exhibitions rather than simple store display. Such galleries generally specialize in works of unusual or innovative design and technique, and appeal more to the collector who is interested in buying one-of-a-kind esthetic objects rather than multiple-produced functional objects.

Whether a particular piece of work is unique becomes a major factor in a gallery owner's consideration. If something very similar can be bought at a shop around the corner or in the local department store, it is not likely to find its way into a gallery. Galleries do not depend primarily on walk-in customers who are attracted by a window display or a big ad in the papers, but rather on a carefully developed list of clients who respond to invitations to an exhibition. To build such response, a gallery owner must offer customers something that is either unusually artistic, unusually unique, or unusually innovative.

To accomplish this, many galleries build their reputations and clientele by specializing in certain types of work, certain artists, certain periods, certain schools, and so forth.

From a craft artist's point of view, a gallery show includes many benefits beyond the possibility of selling the work. Since competition for gallery acceptance is very keen, a great deal of prestige attaches to having such a show, even at a nonselling gallery in a museum. Many gallery exhibitions are reviewed in the press, and this can become an important asset in the craft artist's portfolio when trying to sell to retail stores, obtain special commissions or assignments, or qualify for a teaching position— not to speak of what it does for the ego.

When it comes to selling work with very high price tags—such as a large wall hanging or an expensive piece of sculptured jewelry—gallery selling often is the most effective way to find the customer who has both the appreciation for fine work and the money to spend on it. Once a good gallery connection has been established, it is much easier for a craft artist to find customers for important works in the future.

All of this background is by way of introducing the methods of approaching a gallery and the specific arrangements that should be made.

First, determine whether your work is really suited to gallery selling, according to some of the standards outlined above.

Visit some galleries in your area, or whenever you are on a trip. Walk in as a spectator and try to visualize your work in that setting. Does the gallery's general approach appeal to the kind of customers who might be interested in your work? Does the price structure seem compatible with yours? Do you like the way the gallery exhibits the work and prepares the show catalogue? Can you find some reason why that particular gallery should be interested in handling your work?

The initial approach to a gallery, unless you know the owner or have a personal introduction, is to send a letter, enclosing a brief resumé which outlines your background, describes your experience, and includes some reference to exhibition or competition experience. Indicate in the letter that you will call in a week or so for an appointment to show slides or samples of your work.

Don't be discouraged if gallery owners don't fall all over themselves to see you and sign you up. They often have contracts and commitments for many months in advance. Unlike retail shop owners, they don't work under intense daily pressure, and their concern is not how many units of a given item they can sell tomorrow. On the other hand, they are in business to make a profit, and anything you can tell them that would lead them to believe in the possibility of a profitable connection if they handle your work is an obvious advantage. For example, if you already have a list of potential customers who came to another exhibition of yours and could be invited to an opening, the gallery owner should be interested.

The basic decision, of course, will be made on the quality of your work. When you finally do have the appointment and meet with the gallery owner, be prepared with a good set of slides or a representative group of pieces to show. No need to bring a slide projector; most galleries have their own. If your presentation is made by mail to a gallery in a distant city, then superb slides are even more important. It is best to start locally until you have some experience and credentials under your belt.

Be prepared, also, to discuss price. The overwhelming bulk of gallery work is sold on consignment, especially in the higher price levels. Depending on a gallery's financial capabilities and its experience with a particular craft artist, some work is bought outright.

In a consignment arrangement, you determine the ultimate retail price and get a percentage of the sale after it is made. The percentage generally runs between 50 and 66 percent. Galleries occasionally expect the artist to help defray some of the costs of a reception for an opening, or advertising for an exhibition. In that case, the percentage the artist receives should be around 66 percent since the artist has made an investment in his own show. If the gallery is responsible for all the costs, then it generally keeps 40 to 50 percent of the ultimate selling price.

The concept of artists or craftspeople paying for some of the costs of an exhibition, also known as charge backs, is a subject of considerable controversy. What control, for example, do artists have over the quality and cost of the activity to which they are expected to contribute a share of the expense? Should such expenses more properly be a responsibility of the gallery as part of its normal operating expenses?

If you are approached with such a proposition as a condition for selling your work, ask yourself whether the gallery is really convinced that your work will sell, or whether you are just being used to bring people into the gallery where they are exposed to other artists' work as well as your own. Each situation should be evaluated on its own. Sometimes this arrangement can benefit the craft artist, especially for a first show which you may need in order to establish some credentials. If you do agree to share some of the costs, be sure everything is spelled out in detail and in writing, especially the amount of money involved, and what control you have over how it is spent.

Several other thoughts should be kept in mind on the subject of pricing. First, it should be clearly understood that the gallery cannot change the price of consignment items downward without your prior agreement.

Second, pricing of one-of-a-kind objects differs somewhat from pricing production crafts. Raw materials, labor, and overhead must be calculated, of course. But the elements of originality, exclusiveness, and artistry are much more important in selling gallery items than in the kind of work that might be sold at a craft fair or department store. The price can therefore be relatively higher to compensate you for these intangible elements.

Since it may take longer to sell a major work in a gallery than to sell production craft items to a store, the price should reflect the fact that your time and money are tied up for longer periods in an unsold work.

The price must, of course, still be competitive, although the nature of the competition may have changed. Unless you are a big star, the market and the price range of the particular gallery must be considered if you hope to sell your work. These are subjects you can discuss with the gallery owner who knows what type of work his clients will buy and what kind of price they'll pay.

The question of how long a gallery can keep your pieces if they remain unsold is a matter of negotiation. If the gallery spends considerable sums to mount an exhibition and pay for the promotion, then it will want the opportunity to recoup its investment. The most common time frames are between six months and a year.

Another important question is insurance. Is the gallery properly insured to cover consigned work which is on its premises but is still your property until it is sold? Who is responsible for damage or theft? Who is responsible for bringing the work to the gallery and returning unsold work to you? This is particularly important when objects have to be shipped rather than hand-delivered locally.

You may want to ask yourself (and the gallery owner) a few other questions: do you have any say in the manner in which your work is displayed, or what is shown near yours; what happens if you and the gallery owner don't see eye to eye; how are you protected if the gallery goes bankrupt; does the gallery have the right to put your work out on loan; does the gallery's sales contract with its customer include a clause that gives you a share in any increased value if the work is later resold by the customer at a higher price; does the gallery want your work exclusively or can you sell to and through anyone; when and how does the gallery pay you, and what kind of records does it keep?

These are only a few questions, some of which may be of no concern to your situation at all, others of which may be a significant factor in your relationship with a gallery.

Whatever arrangements you make on consignment, contributing to expenses, manner of payment, insurance, time, etc., should be put into writing to avoid any future misunderstandings and controversies.

(*See also: Consignment, Fine Arts Floater, Insurance, Portfolio, Resumé, Retailing*)

Government Activities

Dozens upon dozens of craft-related activities are hidden in the various nooks and crannies of federal government agencies and departments.

Perhaps the best known of these are the programs of the National Endowment for the Arts, which has a crafts coordinator in its visual arts department and provides grants running into the millions. Craft categories for which grants are available include craftsmen in residence, artists-in-schools, craftsmen's fellowships, crafts workshops, master craftsmen apprenticeships, and others. (See entry, "National Endowment for the Arts.")

Equally active, though not engaged in funding, is the Craft Development Program of the U.S. Department of Agriculture. This, too, is conducted by a crafts specialist and is engaged primarily in helping local and regional groups expand the economic development of crafts and craftspeople in their areas. The crafts specialist helps in the establishment of craft groups, cooperatives, and other associations, in providing management and technical advice, educational materials, marketing information, and other assistance. (Crafts Specialist, Farmer Cooperative Service, Department of Agriculture, 500 12th St., S.W., Washington, DC 20250.)

Other divisions of the Agriculture Department also include a variety of craft activities in their programs: the Extension Service through community resource development and 4-H youth programs; the Farmer's Home Administration through loans for industrial and business development and community facilities under the Rural Development Act; the Rural Electrification Administration; and various research and education programs of the Forest Service.

The activities of the Small Business Administration, while not specifically craft-oriented, have had an immense impact on craft producers both through direct small business loans or guaranteed loans, and through the extensive series of publications on a wide range of business subjects.

Other government agencies involved in art and craft activities are the Department of Health, Education, and Welfare, Commerce Department, Interior Department, Department of Justice (through its Prison Arts Program), the armed forces, Smithsonian Institution, Tennessee Valley Authority, National Park Service, Appalachian Regional Commission, even the State Department with its Art in the Embassies and Graduate Study Abroad programs.

Many of the programs do not deal with individual craftspeople (Small Business Administration and National Endowment for the Arts are the major exceptions), but are more involved with institutions or organizations. Of course, in most of these agencies the art and craft interest is a very minor one. But whatever it is, it often provides opportunities, directly and indirectly, for economic support to crafts.

Complete details about federal funds and services available to arts or crafts can be found in an excellent 340-page *Cultural Directory* published by the Associated Councils on the Arts. This volume can probably be found in most good libraries, and should also be on the shelves of well-informed craft organizations. Single copies can be ordered at $4 each from ACA Publications, 1564 Broadway, New York, NY 10036.

(*See also: National Endowment for the Arts, Small Business Administration*)

Grants

A grant is a specific sum of money given to an individual, organization, or institution for a specific project which has a useful purpose and requires more money than the recipient has available.

The major sources for grants are:
1) Government agencies such as the National Endowment for the Arts and state arts councils;
2) Private organizations or institutions such as museums or foundations;
3) The business community, such as major corporations.

Most grants are given for very well defined purposes. Some foundations, for example, specify that they will give grants for medical education only; some corporations support symphony orchestras, and so forth.

The largest single source for grants in the crafts field is probably the National Endowment for the Arts, which has a separate visual arts department with a crafts coordinator. Its annual "Guide to Programs," published in August, outlines in detail the eligibility requirements for various grants. Fifteen categories involve grants of interest to craftspeople.

The other major sources are state arts councils or arts commissions. They can usually be located in each state capital. Both the size and the nature of grants vary from state to state.

Some major cities have their own arts councils or arts commissions which also have funds for grant purposes.

A number of federal agencies, notably the Department of Health, Education, and Welfare, give grants for specific educational purposes. A complete list of federal funds for cultural activities is found in the *Cultural Directory* published by the Associated Councils of the Arts, available for $4 from ACA Publications, 570 Seventh Ave., New York, NY 10018.

A major source of information about private funding is the *Foundation Directory*, published by Columbia University Press (136 South Broadway, Irvington, NY 10533). This volume costs $30, and is available in most good libraries.

Scholarships and fellowships for elementary and advanced university study are closely related to the concept of grants. The best approach is to decide which particular university offers the most suitable curriculum, and then inquire what scholarship aid is available at that institution. A good source for information is the *College Blue Book*, a three-volume reference work revised every two years. It includes supplements on fellowships, grants, and loans for study at both the undergraduate and graduate level, and is cross-referenced by institution and by subject matter. The whole thing costs $125; it too is available in most libraries.

The Office of Education of the Department of Health, Education, and Welfare is a major source of funding for educational institutions and students. In fiscal year 1975 its budget provided almost $7 billion for funding purposes. Among the major programs of assistance to individual students are Basic Educational Opportunity Grants, Supplemental Educational Opportunity Grants, College Work Study Program, National Direct Student Loans, and Guaranteed Student Loans. Information and application forms for the basic grants are available through colleges, libraries, or by writing to PO Box 84, Washington, DC 20044.

Every institution of higher learning also has its own student financial aid office. If you've already determined which institution you want to attend, consult with the financial aid office to find out what kind of scholarship, fellowship, grant, or loan assistance is available at that institution.

There are no prescribed general rules about how to apply for a grant, although many grant application forms outline in specific detail what type of information is required. Since a grant always has a purpose, the information the applicant furnished should stress how the use of the funds, if they are granted, will help accomplish the purpose of the grant.

(*See also: National Endowment for the Arts, State Art Agencies*)

Gross

This word has three meanings for craftspeople:
1) In poor taste, unrefined, ugly, coarse, garish;
2) 12 dozen, 144 pieces;
3) As applied to financial terms to indicate that deductions have not been taken; e.g., gross income is the total amount of dollars received, before deducting such costs as production, materials, labor and selling; gross profit is the total profit before taxes are deducted.

The opposite of gross is net, which is used when the deductions have been calculated.

(*See also: Net, Income, Profit*)

Group Insurance

Life, medical-hospital, and disability income insurance policies can be bought at comparatively low rates when a single policy is issued to a group to cover members of that group, and the group pays one premium to the insurance company on behalf of the enrolled members. A group can be formed by a business firm, an organization of craftspeople, or any similar organized entity.

Most such policies require that the group consist of at least ten members, and that a certain percentage of all members participate in the group policy. Premiums can be paid by the employer or the organization's treasury, or they can be paid by the members through the employer or the organization. Most major insurance companies offer group plans. Among the better known in the hospital and medical field are Blue Cross and Blue Shield.

Members generally need no physical examination to qualify, even for life insurance. When a member leaves the group, he or she usually has the right to convert to an individual policy within a specified period, generally thirty days, again without physical examination.

Group insurance policies do not accumulate cash values as other life insurance policies do, members cannot select their own amount of coverage, and the insurance company cannot cancel an individual member's participation in a group policy.

Group insurance is used by many companies as an added form of compensation and to induce employees to remain with the firm; organizations offer it as a service to members and to attract new members.

(*See also: Insurance, Life Insurance*)

Guaranty

A guaranty is a seller's promise to repair or replace a product if it is found defective. Guaranties are normally made in writing (though the law sometimes recognizes oral guaranties) and generally stipulate the conditions under which the guaranty will be performed. There may be a time limit, such as replacing defective parts during the first ninety days; or a condition imposed on the customer, such as not having used the product improperly (e.g., plugging an AC motor into a DC outlet); or specific restrictions, such as guarantying the working parts but not the exterior finish of a product.

The words guaranty and warranty are often used interchangeably, but there are several important differences, both from the seller's and the buyer's point of view.

(*See also: Warranty*)

Health Hazards

(*See: Safety*)

Import

(*See: Customs*)

Income

The financial gain resulting from any business activity, investment, labor, personal service, or other source is known as income. Income includes:

Wages which are paid for labor performed, usually by skilled and unskilled workers, on an hourly basis or on production output.

Salaries which are paid for services over a specified period of time or for a specified function, such as annual executive salaries, a movie star's salary for a particular film, etc.

Dividends which are paid as a return on investments.

Interest which is paid as a return for the use of money.

Rents which are paid as a return on the use of property.

Royalties which are paid for the right to use the creative work or natural resources owned by others.

Sales Receipts which result from the sale of products or services (also known as gross income).

Commissions which are paid on the basis of performance, such as sales commissions earned as a percentage of sales produced.

Fees which are paid for legal, accounting, medical, and other professional services.

Within many of these categories there are refinements and secondary definitions which are described more fully under the appropriate headings in this book.

Income Averaging

Income averaging is a special income tax situation for individual taxpayers who suddenly find themselves with an annual income far in excess of their annual income during the four preceding years. This can happen if you have an unusually good selling year, or sell a piece of valuable property, or write a best seller, for example.

Rather than pay taxes in the much higher bracket for that year, under certain circumstances the law allows you to spread the income over the immediately preceding four years and pay at a lower tax rate.

Three basic conditions must be met:

1) You must have been a citizen and resident of the United States

during all of the years to which you apply the income averaging computation.

2) You must have contributed at least 50 percent of your own support during each of those years. This prevents brand new taxpayers, such as young people just out of schools, from applying income averaging to years in which they had almost no income and were supported by their parents.

3) Your income during the great year must be at least $3000 above 30 percent of the total preceding four years. Here's how that works in dollar and cents: suppose your taxable income for the four preceding years totaled $20,000; 30 percent of that is $6,000. Now you find yourself with an income of $16,000 last year. If you subtract the 30 percent average ($6,000) from the $16,000 figure, you wind up with a figure of $10,000, which is more than $3,000 over the base figure of $6,000. In this example, income averaging would most likely move you into a lower tax bracket if all your other taxpayer qualifications are the same.

Suppose you made $14,000 last year (still a hefty jump over the preceding years). Subtracting $6,000 from $14,000 leaves $8,000, or only $2,000 above the 30 percent base figure, not enough to meet the $3,000 difference demanded by the tax laws.

In all cases the figures are based on taxable income, not gross income. Unless you're a wizard at math and the tax laws, it is probably wise to get professional help if you think you might qualify for income averaging. Free advice is available from your nearest Internal Revenue Service office. If you feel more comfortable discussing this with an accountant, consider that the fee you pay might save you hundreds of dollars.

(See also: Income Tax)

Income Statement

A summary of the income and expenses during a given period, at least once a year, is known as an income statement.

It lists various categories of income and various categories of expense. By deducting the expense total from the income total, the net income for the period is determined. If expenses were larger than income, the statement will show a net loss.

An examination of the income statement, and a comparison with income statements of previous years, can be helpful in pinpointing improvements or shortcomings in specific areas of income and expense.

An imaginary income statement for an imaginary craft business is illustrated herewith. In this example, the owner of the business put himself on the payroll for $6,500, which is part of the wages expense. His total income for the year (wages plus net income) was therefore $11,432.37.

```
                    POT LUCK POTTERY

                    INCOME STATEMENT
         for the year ended December 31, 1975

  INCOME
      Retail Sales                $ 2,815.76
      Wholesale Sales              15,972.15
      Shows and Fairs              1,721.88
                              Total Income      $20,509.79

  EXPENSES
      Raw Materials               $ 3,018.11
      Wages                         8,400.00
      Payroll Taxes                 1,214.50
      Rent                            600.00
      Utilities                       396.74
      Insurance                       240.00
      Telephone                       142.68
      Depreciation                  1,060.00
      Sales Expenses                  315.46
      Miscellaneous                   189.93
                              Total Expenses    $15,577.42

                              Net  Income       $ 4,932.37
```

(*See also: Balance Sheet, Expenses, Income, Statements*)

Income Tax—Business

The federal income tax laws require different things from different types of business organizations. Sole proprietors and partnerships do not pay a business income tax on their firm's profits; those profits are taxed on the individual's income tax return. Of course, in both instances special returns have to be prepared to declare the firm's income and expenses and reach a taxable figure: Schedule C with Form 1040 for individual owners, Form 1065 for partnerships.

Corporations are another matter. For a number of years they were taxed by the federal government at the rate of 22 percent on their first $25,000 in profits and 48 percent on everything above $25,000. In 1975 the law was changed temporarily to a formula of 20 percent on the first $25,000 in profits, 22 percent on the next $25,000, and 48 percent on everything above $50,000. That law was extended into 1976, and may well be extended again, though there's no guarantee that the old formula is dead forever.

The corporate tax is, in effect, a double tax. First the corporation's income is taxed, and then, when the income has been distributed to stockholders, it is taxed again on the stockholder's individual income tax return.

All states, and many cities, impose their own taxes on corporate profits. Some even tax the incomes of unincorporated businesses. That tax is often called a franchise tax though it goes by a variety of names. It is, in effect, a tax on the right to conduct a business. An accountant or the applicable taxing authorities should be consulted to determine the specific tax requirements in your area.

The Internal Revenue Service has published an unusually clear "Tax Guide for Small Business" (Publication 334), which is revised annually and is available without charge from the nearest IRS office (see telephone white pages under "U.S. Government, Internal Revenue Service") or by writing to the IRS in Washington, DC 20224.

(*See also: Accounting, Estimated Tax, Income Tax—Personal*)

Income Tax—Personal

For tax purposes, almost everything you earn from any source is considered income: wages, fees, dividends, interest, rent, profits, pensions, annuities, alimony, prizes and awards, jury duty, tips, profit from the sale of real estate, etc.

Income that does not have to be reported includes: Veterans Administration benefits and disability payments, Social Security benefits, life insurance sums received at a person's death, workmen's compensation or other benefits paid for injury or sickness, interest on certain state and municipal bonds, and money or other property you inherited.

Who Must File?

Federal income tax returns must be filed before April 15 each year by everyone whose income in the previous year exceeded a certain minimum, depending on the taxpayer's status. For 1976, the IRS provided the following list of minimum gross income at which you have to file a return:

Single under 65	$2,350
Single over 65	3,100
A person who can be claimed as a dependent on parents' return	750
Widow(er) under 65 with dependent child	2,650
Widow(er) over 65 with dependent child	3,400

Married, filing jointly, both under 65 and living together at end of 1975	3,400
Married, filing jointly, one spouse 65 or older	4,150
Married, filing jointly, both 65 or older	4,900
Married, filing separately or not living together at end of 1975	750

If income was from self-employment a return must be filed if the net earnings from self-employment were at least $400.

Even if you are not required to file an income tax return according to the figures shown above, it is necessary to file if you worked during the year in order to get a refund of income tax that was withheld.

Long Form or Short Form?

Taxpayers in income brackets below $15,000 whose income was solely from wages and who have no unusual deductions to itemize will generally find it easiest to file the short form 1040A as their federal income tax return. All you need do is to record the amount of income and tax withheld as shown on the forms which are provided by the employer(s) to every wage earner in January. The Internal Revenue Service allows a standard 16 percent deduction and calculates the tax due or the tax refund based on the number of dependent exemptions claimed.

Persons with larger incomes, self-employed income, or deductions beyond the standard 16 percent allowance must fill out Form 1040, calculate their tax, and send a check for the payment due or claim a refund.

Estimated Tax Declaration

Taxpayers who have income from sources other than wages subject to payroll deduction must file a declaration of estimated tax when they file their income tax return. Estimated taxes have to be paid in equal quarterly installments on April 15, June 15, September 15, and January 15. There are several ways to calculate the estimated tax, the most convenient being the use of the previous year's self-employed income as the basis for estimating the current year's tax obligations.

On Telling the Truth

Intentional falsification of tax returns, or even negligence, can lead to severe penalties. Unintentional errors, or deductions subject to interpretation, may lead to a tax examination by the Internal Revenue Service. If you're not trying to defraud the government, the worst that can happen in such circumstances is that you'll be required to pay the shortage plus a penalty. The best that can happen is that the IRS tax examiner agrees that your tax return is correct.

The secret here is to have all the documents available to prove the claims you make. The initial examination of a federal tax return is usually made by a computer. If the computer finds something unusual, it refers the return to a pair of human eyes. For example: if you claim $5,000 in medical expenses and only $8,000 in income, the computer will frown. That doesn't sound right. But if you have the receipts to prove that you really spent $5,000 on doctor bills, all will be well.

Hold on to every scrap of paper that supports your deductions for at least three years after the date of filing your tax return. Thereafter you will not be confronted with a tax examination or a need for those papers except in cases of fraud or if you omitted more than 25 percent of your gross income.

Where to Get Help

Taxpayers who file the short form 1040A rarely need much help, except perhaps in making a decision on whether to file the short form or the long form. This happens if you are on the borderline of $15,000, or if your deductions are on the borderline of the standard 16 percent which the IRS allows automatically.

In most other cases, taxpayers will find that the cost of professional help in filling out the income tax return often represents a saving in tax payments because accountants are more familiar with the latest regulations, what may be deducted and what may not be, and other intricacies of the tax laws. Be sure that whoever helps you knows his or her business. A $5 tax preparer may be worth no more than that. Taxpayers can also get free help and advice from the nearest office of the Internal Revenue Service.

(*See also: Accounting, Income Averaging, Income Tax—Business, Taxes*)

Industrial Design

Industrial design is nothing new. No matter what the product was, it had to be designed before it could be produced by industry. But with the resurgence of consumer demand for mass produced items that also incorporate some element of good design, major manufacturers have begun to seek industrial designers who are also thoroughly grounded in art and design. This has opened up numerous opportunities for craftspeople.

The pure craft artist may find it unacceptable to design a refrigerator or a bath towel or a cookie cutter for mass production. But some believe that by upgrading the appreciation for good design and good taste in such products, limited as the possibilities may sometimes seem, new customers will be developed for truly handcrafted design work. Besides, the fees for industrial design work often help a craft artist to pursue his or her other craftwork under less economic pressure.

In addition to good taste, industrial design also requires an understanding of mass production processes. This often imposes a need to adapt or compromise, which some craft artists find difficult to do.

Some schools, such as Parson's Institute of Design, Pratt Institute, and Fashion Institute of Technology, all in New York City, offer courses in industrial design with special emphasis on textiles and similar consumer goods.

Finding a job or a commission in this field requires a considerable amount of digging and perseverance. If you think you are professionally and emotionally suited to do this kind of work, make a list of manufacturers of consumer goods in your area. It is easiest to start locally until you have a reputation which does not require you to spend a large amount of time and money traveling around the country to introduce yourself.

Send your resumé with some slides or photographs of your work to these companies. Study what they are now producing so that your introductory letter can give them some indication of what you think you can do for them. Don't send any original sketches which haven't been copyrighted. But if you contact a firm which makes dinnerware, for example, indicate that you have had experience both in designing such pieces which have had some sales success, and an understanding of the production problems and processes.

The smaller the firm, the better your chance for an interview. Don't start with the likes of General Motors or Burlington Mills. They have their own staffs of industrial and textile designers.

An industrial design commission should always be put into writing to avoid misunderstandings. The contract should specify what you are expected to do, when you are expected to do it, how much and when you will be paid (a flat fee or a royalty), who owns your design after you've completed it (usually the company that commissioned it, unless you're very famous), and any other details that are important to the particular relationship. Have your lawyer look over the contract; you can be sure the company's lawyers will study it to protect their client.

(See also: Commission)

Inland Marine Insurance

(See: Property Insurance)

Installment

An installment is, by definition, a part of the whole. Thus in an installment purchase or an installment loan, the whole amount is paid off in equal parts. Interest charges are added to the face amount, and the total is then divided into equal payments, usually on a monthly basis for one or two years.

The buyer of an installment purchase does not own the property until the last installment has been paid. The seller can take the property back (repossess it), give no credit for what's already been paid and sometimes claim the entire balance due as well.

Mortgages, automobile loans, and other long-term borrowing for major purchases are, in effect, installment loans, although they're not called that. The real estate, the car, or the equipment, serve as security for the repayment of the loan and can be repossessed if the borrower fails to pay installments when they are due.

Interest rates on installment purchases are usually much higher than on bank loans. In many states such interest can reach 18 percent per year on short-term installment purchases. Many buyers find it more economical to borrow the money from a bank, pay off the purchase in one lump sum, and repay the bank in monthly installments at a lower rate.

Laws and regulations covering installment selling vary from state to state, but it is always wise to read the fine print on installment contracts before signing.

(*See also: Contracts, Loans, Mortgages, Revolving Credit*)

Insufficient Funds

When there is not enough money in a checking account to pay a check drawn against it, the bank marks the check "insufficient funds"and returns it to the recipient who presented it for payment through the recipient's bank. For example: you take a check at a craft fair in payment for a wall hanging. You deposit the check at your bank. Your bank sends it through to your customer's bank for collection. However, your customer doesn't have enough money on deposit to pay the check. Your customer's bank rubber-stamps the check "insufficient funds" (or "no funds" or "no account," as the case may be), and sends it back to your bank which, in turn, sends it back to you. There's some colorful language to describe such checks. Since they've come right back to their starting point, they have bounced and are known as rubber checks. To rub salt into the wound, your bank will add a service charge, normally about 50¢, to your monthly statement for handling such a check.

That's why it is so important to know from whom you accept a check.

112

Usually it is an unintentional error. The person who gave you the check may have written it before a deposit had cleared. In that case you'll be told to deposit the check again, and it will usually clear the second time. If it does not, there's no third chance. Most banks will not handle such a check more than twice.

If the customer offers to write a new check, be sure it includes a reimbursement for the service charge your bank levied against you.

When the shoe is on the other foot—a check you wrote is returned to the recipient marked "insufficient funds"—you may get an angry phone call, even though your intentions were honorable. Make sure you have enough money on deposit to tell the recipient to redeposit the check. If need be, tell him or her to redeposit it in three days or next week, or whenever you know you can cover it.

Intentionally writing a check for which there are not sufficient funds on deposit can bring on a lawsuit. Keeping an accurate checkbook can avoid such difficulties.

(See also: Balance, Checking Account, Collection Problems, Overdrawn)

Insurance

Everything in life is a risk, and insurance exists to reduce the consequence of some risks. An insurance policy, really, is nothing more than a transfer of some of the risk from your shoulders to those of the insurance company, in return for which you pay them a fee known as a premium.

It isn't quite that simple, of course. Some risks cannot be insured, some risks are not worth insuring, and some risks must be insured.

To cite three examples: betting on a horse is a risk which cannot be insured; throwing a pot which may turn out lopsided is a risk hardly worth insuring; driving a car is considered by many states a sufficiently high risk to require insurance by law.

There are some basic things that should be understood about insurance in order to buy wisely. These include the nature of risk, the types of insurance, what to insure, insurable interest, how much to buy, deductibles, telling the truth, and from whom to buy.

The Nature of Risk

Risks fall into two basic categories. One is pure risk, where you have no choice in the outcome. If you own a building and a fire breaks out, there is a loss. Pure risks don't allow any other result but a loss.

Speculative risks, on the other hand, are those in which you have a choice. You have a hand in controlling the risk, and can therefore make a decision whether you want to take it. Going into business is itself a speculative risk. You might make money or you might not.

Pure risks can be insured. Speculative risks cannot.

Types of Insurance

There are two general categories of insurance: personal and property.

Personal includes life, accident, medical and hospital, public liability, and a few others.

Property covers fire, theft, title, and automobile, plus some minor ones of little consequence in a crafts business.

Many of these are discussed in detail in this book under their appropriate alphabetical entries.

Insurable Interest

You cannot insure anything in which you have "no insurable interest"; that is, from which you would suffer no loss. You can insure a building you own against loss through fire, but you cannot insure the Empire State Building (unless you happen to own that too). You have no insurable interest in the Empire State Building.

Similarly, you can insure the life of your family's breadwinner, but you cannot insure the life of the king of England (unless you are the queen of England), again because you have no insurable interest.

The real test of insurable interest is whether you or the beneficiary of the insurance policy would suffer a loss if the risk covered by the policy came to pass. You need not even own a piece of property to have an insurable interest in it. The holder of a mortgage certainly has such an interest in a building on which he's made the mortgage loan. Nor need you be related to the person on whose life you take out a policy. An employer has an insurable interest in a key employee whose death might seriously damage the earning capability of the business.

The insurable interest must exist not only at the time the policy goes into effect, but also at the time a claim is made. If you have a fire policy on a building which you subsequently sell, and it then burns to the ground, you no longer have an insurable interest, even if you paid the premiums.

The exception is life insurance, where the insurable interest needs to exist only at the time the policy is written. Two examples: if you take out a policy on a key employee who subsequently leaves you, you can still collect in the event of his death, even many years later, as long as you continue to pay the premium. Or if you have a big fight with your wife which leads to divorce, and you remarry and live happily almost ever after, the first wife can still collect on your life insurance if you have not instructed the insurance company to change the beneficiary on your policy.

It is sound judgment, therefore, to examine your policies periodically to determine what should remain in effect, what should be added, what can be cancelled, and whether any of the beneficiaries should be changed.

114

What to Insure

On the assumption that craftspeople don't have unlimited funds to spend on insurance premiums, certain priorities must be established when you sit down to determine what to insure.

The first and foremost consideration has to be the risk in relation to your capability to survive it. Fire insurance is clearly a top priority. A serious fire can put you out of business. Even a minor fire can pose a serious loss if your productive activities are interrupted for any length of time.

In automobile insurance, liability takes precedence over collision. If a $3,000 car is totally destroyed, you've lost $3,000. But if that same car gets into an accident without proper liability coverage, it could cost you $100,000. Saving on the latter to pay for the former can be penny wise and pound foolish.

If you work at home, even if it's a totally separate shop or studio in your home, be sure you are properly covered. The ordinary homeowner policy does not include commercial or professional activities in its coverage. You can usually add your craft activities to the homeowner policy at a fairly small premium.

If the worst anyone can steal from you is a few hundred dollars worth of tools, you may not want to buy theft insurance. But if you're a jeweler with a tempting supply of gold and silver on hand, theft insurance may be essential. Every craftsperson has to make his or her own list of priorities. If there are some items you can't afford now, perhaps they can be insured later.

How Much to Buy

A big question always is "How much insurance do I need?" In property insurance, that depends to a large extent on the value of the property, how much of a loss you can sustain without insurance, and how much money is available for premium payments.

Underinsuring serves little purpose, and can be expensive if trouble develops. For example: you own the building where your pottery is located. The building's current cash value is $25,000. Most fire insurance policies require that you insure up to 80 or 90 percent of the value, or else you assume some of the risk yourself.

Now, you insure that $25,000 building for only $15,000. That's 60 percent of the value. But it doesn't mean that the insurance company will pay your losses up to $15,000, and you pay the rest. If the particular policy requires 80 percent coverage, and you buy only 60 percent, then the insurance company will pay only 60 percent of a claim. The rest is your responsibility. That's also known as co-insurance because you are, in effect, insuring yourself for part of the loss. It's rarely worth the risk. Expensive as fire insurance may be, few craftspeople can afford the chance of underinsuring or co-insuring.

115

Overinsuring is wasteful, because property insurance policies do not pay off the face value of the policy, only the actual loss up to the face value. Again, the same $25,000 shop—only now it is insured for $50,000 and you are paying a higher premium for the higher coverage. Even if the shop is totally destroyed you will still collect only $25,000.

The major exception to this rule is life insurance. Since no one can place a dollar value on a human life, the purchaser of life insurance is entitled to determine how much insurance is desirable or necessary, and the entire amount is paid to the beneficiaries when the insured dies.

It is essential that property insurance policies be reviewed periodically to determine whether the face value is still appropriate. You may have installed an expensive piece of equipment, or the property itself may have increased in value, in which case the policy should be increased. If the property has decreased in value you can save some money in premiums by reducing the coverage.

But whatever you do, don't buy a particular policy simply because it seems cheap. Many factors enter into the determination of premiums, including not only fine-print inclusions and exclusions of coverage, but also the insurance company's strictness in claims settlements, its financial condition, etc. Know exactly what you are buying, and compare apples with apples.

Deductibles

Many insurance policies have a deductible clause. This is particularly true in automobile collision insurance and in many medical plans. It means that the policy holder pays part of the claim, say the first $50 or 10 percent of the total, or it establishes a waiting period after which benefits go into effect. Insurance companies do this to weed out the numerous small claims which cost more in paper work than they are worth. In return, the difference in premium costs make it worthwhile. If it costs you $50 extra in premiums to get full coverage and remove a $100 deductible, you are paying a premium rate of 50 percent on that $100 worth of insurance, which is very high.

Telling the Truth

A key ingredient of every insurance policy is that the applicant has told the truth in the application. It's not only what you include in the truth, but even more important, what you leave out.

In official language these are known as representations. The premise is that the insurance company is prepared to shoulder the risk, based on information you furnished. If you leave out anything that could affect their decision, one of two serious consequences can result: 1) the policy can be cancelled, or 2) claims will be denied if the false or misleading statements are discovered after a claim is made.

For example, if you apply for fire insurance and tell the insurance company you've had no fires in the past ten years, they will assume that you take proper safety precautions and are a good risk. So they write the policy. But then you have a fire, and in the course of the investigation it is discovered that you had three fires in the last two years. Had the insurance company known that, they might never have issued the policy, or set a much higher premium. They'll fight your claim tooth and nail, and probably win.

Similarly, even if you are in perfect health, the insurance company still has a right to know that your hobby is skydiving. It could affect the premiums they'll charge, or whether they will write a policy at all. It's better to tell all up front than run into a (losing) argument after the fact.

Where to Buy Insurance

Insurance is available through three sources: agents, brokers, or directly from the insurance company.

The bulk of property insurance is written by agents and brokers. Since they represent a number of insurance companies, they can provide you with the best coverage suited to your needs. They are in a position to issue a binder on your property the moment you telephone them, and you are insured from that moment on. Since they are usually also your neighbors, they can sit down with you and analyze your insurance needs, and are on the spot when a claim has to be settled.

A great deal of life insurance is written directly by the insurance companies through their own salesmen. Obviously, they sell only their own product, and thus are not in a position to give you impartial advice on the merits and demerits of the policies issued by different companies. But settling a claim is a fairly uncomplicated matter. The insured either has or has not passed away.

Automobile and medical insurance can often be bought through the mail, without salesmen. This may save some money in premiums (since there are no commissions to pay), but it removes the personal touch, especially when there's a claim to settle.

Selecting an insurance broker or agent should be done with the same care as choosing a lawyer or an accountant. It should be a professional relationship. The stakes can be very high. Ask around. Consult other craftspeople or business people whose judgment you respect. Settle on one agent or broker to handle all your insurance business. He or she will have a greater interest in you, and you're likely to get better service.

Craftspeople who want to dig more deeply into insurance matters can send for an excellent, nontechnical booklet published by the Small Business Administration. "Insurance and Risk Management for Small Business" (Small Business Management Series No. 30, Second Edition) is available for 95¢ from the Superintendent of Documents, U.S. Government Printing Office, Washington, DC 20402.

An "Insurance Checklist for Small Business" (Small Marketer's Aid #148) is available without charge from the Small Business Administration, Washington, D.C. 20416, or from SBA field offices in major cities.

Not included in this discussion of insurance matters are personal insurance policies such as automobile, medical and hospital, and the like. It should be remembered that some insurance is compulsory (e.g., automobile insurance in most states), while some is voluntary (medical insurance). Almost anything can be insured. You can even buy insurance against bad weather at a craft show, but the premiums are very high because the risk is very great.

(*See also: Disability Income Insurance, Fine Arts Floater, Group Insurance, Liability Insurance, Life Insurance, Product Liability Insurance, Property Insurance, Unemployment Insurance, Workmen's Compensation*)

Interest

This word has both a legal and a financial meaning.

In legal terms it means that you have some claim to a certain property. For example, if you and a partner each invest $1,000 in a craft business, you each have a half interest in the business.

In financial terms, interest is money earned by money. If you think of money as a product which you rent, much as you might rent a car, the interest is the price you pay for the use of that product.

If you borrow $100 from a bank at 8 percent annual interest you are, in effect, paying the bank $8 rent for the use of its money for one year. Similarly, if you put $100 in a savings account at 6 percent annual interest, the savings bank is paying you $6 rent for the use of your money for one year. The same principle applies if you buy bonds. You are lending your money at a specified rate of interest.

Interest rates are usually quoted on an annual basis, even if the period to which they apply is shorter. The interest rate on a department store charge account, for instance, may be quoted at 18 percent a year. However, if your balance is $100 and you pay it off at the end of the month, you will pay only $1.50 in interest (1/12th of the annual amount, which in this case would be $18).

Maximum interest rates are almost always set by state law, although they vary from state to state.

The financial world uses a whole host of interest terminology. For small businesses such as crafts, two terms are of concern: simple interest and compound interest.

Simple interest is calculated on the amount of money involved in the loan, and is either paid to the lender when the principal is repaid at the end of the loan period, or is sometimes deducted from the loan in advance. It does not itself earn interest. This form of interest is most common when you borrow money.

Compound interest is paid on the principal plus previously earned interest. The previously earned interest, in effect, keeps increasing the principal amount. Bank interest used to be calculated quarterly. With the introduction of computers, it is now usually calculated daily, so that the amount in deposit grows every day, and interest is paid on a higher amount each day. That explains why an annual rate of 6 percent will return not $6, but approximately $6.50, on every $100 deposit.

Maneuvering your money to earn the best interest can make a contribution to your profit picture. You may be saving up to buy a new piece of equipment, or you may have just earned a bundle at a craft show. Keeping those funds in a non-interest checking account makes no sense. Even if you deposit them in a savings account for only a few months, the money grows. $500 can earn more than $15 in six months. It may not be much, but better in your pocket than theirs. You'd probably have to sell more than $75 worth of craftwork to clear $15.

The interest rate on charge accounts and credit cards can be deceptive because the monthly amount seems small. If you finance a $1,000 piece of equipment at 12 percent for one year, your finance charges will be $120. If you borrow the money from a bank at 8 percent, pay off the equipment in one lump sum, and repay the bank in twelve monthly installments, the finance charge amounts to only $80.

(*See also: Banks, Checking Accounts, Credit Cards, Loans, Mortgage*)

Interior Decorators/Designers

The two terms are interchangeable, although some people think there's more prestige attached to designer than to decorator. One interior designer said she likes to think of herself as an interior architect since she makes sketches and is consulted on structural situations as they affect interior planning. "Interior decorators," she said, "are suburban ladies who run to antique stores to buy things for their friends at a discount." That kind of snobbery, of course, does not alter the facts.

The facts for craftspeople are that interior designers/decorators can be excellent marketing outlets for craftwork. They are particularly interested in textile design, fabrics, furniture, lamps, and decorative objects. For major projects they may specify particular dimensions, color schemes, materials, design concepts, etc. In addition to the fee they receive from their clients, they usually get a discount on the materials they buy (craftwork included) which ranges between 10 and 20 percent off the retail price.

Interior designers/decorators can be found in the yellow pages of the telephone book. It is best to contact them by letter, enclosing a resumé and several photographs. A personal invitation to visit your shop or studio, to see an exhibition of your work, or stop by at your booth at a craft show often produces interest that leads ultimately to sales. Interior design work ranges from small projects such as a living room in someone's home, to very elaborate assignments to decorate a large hotel or office building. A good connection can therefore turn out to be very lucrative.

Since their stock-in-trade is good taste and new ideas, decorators/designers are constantly on the lookout for imaginative craftwork and innovative design concepts, especially one-of-a-kind objects.

(*See also: Architects, Commissions, Orders*)

Inventory

First, a definition: in the truest sense inventory means everything you own that's movable, and its value. That would include the tools you work with, the chair you sit on, even stationery and paper clips.

For our purposes here, inventory will consist of everything you own that will ultimately become a salable product: raw materials, work in progress, and finished work ready for shipping.

Every item in your inventory started out as a business expense, and will (hopefully) end up as business income. In between it's all part of your assets and has a significant bearing on your money supply and your tax situation.

Million dollar companies can (and have) teetered on the brink of bankruptcy because their millions were tied up in inventories and they couldn't pay their bills. It may be all well and good to buy a ton of clay because it's cheaper than buying a hundred pounds twenty times, but not if that leaves you short of cash to run your pottery. It may save production costs to make a thousand rings at one clip and put them on the shelf, but not if there's no money left to go to craft shows to sell them.

Inventories at both ends (raw materials and finished goods) have to be balanced carefully against available money supply, production capacity, and sales potential.

Inventory of finished goods present a particular set of opportunities and problems.

Here are some of the advantages:

1) Craftwork is always ready to ship; no need to start production when an order comes in.

2) It is usually more economical to make up a quantity of a given item than to make up one or two.

3) You can be ready for a craft show or some other opportunity on a moment's notice.

4) If you sell at retail, you have a wide variety of products from which your customers can choose.

Now for some of the problems:

1) Inventory represents an investment of money.

2) You need considerable storage space.

3) If your type of craft requires a wide variety of sizes or colors or shapes, the inventory will have to be extremely large to be complete.

4) What do you do with the slow sellers that stay on the shelf? How can you get rid of them so that you can invest the money in something profitable?

It becomes fairly evident that a beginning craftsperson is ill advised to build up a sizable inventory. After you have determined that certain items move well, perhaps you can get your feet wet by putting several dozen of these in inventory. But remember that tastes change, the public is fickle, and if it's a trendy object, be careful.

Turnover

The key to a successful inventory is turnover. This means how many times in a given period, usually a year, you sell and replenish your complete inventory, or how often the investment in inventory turns over. That's important in relation to your money supply and the return you get on your investment. Let's assume that you have invested $1,000 in time and material for craftwork which is put on the shelf, waiting to be sold. If everything sells, you get back your original $1,000 plus (for purposes of this example) $250 in profit. The original $1000 goes right back into producing more inventory; no need for more capital. If your inventory turns over twice during the year, you will have made $500. But suppose it turns over five times: in other words, you sell and replenish the stock five times during the year. Now you will have realized $1,250 on that same $1,000 inventory investment.

Obviously it isn't quite that sensational in real life, but the principle is clear.

Inventory Control

Keeping careful records of what goes in and out of inventory is necessary both as a guide to your production operations and to weed out those items which move slowly and therefore retard turnover and put a drain on your money.

Since the dollar value of inventory is needed to determine your annual net income for tax purposes, a *physical inventory* should be taken at least once a year, as close to the end of the taxable year as possible. That involves the actual counting of all the pieces that are in inventory, and recording the count together with the value of the pieces at what it cost to produce them (not counting the potential profit if they are sold).

To keep abreast of your inventory from day to day or month to month, a *perpetual inventory* control system is extremely useful. This need not be a complicated affair. If your inventory consists of a wide variety of items, it is best to use a looseleaf book with one page for each item, or even for each color or size of an item which is produced in various colors and sizes. Divide the page into four columns: Date, In, Out, Balance. Whenever you put items into stock or take them out of stock you list the quantity under the appropriate column, and the new balance in the final column. Now you can see at a glance how much is in stock at all times, and how fast each item is moving. If you mark a reorder quantity at the top of the page, you can compare that number with the current balance and know whether it's time to make more of the same.

This will help not only in controlling what type of item goes into stock, but in determining if particular colors or sizes of one item move better than others.

Why take a physical inventory if you keep a careful perpetual inventory? Experience has shown that the two almost never agree. Breakage, theft, small errors in record keeping inevitably occur during the year. The physical inventory is the only one that comes close to 100 percent accuracy, and that's what's needed for tax purposes as well as your own business information.

Let's examine the tax situation a little more closely. Since inventory represents the cost of work that was not sold, it becomes part of your final gross profit and can therefore increase or decrease your tax liability.

An example might demonstrate this point:

Suppose your total receipts during the year were $20,000. Your inventory at the beginning of the year was $2,000, and at the end of the year, $2,500. Your cost of production during the year (raw materials, labor, overhead, etc.) totaled $8,000. We can construct a table like this:

Total Receipts		$20,000
Beginning Inventory	$ 2,000	
Cost of Production	8,000	
Total	10,000	
Less Year-End Inventory	2,500	
Net Cost	$ 7,500	– $ 7,500
Gross Profit		$12,500

Now, by controlling inventory carefully, you can change your tax liability by changing your gross profit. Let's assume all the other figures remain the same, but you decide to produce less during the latter part of the year, and thereby reduce your year-end inventory. Now you have this set of figures:

Total Receipts			$20,000
Beginning Inventory		$ 2,000	
Cost of Production		8,000	
	Total	10,000	
Less Year-end Inventory		1,000	
	Net Cost	$ 9,000	– $ 9,000
	Gross Profit		$11,000

In other words, the lower your year-end inventory is, the lower your gross profit (and therefore your tax liability) will be. The actual physical count at the end of the year allows you to remove shopworn, broken and pilfered items from inventory, write them off as a loss, and reduce your inventory even further in terms of dollars. This is also valuable to reduce taxes for craftspeople in states or localities which impose an inventory tax.

A few other important points to remember:

The value of an item in inventory is established by law according to its fair market value or the cost of production, whichever is lower. In other words, the price tag you put on an item is usually not the determining factor since it is generally higher than the cost of producing that item. Only when you sell work below what it actually costs to produce (seconds, and the like) can the market value be used.

While direct labor costs are part of the costs of production, and even some management expenses can be included, selling expenses can never be counted as production costs for inventory purposes, although they are deductible as other expenses.

Since the government requires that inventory be counted for tax purposes, it is clearly to the advantage of craftspeople who maintain a sizable inventory of finished work and raw materials to use inventory methods that help them realize the best tax advantage under the law.

This can be a complicated business. It is wise to consult an accountant before the end of the year when there's still time to do something about it.

(*See also: Multiple Production, Production, Turnover*)

Investment

The money you put into some property with the expectation of a financial return is called an investment. The return can take various forms: stock dividends, an increase in the value of real estate, profits from the use of equipment, and others.

Investments have two basic characteristics: 1) they are generally of a long-term nature; and 2) they generally expect a reliable return at relatively low risk. It doesn't always work out that way (look at the stock market), but that's the hope when the investment is made.

Speculation is the opposite of investment. Speculation can bring a high return, but always at great risk of loss. Buying a race track is an investment; putting money on a horse is speculation.

The essential difference between investments and other ways of spending your money is that ordinary expenses are expected to produce satisfaction for some want or need, and investments are expected to produce more money.

The quality of an investment is measured by its return—how much money you make on every dollar you invest. An ordinary savings account may pay 6 percent, or bring a 6 percent rate of return. A corporate stock may bring 8 percent. A bigger kiln may enable you to make more pots and increase your profit by 10 percent. This is a simplistic way of stating the case, but it serves to illustrate the point. Calculating the actual return on investment is best left to an accountant.

A consideration when making investments is how easily the investment can be reconverted into cash if the need arises. A savings account is easily convertible: just take the money out of the bank. A corporate stock may increase or decrease in value, and you may not be able to sell when you want to. Used equipment is an even more difficult investment to convert into cash.

All of these factors influence whether or not you make a particular investment, and also the rate of return. If you want to keep your cash position liquid—that is, if you want to be able to get your hands on the money quickly—a savings account is obviously the best investment, even if it doesn't bring the best return. If you must invest in a new piece of equipment or go out of business, then other considerations such as risk or rate of return are laid aside.

Unfortunately, the investment of creative energy, artistic skill, devotion, and love which you make in your craftwork is never calculated by accountants—or you'd be rich.

Invoice

The invoice (also called bill) serves two purposes: 1) it lists in precise detail what was sold, at what prices and under what conditions, how and where it was shipped, and 2) it is the official request for payment.

Whether you use an elaborate printed invoice form with many duplicate copies, or simply use your letterhead or a plain sheet of paper (with at least one carbon copy), every invoice should contain the following information:

1) An invoice number. These should be numbered in sequence.

2) Your name, address, telephone number.

3) The date of the invoice.

4) The name and address of the customer. Be sure to follow instructions if an order specifies that an invoice be directed to a particular department, such as the accounting department of a large store.

5) Where the merchandise was shipped.

6) When and how the merchandise was shipped (UPS, parcel post, etc.).

7) Payment terms, such as 2/10– net 30.

8) Claims limitations, such as accepting damage claims only if made within ten days of receipt of the merchandise.

9) The quantity, exact description, unit price and total price of each item shipped. Where the same item is shipped in different sizes or colors, list each one separately.

10) The total price for all items.

11) Sales taxes, if any.

12) Shipping charges, if any.

13) The Grand Total.

The original copy of the invoice is sent to the customer. You keep at least one carbon copy in numerical order in an unpaid file. Mark the date you receive payment on the bill and transfer it to the paid file when the bill has been paid. This provides a quick and easy check on what bills are outstanding, and which ones are past due.

If you have a large volume of business that is billed, you may want to keep two carbons: one to file under unpaid or paid, the other to file in a separate folder for each customer. That provides you with a handy reference on the purchasing record of each customer. Checking such files periodically may also remind you that it's time to call about a reorder.

Some large stores often require a blind copy of the invoice to be included in the shipment as a packing slip so that the store's receiving department can check the shipment against the packing slip. Blind means that the packing slip copy of the invoice shows everything except the prices. When the shipment has been verified, the packing slip is sent along to the accounting department as proof that the merchandise was received in good order and payment can be made.

Where numerous copies of an invoice have to be prepared, it is usually best to get them in preprinted carbon sets. These sets normally provide a different color for each copy and also block out the price area on the packing slip copy. They also indicate who gets each copy: customer, file, packing slip, etc.

Numbering is essential for a great many reasons. It makes it easy to identify the particular invoice when you need to speak to a customer about it. It enables you to match up a check with the invoice which is being paid. Checks from stores or other business firms almost always indicate the invoice number for which the check is drawn. If a packing slip is used, it will enable the accounting department to coordinate the receiving department report with its outstanding invoices, and expedite payment to you.

The grand total should never reflect such discounts as a 2 percent allowance if the bill is paid within ten days. Mark your copy of the invoice when payment is received to indicate that the discount was taken.

The conditions you set for returns or damage claims protect you against an occasional wise guy customer. Say a store buys four dozen appliqué pillows from you. Two weeks later, the buyer finds a source for pillows less expensive than yours, so he returns your pillows with hardly an explanation. The "returns within five days" clause protects you. Of course, if it's a good customer you may not want to make a fuss and just take the pillows back. Then again, you may tell him nothing doing, and have the law on your side. If the customer has a legitimate gripe—the pillows aren't the color he ordered, for example—he should be able to discover that within five days.

The reverse of this situation applies when you receive a bill from a supplier for materials you bought. Examine the merchandise right away. Read the invoice carefully to see what your claim and return privileges are, and what kind of cash discounts you're entitled to.

The cash discount policy is one you have to be tough about. If you allow 2 percent for payment within ten days, then that's it. Some customers try to take the discount even when they pay in thirty or more days. Money is too hard to come by to allow that sort of thing. A few daring souls have even begun to add a 2 percent surcharge if the bill is paid later than thirty days, but that's quite uncommon.

Again, there's an exception. If you have a regular store customer to whom you make shipments every month or so, and it is that store's policy to pay bills on the fifth of every month, then you'll probably have to allow the 2 percent discount even if it isn't within ten days. You could, of course, send the bill on the twenty-fifth or thereabouts, but whenever you send it, as long as the customer sticks to his regular payment date you have accomplished the same purpose.

(*See also: Business Forms, Orders, Sales Conditions, Sales Tax, Shipping, Statement*)

Job Ticket

The term job ticket comes from the printing craft and has been adapted to many activities where a variety of items is produced for a variety of customers.

A numbered job ticket or production envelope is prepared for each order. It enables the craft producer to keep track of all the details and expenses connected with that order. If you decide to make 100 pots for inventory, treat that like an order as well.

The front of a 9"-x-12" manila envelope lists the customer's name, address, order number, shipping information, delivery date, and the specification of the order, e.g., thirty wooden bowls #12.

The job ticket travels with the order through all the stages of production right to the shipping table. The back of the envelope is used to record the materials used (as they are used), the time spent (as it is spent), and any other factors which influence the cost of filling that order. When the time comes to add up all the costs in both labor and materials, a glance at the job ticket brings all the cost factors into sharp focus.

Any papers connected with the production of that order can be stuffed into the envelope. Each job ticket has its own number, and that number is associated with the order all the way from the moment it comes in until shipment is made.

If the job tickets are filed in numerical sequence after the order is completed, and the number is indicated on all other records such as invoices and shipping receipts, it is easy to trace the entire history of a specific order at one point, and to determine what was involved in filling that order.

A simplified version is to set up a looseleaf notebook, with each page serving the same purpose as the job ticket. This may be useful in a small craft business where it is not necessary to have the job ticket move through the shop or studio with the order, or where there's no necessity to keep papers in the envelope.

The point of this system is not to create more paperwork, but to arrive at more accurate pricing through more accurate cost records, and also to reduce the amount of information you have to remember and search for, and thus clear your head for more creative and productive pursuits.

(See also: Production, Systems)

Joint Venture

A joint venture is a particular form of partnership in which the scope of the business and liabilities of the participants is limited. It can be used only for certain kinds of activities. For example, a leather worker and a buckle maker could form a joint venture to produce complete belts. In order to avoid accidentally becoming full partners, joint ventures need good legal advice before beginning operations.

Craftspeople who work together, or situations in which a craftsperson works very closely with a store or gallery in common enterprises beyond the normal supplier-retailer relationship, require great care so that their activities are not conducted as joint ventures, and the specific nature of their relationship should be spelled out in writing. If you help to finance an exhibition of your work at a gallery, for example, be sure all the conditions are set down on paper. Verbal contracts are legally binding but easily misinterpreted.

(*See also: Contracts, Corporation, Partnership, Sole Proprietorship*)

Journals

(*See: Ledgers and Journals*)

Keogh Plan

(*See: Pensions*)

Labeling

(*See: Textile Fiber Products Identification Act, Wool Products Labeling Act*)

Labor

(*See: Apprentices, Employees*)

Lawyers

"I want to see a lawyer!"

That plaintive cry is heard most often when someone gets into a peck of trouble. But most lawyers are not Perry Masons, keeping people out of jail by dint of clairvoyant detective work and facile courtroom oration. And most people fortunately do not need lawyers for so serious a purpose.

However, it is a rare individual who can get through the complications of an entire twentieth-century lifetime without ever having a need for a lawyer, particularly if you conduct business activities. Lawyers, like doctors, are needed not only to solve problems, but to prevent them before they arise.

Like doctors or craftspeople, lawyers specialize. Because the law has become so intricate, some handle only corporation law, others specialize in divorce, still others take only criminal cases. Yet there are still thousands of general practitioners who are well versed in the ordinary problems many of us face sooner or later: buying a house, signing a contract, making a will, setting up a business venture.

Of course, you don't need a lawyer every time you sign something. A contract for a booth at a craft fair, for example, is rarely worth the expense of legal advice.

The New York State Bar Association provides this rule of thumb: "Get a lawyer's advice whenever you run into serious problems concerning your freedom, your financial situation, your domestic affairs, or your property."

"Serious" is the important word in that sentence.

Legal matters fall into two basic classifications: civil cases and criminal cases.

Civil cases concern disputes between two parties, such as breach of contract, nonperformance of an obligation, and the like. A lawyer is necessary in such cases to protect your rights. In the proper conduct of your business and personal affairs, a lawyer helps to prevent complications which could end up in court as civil cases.

Criminal cases concern violations of the criminal law, such as murder, theft, and forgery. In such cases the government accuses a person of committing a specific crime.

The U.S. Constitution presumes that a person is innocent until proven guilty, and provides that every criminal defendant is entitled to a lawyer, even if the government has to pay the lawyer's fees in the event that the defendant does not have the resources to hire a lawyer.

If you are ever confronted with a criminal matter which could lead to loss of liberty or property, the first call you should make is to a lawyer. Don't ever plead guilty to anything (except perhaps a parking ticket) without consulting a lawyer first. What may seem like an insignificant situation to you could well lead to serious consequences if you don't have proper legal advice.

This applies to civil matters as well. The wording of a long-term contract that you sign may seem plain enough to you, but do you know how a court would interpret it?

When you discuss a case with your lawyer, do not hesitate to discuss the fee as well. Fees depend generally upon the amount of time and research that is involved in the case. On simple matters, such as incorporating a business or drawing up a will, the time element is well established and a fee can easily be determined. More complicated cases may require an estimate which will give you a general idea of the possible cost.

Some cases, especially law suits involving the recovery of money in accident cases, are often handled on a contingency fee basis. This means the lawyer gets 25 to 50 percent of the amount if the case is won, and gets nothing if the case is lost. But even in such cases the court costs have to be paid by the client.

The relations between a lawyer and a client are held by law to be confidential. A lawyer cannot be compelled—indeed, is not permitted—to reveal what you discuss unless you give your permission. But you should realize that this confidential relationship exists to enable your lawyer to get all the information, even such information as may be unfavorable to you. It's the only way the lawyer can properly prepare a case and can properly represent a client.

Finally, where do you find a good lawyer?

Since all lawyers are licensed, it is a matter of finding someone in whom you can have confidence, much as you would find a doctor or any other professional in whom you trust. Ask your friends or business acquaintances to recommend someone they have found satisfactory. You may want to talk to several lawyers before you settle on someone with whom you can establish that special relationship of confidence. The local bar association may be able to recommend someone if you have a particular problem which requires specialized legal experience. If your resources are very limited, the Legal Aid Society (or its local equivalent in your area) may be of help.

For information, and possibly free legal service, on problems related specifically to your work as a craft artist, contact Volunteer Lawyers for the Arts, which has chapters in many states. If you can't find them in your phone book or through your local bar association, write to Volunteer Lawyers for the Arts, 36 West 44th Street, New York, NY 10036, for the address of the nearest group.

The better part of wisdom is to have a lawyer before you need one. And sooner or later you probably will.

(*See also: Contracts, Corporation, Joint Venture, Partnership, Patent*)

Lease

Reading the fine print is never more important than when you sign a lease. It's harder to get out of than a marriage contract.

A lease is a contract between landlord and tenant, and like any other contract it spells out the responsibilities and benefits of both parties. But if you are renting, it is good to remember that leases are generally drawn up by the landlord's lawyer. They are usually weighted heavily on the landlord's side.

Some clauses should be obvious: how much is the rent, when does it have to be paid, a description of the premises you are renting, the term (length) of the lease, and so forth.

But then we come to dozens of fine print clauses. Who is responsible for painting the place? What restrictions are there on remodeling? (Some leases don't even allow you to put a nail in the wall without the landlord's permission.) Who pays for heat and hot water?

As a crafts professional, it is important that you carefully inspect the premises you are renting *before* you sign a lease. Will the floor sustain the weight of heavy equipment if you need it in your work? Can the electric wiring carry the load of heavy duty equipment such as kilns? If it can't, whose responsibility is it to install the proper wiring? Are there any zoning, pollution, noise or other restrictions that would affect your use of the premises?

Such an inspection should also raise other questions. Don't take for granted, for example, that the air conditioners in the windows will stay there after you move in, or that you won't be surprised with an extra charge above the stated rent to keep them.

If the lease specifies that you pay for your own utilities such as gas, water, and electricity, make certain that separate meters are installed for your premises. Sharing the landlord's meter almost always leads to arguments when the bill comes in.

Inspect carefully to see that everything is in good repair: water supply, radiators, bathrooms, windows, floors, ceilings. The lease should specify whose responsibility it is to fix such things if they break during the course of your lease. A tenant must realize that the more responsibility is on the landlord's shoulder, the higher the rent is likely to be.

That is true of maintenance and remodeling as well. If you want to fix up the place by putting in walls and partitions, new wiring, light fixtures and so forth, your right to do that must be spelled out in the lease, providing only that the end result meets all legal standards such as fire and building regulations, and that it doesn't lower the value of the landlord's property or increase his insurance rates.

Having the landlord do all the repair and improvement work doesn't necessarily save you money. He'll get it back in the rent by charging you more. If you do it yourself, you have to make the financial investment directly. Before you sign a lease, calculate which is the more practical approach for your particular financial situation.

Remember also that every request for repairs or improvements carries the possibility of lengthy debate and argument with the landlord. He or she will obviously want to save the money. If the lease gives you the right (and the responsibility) to do such work, be certain that you do not need to obtain the landlord's permission for every dab of paint you put on the wall.

The basic quid pro quo in such situations is only that you do not depreciate the landlord's property, and that you leave it in the same condition, excepting normal wear and tear, when you move out.

One area of landlord responsibility that the tenant should rarely assume is the basic structural condition of the premises, or other conditions required by law. If it rains through the roof, the landlord should fix it. If the fire department issues a structural violation, it is the landlord's responsibility to fix, unless the tenant created the violation. The lease should be very specific on this subject.

If the lease does not otherwise specify it, any permanent installation by a tenant—new wiring, for example, or a new sink—usually becomes part of the premises. You can't just rip out the wiring when you move out. If you plan to install permanent fixtures that you want to take with you, make sure the lease allows it. Determine also whether everything you see on the premises before you sign the lease will still be there after you sign it; the previous tenant may not have removed all of his property. Verbal promises by the landlord mean nothing. Get it in writing in the lease.

Some craftspeople have found themselves in a barrel of hot water when they opened workshops or studios in premises leased for residential purposes. If it's a small and quiet affair, there's usually no trouble. But if the lease or the zoning regulations prohibit such activities, you can run into difficulties on two counts: 1) the landlord may want more rent for the commercial use of the space; and 2) neighbors may complain if extensive noise, odor, refuse, or other objectionable conditions are associated with the improper use of the premises.

The end of the lease is as important as the beginning. Every lease includes a clause that the tenants leave the premises in the same condition as when they moved in. The deposit required by most landlords is one way in which they make sure that you pay for repairs which have to be made after you move out to restore the place to its original condition.

A sublease clause is also important. If you find it necessary to move out before the lease expires, do you have the right to find a new tenant to fill the remaining term of your lease? If you have that right, does the landlord have veto power? Can he, for example, determine that a certain type of tenant is undesirable?

Finally we come to the renewal clause. Suppose you sign a two-year lease with an option to renew. Does it specify at what rent you renew? When you have to exercise the option? What happens if you don't exercise the option?

In some states, the law assumes that you have renewed the lease and all its terms if you have not notified the landlord otherwise in writing by a certain date.

In other cases, your lease may have expired, but you remain on a month-to-month basis. In the absence of a lease at that time, the landlord can charge you anything he wants, unless the original lease specifies otherwise.

It is obviously impossible to discuss every fine print clause of every lease without making this chapter a casebook study only lawyers would understand. Nor is it possible to predict every eventuality that is left unmentioned in the so-called standard lease.

The basic purpose here is to alert you to the necessity of reading all the terms very carefully, taking nothing for granted, assuming nothing that isn't put down in writing, and taking the time to think carefully about the implications of everything you sign.

If the lease is of any extensive term, or if you intend to make a major investment in improvements, it is advisable to spend $50 or $100 to consult a lawyer. Tell him or her what your requirements are, what you want to do and don't want to do, and let the lawyer analyze the fine print to make sure that your interests are properly protected.

Ledgers and Journals

Ledgers and journals are bookkeeping records in which the various financial transactions of a business are indicated.

The journal is the initial method of keeping the records, and no extensive bookkeeping expertise is required. Many businesses keep several journals: one in which to list all sales, one for expenses, one for wages, one for accounts receivable, and so forth.

While some large firms with complicated financial dealings may also keep several ledgers for different purposes, a crafts business usually has only one: the general ledger. The information recorded in the general ledger is based on the entries in the journals, and is listed side by side in columns marked "debit" (expenses or liabilities) and "credit" (income or assets), according to the nature, type, or source of the transaction. While an experienced bookkeeper can maintain a satisfactory ledger for an uncomplicated business operation, it is usually wise for a small business to engage the services of an accountant to keep the ledger up-to-date periodically on the basis of journal entries or other records which the owner maintains.

(See also: Accounting, Bookkeeping)

Legality

(See: Lawyers)

Letter of Credit

A letter of credit is a special bank document in which a bank notifies its agent or correspondent bank that funds are to be paid immediately to the person named in the letter upon proper identification and evidence that the purpose for which the funds are to be paid has been accomplished, e.g., a bill of lading to prove that shipment was made. This document replaces the use of a check for payment, and makes the money immediately available. In effect, it establishes a credit line for the recipient upon which he can draw as soon as the specifications of the letter of credit are carried out. Letters of credit are used primarily for very large transactions and for foreign payments.

Liabilities

Liabilities are what you owe others, in terms of money, goods, or services. Bills you haven't paid are liabilities. So are goods you haven't shipped to customers when you've already been paid for them.

There are basically two types of liabilities: current and long term. Current liabilities include all obligations that are due in the current fiscal year. Long-term liabilities are obligations that stretch over a number of years: a mortgage, a bank loan, or the pay-out on a piece of equipment such as a car.

Liabilities and assets appear together on the balance sheet, which is prepared at least once a year. In a sound and healthy business, assets are larger than liabilities. The difference can be taken as profit or, if it remains in the business, becomes an addition to your investment.

(*See also: Assets, Balance Sheet*)

Liability Insurance

Any injury for which you or your business can be sued can be covered by liability insurance. Such insurance also covers injury caused to others by the negligence of your employees, but it does not cover the employees themselves.

There are several forms of liability insurance of concern to craft producers:

1) *Personal Liability.* This can protect you as an individual; for example, if your dog bites the mailman or someone slips on the ice in front of your house.

2) *Public Liability.* This protects you as a business owner; for example, if a customer suffers an injury while visiting your studio or workshop.

3) *Product Liability.* This protects you if a defect in a craft object you made causes injury to the user of the product.

Some craftspeople buy specific short-term liability insurance to cover themselves at a craft show or fair in case a visitor is injured at their booth.

(*See also: Insurance, Product Liability Insurance*)

License

A license or permit is the granting by a governmental body to do certain things which are regulated by law. Most craftspeople are not subject to license requirements, although it is necessary in many communities to obtain a license or permit to store flammable liquids, operate potentially dangerous equipment such as acetylene torches used in metalworking, open a retail store, and conduct similar craft-related activities. While many licenses and permits are little more than a device to collect a fee for the municipal treasury, license requirements related to health and safety are essential for the protection of the entire community, and should be carefully observed.

Lien

A lien is a legal device by which your real estate is held for the satisfaction of some debt. If the debt is not paid, the property can be foreclosed, or sold for the benefit of the debtor. In that respect it is similar to a mortgage.

Here are two types of lien:

1) *Mechanic's Lien.* If you hire a carpenter to erect an addition to your pottery, and a plumber to connect the gas pipes for your new kiln, and then you don't pay them, they can file a lien against your property in the county clerk's office. A mechanic's lien usually takes precedence over all other obligations the property may have, including a mortgage. Banks and other mortgage lenders find out about such liens very quickly, and you'll hear from them just as quickly because their loan is endangered if the lien leads to a foreclosure.

2) *Judgment Lien.* If someone sues you and wins a judgment for damages, they can also place a lien on your property, even though the cause of the lawsuit is totally unrelated to the property (unlike a mortgage or a mechanic's lien). The same procedure, and the same results, apply as in a mechanic's lien.

(*See also: Mortgage*)

Life Insurance

Life insurance doesn't guarantee that you'll live, only that the financial impact of your death will be lessened. Life insurance is not based on the same kind of risk as property insurance. Medical examinations weed out the poor risks, but once a policy is issued, the risk is 100 percent. True, the premiums are related to risk. If you are twenty years old the risk of your dying anytime soon is substantially less than if you are eighty. Statisticians have figured out those risks, and have calculated the premiums so that, on the average, you're paid up by the time you die.

It also differs from property insurance in several other important respects:

1) The amount of coverage is not related to the value of the insured item since no dollar value can be placed on a human life. Everyone can choose his or her own dollar value in terms of how much money becomes available to the beneficiaries and what the premium payments are.

2) Most insurance policies have two parties: the insured and the insurance company. Life insurance has a third one: the beneficiary. The insured usually has the right to change beneficiaries at any time through proper notice to the insurance company. There are exceptions, such as a business which carries life insurance on a key employee, with the business as the beneficiary. The employee whose life is insured cannot change the beneficiary in a situation like that.

3) Most life insurance policies cannot be cancelled by the insurance company after a stated period of time, generally two years, except when the premiums are not paid or misrepresentations were made as to age and other important factors when the policy was issued.

4) Most life insurance policies have a cash value which increases with the years. This cash value is paid to the insured if the policy is cancelled or lapses for nonpayment of premiums. The cash value can also be borrowed against. If a loan is outstanding at the time the insured dies, the loan is subtracted from the benefits and the balance is then paid to the beneficiaries.

5) Most life insurance policies pay annual dividends based on the cash value of the policy and the earnings of the insurance company. They therefore represent not only protection, but also investment.

There are literally dozens of varieties of life insurance, but they fall into four major categories: Ordinary (Straight), Limited Payment, Endowment, and Term.

Ordinary (Straight) Life is a policy on which the same premiums are paid every year as long as you're alive, and the face value of the policy is paid to your beneficiaries after you're dead.

Limited Payment is a policy under which premium payments are made for a specified period. Thereafter you stop paying but the policy is in full force and the benefits are paid to your beneficiaries when you die. It is more expensive than ordinary life in terms of the individual premium payments, but may be less expensive in terms of total premiums paid, especially if you are very young when the policy goes into effect.

Endowment policies are really savings plans with life insurance added (or vice versa). You pay premiums for a stated period of years. At the end of that time, if you are still alive, you are your own beneficiary. The face value of the policy is paid to you. If you have died in the meantime, your beneficiaries collect.

Term insurance is pure life insurance for a specified period of time, generally no more than ten years. Then coverage ends. Term policies have no cash or loan value, but their premium rates are very low compared to other types of life insurance. Term insurance is used primarily to protect unusually heavy responsibilities during a limited period of time. For example, if you have teenagers, a five- or ten-year term policy can make sure the money is available to get them through college in case you're not around to pay the tuition. Mortgage insurance is, in effect, a form of term insurance on the life of the mortgage holder for the unexpired portion of the mortgage. If you die before the mortgage is paid off, the insurance policy pays the rest. There are no other benefits.

Life insurance policies cannot be bought in the names of other people unless there is an insurable interest. A husband and wife can insure each other, and so can two partners. A corporation can insure the lives of its executives, and a baseball club can insure the lives of its players. In all instances there would be a demonstrable loss if the insured dies, and therefore an insurable interest.

Unlike property insurance, where the insurable interest must exist both when the policy is issued and when the claim is made, in life insurance that interest must exist only when the policy is issued. It becomes important, therefore, to examine your life insurance policies periodically to see if the beneficiary needs to be changed. Such instances occur when the beneficiary dies before you do, when there's a divorce, when a partnership is dissolved, or whenever some other reason for which the beneficiary was named no longer exists.

(*See also: Group Insurance, Insurance*)

Loans

Very few people, and even fewer businesses, get through life without finding the need to borrow money sooner or later: whether it's a car loan, a mortgage to buy a house, funds for expansion of a business, an installment purchase of a piece of equipment for craft production, or cash to tide a business over a slow period until sales pick up again.

Borrowing money is as American as apple pie. And like apple pie, some specific ingredients are involved to make the thing come out right.

Loans can come from a variety of sources: friends and relatives who have confidence in you or share your crafts enthusiasm, your own life insurance policies (if they have loan values), and lending institutions such as banks, credit unions, and the like. Even the credit extended by your suppliers is, in effect, a form of loan.

The major source of money which is *not* a loan is the equity capital which investors put into a business. Unlike all other sources of funds, equity is never paid back unless the business is dissolved. Rather, it serves as the basis on which the investor is paid a share of the profits.

The basic characteristic of a loan is that it must be repaid at some specified time, and that interest is charged for the use of the money.

The first question that will go through a lender's head, then, is whether the borrower can pay back the loan. That involves a whole host of questions. A bank may want to know why you need the money, what you plan to do with it, how and when the loan will be repaid, what your credit rating is (how you've repaid previous loans), whether you can put up collateral (such as real estate) as a guarantee, and so forth. These are not idle questions on the bank's part. When a bank lends money, it has to be as sure as possible that the loan will be repaid. The answers to questions such as these determine not only whether the loan will be granted, but how much interest will be charged. The greater the risk, the higher the interest.

To sum up, there are three basic sources of funds, other than your own:

1) *Equity capital:* the money which investors provide. This does not have to be repaid. The equity capital is the basis on which investors share in the profits.

2) *Trade credit:* the terms on which you can buy supplies without paying cash. You are, in effect, borrowing money for a short term until you pay your bill.

3) *Loans:* the money provided by friends, relatives, or outside lending institutions such as banks, with a specific understanding of how and when the loan will be repaid, and subject to interest charges.

There are two basic types of loans:

1) *Short Term.* These are loans for a period of one to twelve months which are expected to be repaid from the proceeds of the activity for which the money is needed. For example: you suddenly receive a large order which necessitates the purchase of $3,000 worth of raw materials. If you don't have the $3,000 readily at hand, you can borrow it for a period of a few months because the bank expects that you will repay the loan as soon as you have been paid for the order.

2) *Long Term.* These are loans which you expect to repay from your profits over a fairly long period of time, usually in monthly or quarterly installments. Such loans are made for major expenditures such as the purchase of equipment, not for immediate operating cash needs.

Short-term loans can often be made as unsecured loans, which means that your signature and your credit reputation are sufficient. Long-term loans, on the other hand, usually requires some sort of collateral, the pledging of some assets which the bank can claim and sell if the borrower fails to repay the loans. The most familiar of these is a mortgage in which the building itself is the collateral. Other forms of collateral are stocks and bonds, life insurance policies, accounts receivable, and signatures of comakers or endorsers who agree to be personally responsible if the borrower defaults.

A bank does not really lend you its own money, but the money which its depositors have placed in the bank's trust. To safeguard those deposits, banks ask many questions, as noted above. It must be remembered, that a bank is not in business to turn down loan applications. Banks make their profits primarily by lending money.

What the bank wants to know, therefore, includes some or all of these points:

1) How solvent are you?

2) Are your books and records up-to-date and in good order?

3) How much do the owner or owners take out of the business in salaries?

4) How many employees do you have?

5) How much insurance coverage do you have?

6) How large are your accounts receivable?

7) How large is your inventory?

8) What is the age and value of your fixed assets such as equipment? How are they depreciated?

9) What are your plans for the future?

For a business loan, the balance sheet and the profit and loss statements are the most important documents the bank usually requires, especially for long-term loans. They indicate your financial condition and your profit picture. A series of such statements covering several years will indicate the borrower's business growth and indicate to the bank how much of a risk it is taking by lending the money.

That's why it is so difficult for brand-new enterprises to raise funds through borrowing. It's the age-old chicken-or-the-egg theory. If you are already established, if you already owe money or have paid back previous loans, it is much easier to borrow more money.

How much money to borrow is another important consideration both for the borrower and the lender. Here again the borrower's financial statements are a key factor because they reveal if they are up to date, what the borrower's financial capacity to repay the loan is likely to be.

Suppose you have been quite successful as a potter, and you want to expand: buy another wheel, a larger kiln, remodel a bigger workshop, and hire someone to help you. If you can prove to the bank that your past financial performance is sound, that you have established some good connections with major retail outlets that bear great promise for the future if you expand, then the likelihood of getting the loan is quite good.

On the other hand, if you've done well in your own little workshop, have sold well at craft fairs, and now want to hire a dozen potters and spend $20,000 on equipment because you feel the magic spell of success in your bones, the bank will think twice, or three times, and may suggest that a smaller loan for more modest expansion is more in order for your particular situation. You may hate the bank for being so tight with its money, but since banks lend money on facts, not enthusiasm, it may even be doing you a favor by turning down an application which, on strictly financial terms, is not likely to succeed.

Another factor which banks take into account is your willingness to invest in your own business. If you make a long-range plan for expansion which will require a bank loan, it is wise to save up some money of your own. Then, when you go to the bank with your loan application, you can indicate that you are ready to invest $2,000 but need another $3,000, and you'll probably get much more sympathetic attention. The bank will be more inclined to take the risk if it knows that you are also taking a risk. Planning ahead through saving is itself an indication of good management which will impress the bank.

The limitations a bank sets on its borrowers, the size of interest it charges, and the terms of repayment are all related to the bank's interpretation of how great a risk it takes. That does not mean, however, that every bank interprets the same set of facts the same way. Some are more conservative than others. Some have had good experience with small business loans or may have a policy of encouraging small local business to develop. Some may consider a particular type of collateral very secure, while others may frown on it.

All of this influences the borrower's experience with a particular lender, and if the first approach does not succeed, or if the limitations and interest rates are not acceptable, it is perfectly reasonable to approach another bank.

As an example of how easy it is to obtain a loan when the risk is low is the passbook loan, offered by many savings banks. The bank lends you any amount up to the balance in your bankbook. It also takes possession of the bankbook, and you can touch only the amount of money in excess of your loan balance. You pay your loan back regularly, and the interest rate is generally only 1 to 2 percent above the interest the bank pays you on your savings (including the frozen funds which continue to earn interest). If you don't repay the loan, the bank simply takes the money out of your savings account. Since the risk to the bank in this transaction is zero (there's no way to lose), you need show no financial statements, provide no documents of your credit worthiness; just sign the loan papers which authorize the bank to take the money it already has in its possession to repay the loan if you fail to do so.

This is a good device for borrowers who have some cash in a savings account but don't want to use it because they fear that they don't have the self-control to repay themselves as regularly as they would the bank. And since interest charges are very minimal, many borrowers consider the cost worthwhile.

In addition to the financial documents which the bank wants to see, a carefully thought-out loan proposal also contributes a great deal to the application. The proposal should indicate how you expect the loan to perform the functions for which it is made, what the conditions in your own enterprise and in the craft field in general are, how you forsee your own production and sales plans, what new products you plan to develop, how your business is managed, and so forth. Here again, the loan proposal not only provides the bank with a picture of how safe the loan might be, but how thoroughly you have considered the need for the money and how competent your own understanding of your business situation is.

This end of the application is yours. The financial documents should be prepared by an accountant.

Borrowing money is such an extensive subject, with so many ramifications, that this chapter can provide only a general overview. Discussion of your financial needs with your accountant or your bank often provide much valuable information on the most economical and practical way to solve those needs through a wide range of borrowing opportunities.

Two excellent booklets on the subject are available without charge from the Small Business Administration: "The ABCs of Borrowing" (Management Aid #170) and "Sound Cash Management and Borrowing" (Small Marketers Aid #147). You can get them through any of its field offices or the SBA headquarters, Washington, DC 20416.

(*See also: Banks, Capital, Credit Cards, Mortgages, Trade Credit*)

Loss Leader

An item which is sold below cost in order to attract customers to buy profitable merchandise is known as a loss leader. This practice is against the law in many states where items must be sold at no less than their actual cost plus a small percentage for sales expenses. Such laws do not affect sales and other price reductions on which some profit is realized.

(*See also: Pricing*)

Magazines

(*See: Periodicals*)

Mailing Lists

Whether you use the mails to make announcements that will bring customers to your store or studio, or whether you use the mails to generate mail-order purchases of your craftwork, the mailing list is the most important ingredient.

Mailing lists come from two sources: your own lists of customers or prospects which you compile over the years, and lists which you can buy from list brokers whose names you will find in the yellow pages of the telephone book.

Your own list is, of course, the most effective. Since the quality of a list is measured by how many names on it can be expected to buy from you, a list of your former customers or others who have seen your work is one of your most valuable possessions.

Keep that list up-to-date. A card file maintained in alphabetical order is the most convenient. Whenever you have a new customer, whenever you come across an interested name, add it to the list.

Depending on your needs, that list may be sufficient for your purposes. An invitation to a gallery opening, for example, may produce enough attendance from just such a list.

However, there are occasions when you want to make a large mailing. There are literally hundreds upon hundreds of specialized lists available. The usual procedure is to buy the one-time use of such a list.

The cost depends on the nature of the list, and always includes a complete set of mailing labels. Costs generally run between $25 and $40 a thousand, though some are higher.

There are lists of doctors, society matrons, plumbers, and business executives. A list of business executives is even broken down by their titles, or the size of their businesses. You can buy lists of art patrons, museum trustees, members of particular organizations, and many others.

Discuss your list needs with a large, reliable list broker. He will usually be able to give good advice and obtain special lists for you.

If you can't find a satisfactory list broker locally, an inquiry to any of the following may be helpful: Dependable Lists, Inc., 257 Park Ave. South, New York, NY 10010; R.L. Polk & Co., 551 Fifth Ave., New York, NY 10017; Fred Woolf List Co., 309 Fifth Ave., New York, NY 10016; Alan Drey Co., Inc., 600 Third Ave., New York, NY 10016; Fritz S. Hofheimer, Inc., 88 Third Ave., Mineola, NY 11501; Noma List Services, 2544 Chamberlain Rd., Fairlawn, OH 44313; Names Unlimited, Inc., 183 Madison Ave., New York, NY 10016. There are others, of course, and several of the above have branch offices in major cities.

If you want to make a mailing to the members of a specific organization, or the subscribers of a specific publication, a direct inquiry may be useful. For a fee, some of them make their lists available to reputable firms.

You can also exchange lists with other craftspeople who are not competitive with you.

The size and nature of a list is not the only consideration, however. How "clean" a list is must also be considered. Clean means how many names will actually be reached by your mailing piece. During the course of a year people move away, or die, or change jobs. On a list which has not been used and cleaned in a year you can expect as much as 20 percent or more of undeliverable mail. That's an expensive proposition when you consider that even a simple mailing piece can cost 25¢ or more. Ask a list broker how recently a list has been used. If that wasn't very recently, ask for a refund on any undeliverable returns over 5 percent. Of course, the only refund you'll get is on the cost of the names you rented, but that's better than nothing. And most reputable brokers will stand behind their promises of clean lists.

Before you make a commitment to rent a large list, test it first. Suppose a broker has four lists, each of which has 10,000 names. All four look good to you, but you can never be sure. Instead of buying 40,000 names and discovering that some of the lists were not suited to your purpose, buy only a representative sample of each list at first—say 1,000 names. Now you have a mailing of 4,000 pieces which will cost much less than taking a chance on 40,000.

There's another use for testing as well. Suppose you have two kinds of possible offers to make in a mailing piece. Buy a representative sample of the list and mail one offer to half the list, and the other offer to the other half. If one pulls better than the other, you know what to send to the whole list.

Careful record-keeping is necessary when you test, or when you do any sort of mail promotion. There's too much money tied up in using the mails to skimp on tracking down the results.

What kind of response can you expect from a list? That depends on the quality of the list and the nature of the offer. Under normal circumstances, a list user considers 2 percent a satisfactory response. In other words, if you send out 10,000 pieces, 200 sales or inquiries would be considered acceptable. A response of 10 percent or higher could be expected from an unusually good list, such as your own customer list.

But all of that has to be related to costs. To send out 10,000 pieces at a total cost of $2,500, for example, and wind up with a 2-percent response or 200 orders of $10 each, doesn't even pay for the cost of the mailing. On the other hand, if the orders are $50 each, you take in $10,000 on a 2-percent response. That should leave a nice profit if you've priced your work properly.

You may never see the names on the original list since most list owners will make labels available directly to your printer for mailing purposes only, but you do have the names of people who respond. Add them to your own customer list for future mailings.

(*See also: Advertising, Catalogues, Mail Order, Post Office*)

Mail Order

Mail-order selling is a hazardous exercise which only the most persistent and hard-headed business people survive. It's not as easy as it looks, and requires a combination of marketing skill, media selection, and a considerable sum of cash. When that combination works, it can be extremely successful. When it doesn't: disaster.

A profitable mail-order program is built on two operations that work in tandem: 1) getting the customer's names through the sale of a single item, and 2) following up those names with catalogue mailings for future business.

Except for rare hits, a single-item mail-order campaign rarely pays off. The cost of advertising and shipping normally eats up most of the income. Unless it is an item with an unusually high markup, don't be disappointed if the first order merely pays for itself. The real profits come when those customers order other merchandise from a catalogue. That's why the initial mail-order ad is often known as a list builder.

Let's examine the four major components of initial mail-order items one by one: how to choose, how to price, where to advertise, and the follow-up.

How to Choose Items for Mail Order

Almost all mail-order items have several things in common. They cannot be bought in the usual retail store, they are familiar types of objects, they can be bought sight unseen, they can be produced in quantity, they can be shipped easily, and they are easily described and illustrated in advertising or sales literature.

A pendant is a perfect example. It can be unique and not sold at retail; it can be crafted in quantity if the advertising results require it; it can be clearly illustrated; everybody knows what a pendant is, so the description need only state the actual size and the material of which it is made; and it is unbreakable and lightweight, therefore easy and inexpensive to ship.

As any of these components become complicated, the problems multiply. A very fragile craft object, for example, will sharply increase the shipping costs. An object that comes in seven sizes and ten colors presents considerable inventory and ordering difficulties. An object so strange that it requires reams of explanation does not generally produce good mail-order response. And if you're not ready, willing, and able to produce in quantity, forget about mail order altogether.

This is an appropriate point at which to mention a recent federal regulation designed to prevent abuses in mail-order selling. The Federal Trade Commission requires that all mail orders must be shipped within thirty days or customers are entitled to a refund. Mail-order sellers must notify customers if an order cannot be shipped within thirty days (or another specified time period), and furnish customers with postcards on which they can indicate whether the order should be cancelled. This rule applies only to orders accompanied by payment, which is the most common procedure in mail-order selling. Inventory and production capabilities become even more important in order to comply with this rule.

How to Price Items for Mail Order
The public is naturally reluctant to send a large sum of money to an unknown firm in response to a small ad in a newspaper or magazine. The initial mail-order item, therefore, has to be priced fairly low and give the impression of being a good buy. Mail-order specialists consider $10 to $20 to be the maximum range that will produce good results. Depending on the costs of advertising space and the expected response in orders, a mail-order item should be priced at least five times what it costs in materials and labor to produce. A leather belt that will be advertised for $14.95, therefore, should not cost more than $3 to make.

And yet, the price has to remain competitive with retail prices. If other belts, though admittedly not as unique or beautiful as yours, can be bought in a local department store for $7.95, it will be difficult to convince many readers that the advertised belt is truly worth twice as much.

Pricing immediately rules out various types of craftwork which cannot compete with that kind of markup unless they skimp on the quality of raw materials or the labor involved in creating a handcrafted piece.

The unusual markup is also necessary to meet very substantial increases in overhead: handling the orders; packing, shipping, postage; maintaining the lists; returns of broken goods; answering complaints, correspondence about lost shipments, and so forth.

Where to Advertise
Picking the right medium for mail-order selling is often the key to whether even a good product at the right price makes it. An item that appeals especially to women or is bought as a gift can do very well in the

women's magazines, many of which have special "shopping mart" sections full of mail-order offerings. Select the magazines or newspapers carefully so that your advertisement reaches the audience which will include the most likely prospects for your craftwork. Indeed, determine what kind of audience you want to reach and then find the publication that reaches it.

Advertising in national magazines can be very expensive. It is worthwhile, therefore, to get professional advertising help, both to select the right publications and to prepare an effective advertising message.

An essential ingredient of any mail-order ad is to "key" it; that is, to identify it in some manner so that you can keep track of the source of the returns. If it is a coupon ad, place a number or letter in some inconspicuous place in the coupon. That way the letter "A" will identify an ad that ran in one publication, and the letter "B" an ad in another publication.

This can be refined even further by adding a number or two. "A56" might identify magazine "A" and the issue of May, 1976.

This technique works even if you don't use a coupon. You can simply add a "Dept. A" or "Dept. B" identification to your name and address and keep track of the source that way.

Keying the ads is also important if you want to test some variables in the same publication. Does one type of headline produce better results than another? Does one type of product outsell another? Does $6.95 bring in sufficiently more business than $7.25 to make the lower price profitable? If you're trying to build a list, these tests take on even greater importance than the dollars-and-cents results alone.

When you test, change only one ingredient at a time. If you change both the headline and the price, for example, you can never know for sure what might have caused the difference in the results.

Finally, we come to countdown time. Keeping accurate records of the results is the only way you can know whether one type of ad produces more than another, whether one publication pulls better than another, which publication produces results for what kind of product. With accurate records you can put your money where the best results are.

The Follow-up

It isn't often that a mail-order campaign is successful solely on the basis of offering a single item in a magazine ad. The real payoff comes through building a list of customers who respond to the ad, and then producing additional orders from those same customers via catalogues or other sales literature.

Many craftspeople start their mail-order efforts at this point because they already have a list, or know where they can buy an outside list that has been tested and found productive. This avoids the huge gamble of investing in magazine advertising.

Now you may be able to afford a catalogue or sales brochure which offers a range of items. Illustrations can be larger, descriptions more extensive, and price ranges higher. The assumption is that the recipients of the catalogue already know you, whether they've bought from you before, or signed their name to a guest book at your craft show booth, or whatever the source is.

Preparing a catalogue can be a reasonable or an expensive proposition. Much depends on how large the catalogue is, whether it is a simple black-and-white printing job or an elegant full-color production, what kind of paper you use, and, most important, the size of the press run. The initial costs of preparing sales literature is the same, whether you run 1,000 copies or a million. On small quantities the initial cost is usually the largest ingredient of the whole job. If you have a list of only 5,000, for example, a color catalogue is usually out of the question; a four-page brochure would probably fit into your budget. But you might be able to join forces with another, noncompetitive craftsperson, and produce a joint catalogue which saves each of you some money. It also offers the recipient a wider choice of items from which to choose, which is always an advantage in selling.

When you get ready to prepare a catalogue or other sales material, talk to your printer first. He may be of great help in finding the most economical way. Consider the weight of the piece also. Trimming a quarter-inch off the size of a catalogue before you design it may bring the total weight into a lower postage category. Have the printer make a sample, called a dummy, and take it to a post office to be weighed on their scale. Your postmaster may have some suggestions on how to mail the material most economically.

The basic principles of copywriting, illustration, type selection and reader appeal discussed under "Advertising" apply to mail-order promotions as well.

But there is one additional point that is absolutely essential in mail-order selling. The specifications have to be spelled out in the minutest detail: sizes, colors, shapes, materials. Are shipping costs included, or how are they calculated? What sales taxes, if any, are due? And the order form (there's no point in sending a mail-order promotion without an order form) must provide space in which the customer can note all the specifications.

A money-back guarantee is also almost universal in mail-order selling. It serves to reassure the customer who, after all, cannot examine the merchandise until after it is bought and delivered.

A mail-order catalogue provides one other advantage which few other forms of advertising have: you can enclose an order envelope which makes it easier for the customer to respond and order. This is especially useful since you expect payment with the order (billing is a complicated procedure in mail-order selling and is rarely done).

If much of this section sounds discouraging to craftspeople, it is designed that way. Mail-order selling looks so simple, but it's a tough business. If the warnings have alerted you to the dangers, if you have examined them carefully and found them worth the risk, then your chances of success are much improved. By all means look before you leap.

(*See also: Advertising, Catalogues, Direct Mail, Mailing Lists, Post Office*)

Manufacturers Representatives

(*See: Sales Representatives*)

Margin

Margin is often confused with markup, particularly since both can be expressed in similar percentages. Margin and markup both represent the difference between the cost of products and their selling price. Out of this difference come all other expenses plus the profit.

But while markup is simply a percentage figure designed to determine a selling price, margin is the actual percentage realized on sales. Margin has to take into account a variety of factors which don't concern markup at all: defective pieces, unsold items, a disappointing craft show, loss through damage or theft, etc.

Thus, in theory, margin and markup percentages would be identical if every last piece were sold. In real life it rarely happens that way, certainly not over a period of time.

It may be easier to understand this difference if it is expressed in dollars. Suppose you make a hundred pots which cost $5 to produce and are marked up to sell for $10. If every last one were sold, you would realize $500. That would also be your margin. But more than likely a few will break or come out of the kiln in unsalable condition. You sell only 90. You clear $450 after the cost of production. That's your real margin, and it is lower than the intended markup.

To think of markup in the same breath as margin can be misleading if you consider them both in terms of profit. Craftspeople often work on two kinds of margin if they sell at wholesale to stores and galleries, and also sell at retail directly to the consumer. The first margin is the difference between the cost of production and the wholesale price; the second margin is the difference between the wholesale price and the retail price. The two margins need not be the same. Much depends on what's needed for expense and profit in each case.

Suppose your wholesale margin covers all your overhead, and wholesale profit, and is set at 50 percent (half the wholesale price). The second margin may need to cover only your show expenses and selling time. That margin could well be 30 or 40 percent and still turn a fine retail profit.

Margin must be calculated carefully. Your accountant can tell you at what point your margin is too low to make money. You may be doing a record business, the money rolls in, everything looks rosy. But if the margin isn't right, you may find yourself out of business in no time at all.

(*See also: Markup, Pricing, Profit*)

Markdown

There comes a time when you have some items on hand which you have to sell below the regular price. This is called a markdown.

Markdowns are taken for a whole host of reasons. Sometimes a product is simply overpriced, and you want to move the stock out of inventory. Markdowns are occasionally made toward the end of a show to avoid the need for carting unsold merchandise home. Seasonal items are often marked down at the end of the season in order to clean out inventory and raise cash. Sometimes a specific item is marked down as a loss leader to bring customers to your store or booth where they can then see (and hopefully buy) other items at regular prices.

Markdowns are a legitimate business practice if they are taken for legitimate reasons. If everything is constantly marked down from the regular price then there is, in truth, no regular price at all; your business becomes simply a discount or price-cutting operation. Advertising regular prices that never existed may even become deceptive or fraudulent advertising.

(*See also: Loss Leader, Markup, Pricing, Profit*)

Marketability

A line of hand-built ceramic hanging pots was displayed at a New England craft show recently. The craftsmanship was superb, the colors interesting, the glazes impeccable, and the price rational. Such pots were very popular at the time, and this particular line was shown in various shapes and sizes in an attractive display.

Yet only one pot was sold during the two days of the show. What was wrong?

Each pot was designed as a face which could only be described as either a death mask or a gargoyle. From an artistic point of view, the design may have been superb. From a marketing point of view it was a disaster. Gargoyles to ward off demons in the upper reaches of a cathedral wall are one thing; as planters hanging in a living room they are quite another.

Marketability, then, is the simple question of whether a given object or product can be sold to a customer.

The most common (sometimes the only) thought that occurs to a seller is price. But this can be misleading, since price is not the only concern. Indeed, price is rarely the first concern. Before a customer asks how much, a tentative decision has already been made that it might be nice to have the particular craft object. If a customer has absolutely no interest in buying a ring, he or she is not likely to ask what a particular ring costs. In that case it doesn't matter whether it's $10 or $100, or if the price is reduced from $10 to $5. Price follows the determination of need or desire; except on certain occasions, such as Christmas, when a customer might say "I want to spend $10 on Aunt Susie's gift. Let's see what I can get for her."

None of this suggests that price is not an important factor in marketability, but that it is not the only factor.

Before a product can be sold to a customer—and this applies to all products, including craftwork—it must fill a need. The need may be functional, as in a chair to sit on; or emotional, as with an earring that makes the personal appearance more attractive; or prestige, as with a one-of-a-kind wall hanging which the customer's friends can admire; or any number of other reasons.

The next question is how the product or object meets that need. This is where such intangible elements as style, design, color, shape, even current fads or trends, become important. Tastes differ among different people, and change from one year to the next, one generation to the next.

Craftspeople worth the calling need not compromise their artistic integrity for the sake of popular appeal, but to survive economically it is essential to keep a very fine ear to what is marketable, what can be sold, what the customers are buying and what they're not buying (and why). If they're not buying, is it a problem of style, or price, or variety, or being behind or ahead of the times?

Don't play follow the leader, but don't ignore what successful craftspeople are doing. At most craft shows there are always a few booths that have heavier traffic than others. See what's happening there. What's being sold? What's the appeal that draws customers to those booths? What are the prices?

Listen carefully to what's happening at your own booth. What are shoppers particularly interested in? What are they buying and not buying? What are they asking for? Do they want a round pillow when you only have square pillows? Do they want it in green when you have it only in blue? Is price a problem? Don't be shy about asking them directly what's on their mind. It's the only way you can find out what you're doing right, what you're doing wrong, and where you can improve.

Keep an ear tuned also to the popular mood and the current trends. In the mid-1970s, when tennis enjoyed a resurgence of popularity, a New York craftsman produced a finely crafted, tastefully designed line of pendants based on abstract interpretations of a tennis racket. They were advertised as available in silver and gold, and sold quite well at various prices to tennis enthusiasts. During the Vietnam War, the inverted-Y peace symbol was incorporated as a design element in a wide variety of craft objects, ranging from jewelry to stained glass to quilts.

No matter how marketable something is, it will never appeal to everyone. Some people like Beethoven, some like country music, some like rock. From an economic point of view, the importance of being concerned with marketability is whether your work appeals to a sufficient number of customers to enable you to earn a living.

(*See also: Design, Marketing, Market Research, Market Planning, Product Research*)

Marketing

Ask ten marketing experts to explain the term, and you're likely to get eleven answers. One that comes closest, in my view, was formulated by Norbert N. Nelson in his introduction to *Selling Your Crafts*.

Marketing, he said, is "the method of converting merchandise into money."

Note the word "method." Marketing is not a single activity. Marketing and selling are often used interchangeably, but selling is only one part of the process. Other elements of the total marketing operation include publicity, advertising, timing, pricing, the image of the stores or shows through which you sell, so fundamental a matter as design as it relates to market acceptability, a fancy term for "will people buy it?" (All of these are discussed in detail under their own headings in this book.)

Marketing, then, refers to all the things that happen to your craftwork between the time that it is finished in your shop or studio and the time the ultimate customer buys it.

(*See also: Advertising, Marketability, Market Planning, Pricing, Publicity, Public Relations, Sales*)

Market Planning

This term is commonly used in the offices of huge corporations, but the principles can apply to even the most modest craftwork producer. No matter to what scale it is drawn, a market plan is your own guide to what you hope to accomplish in selling your craftwork, how you hope to accomplish it, when and where you need to accomplish it, and how much it will cost.

It is possible to succeed on a hit-or-miss basis, but the chances for earning a living in this fashion are much less secure. It is not simply a matter of taking advantage of opportunities that come along—even a good market plan allows for unexpected opportunities—but whether you even know where to seek out those opportunities and how to fit them into your overall plan once you find them.

A sound market plan can influence what you produce. If your craft is batik, for example, do you want to concentrate exclusively on the creation of large pieces that sell through galleries for hundreds of dollars, or do you want to sell smaller (and therefore less expensive) but equally artistic pieces through a boutique in a major department store?

Assume for a moment that your income in either instance would be the same. The question then is whether you can afford to wait six or twelve months to sell a few large pieces, or whether you need the cash now and therefore want to sell a larger quantity of the smaller pieces immediately. You may even decide that you can do both.

Your market plan must, of course, take into account your creative needs and artistic inclinations. It must also take into account your cash flow needs, your production capability, your sales ability, how much time you have to invest, the nature of your work (will it sell to a very limited market or is it something many people might want to buy), and numerous other very individual factors.

The marketing plan serves the same purpose as a road map. You may want to take all sorts of detours to see the sights, but you know where you're going, you have the itinerary mapped in rough outlines, you have some idea how many miles you want to drive each day, and where you'll stay each night.

Ten people driving to the same spot may take ten different routes. The fact that you have a route to follow is more important than the specific route you choose.

Here are ten major considerations to include in drawing up a marketing plan:

1) How much can I produce?
2) At what price range?
3) Is it of limited or general interest?
4) What are the most logical outlets or combination of outlets in order of importance (stores, galleries, co-ops, craft shows, exhibits, interior decorators, etc.)?
5) Can I produce enough to satisfy the outlets I consider most likely?
6) What will it cost to reach those outlets?

7) What are my cash flow needs?

8) Will my plan, according to points 1 through 7, satisfy my cash flow needs and production capabilities, or what changes are needed to amend my decisions in those areas?

9) Does my plan include enough flexibility to change if decisions prove ineffective? Do I have the will and resources to change?

10) Will this whole plan provide the kind of income and profit I want?

To implement the plan, it is well to draw up a twelve-month outline for the year ahead. This outline should be carefully reviewed at least every three to six months, particularly in the beginning, and updated for the following twelve months.

The plan should note whatever specific events or activities are planned, with dates and locations. What are the major shows at which you want to exhibit? When do you want to issue a brochure? If you produce specific items for a specific occasion, Christmas for example, when do you have to make the sale to the stores? When do you have to deliver?

What are the anticipated costs for each activity? What are the anticipated results? Only by noting these carefully, and also keeping a diary of the events as they occur, can you determine whether your marketing plan is effective or where it needs amending for the future.

Record-keeping is all-important here. Don't trust everything to memory. A marketing plan is only as good as its implementation and analysis. A marketing plan helps you prevent making the same mistake twice. It also helps you to prepare budgets and schedule purchases of equipment and supplies.

Use your marketing plan also to project the price ranges of craftwork you plan to produce. Keep a careful record of how these actually sell. Your plan may call for 100 pieces to sell at $25, and another 100 at $50. Upon analyzing your records, you may find that the market for the $25 item was rather slim and unprofitable, compared to the work you put into it. That will help you to plan on a different price range in the future.

Another example: suppose that three days at a given craft fair brings a profit of $100 after expenses. The show may have been no loss, but if you could have spent those three days producing $200 worth of profits through ultimate store sales by staying in your studio or shop, it may not pay to put that particular fair on your marketing calendar next year (unless the direct contact with the customer is the real reason you go).

Still another example: last year you ran a special show and sale in your studio. You mailed out 1,000 invitations; 100 people came and spent $500. Not bad. But if your marketing plan projects a studio sale of $750 this year, it would stand to reason that you should have a list of at least 1,500 names to mail to, or that you find some other way to attract more people or increase the price of your work. A carefully kept diary of last year's experience tells you exactly what went into the end result, and what you need to do this year to change that end result.

Still another function of the marketing plan is to pinpoint who your good customers are, which prospects merit further attention, what type of items might be added to your line to expand sales to existing outlets which already buy your present line, etc. It is always easier and more profitable to increase sales to existing clients than to develop new ones. If you can make a $1,000 sale on one trip to a retail outlet—making one shipment, writing one invoice—you are obviously better off than making four trips, four shipments, four invoices to four customers who buy at $250 each. Of course, if you can do both, go to it.

(*See also: Marketability, Marketing*)

Market Research

All the customers out there are "the market." Finding out who they are, where they are, how to reach them, how to sell them—that's the problem.

Big corporations call this market research. Call it what you will, the important thing is to find out when and where and how and to whom you can sell your craftwork.

Most craftspeople do this by the seat of their pants, and it usually works out well. Since there are no million-dollar advertising budgets at stake, or expensive tooling-up processes as in mass production, a small mistake need not spell disaster.

But it pays to study which potential retail stores you want to approach to sell your craftwork: do they cater to the kind of customer who might want to buy your work?

It also pays to study the shows and fairs at which you want to exhibit. Taking a line of $500 rosewood cabinets to a $5-and-$10 mall show would be approaching the wrong market.

Other questions present themselves: can you reach enough customers through advertising? Does mail order offer selling opportunities which you can exploit profitably? Is your shop or studio in a high traffic location, which might justify selling at retail to walk-in customers? Or would that interfere with production to the point of being unprofitable?

Do you have any specific customers in mind when you design a particular craft object? What are their tastes? Their ages? Their interests? Their needs and desires?

Marketing opportunities can also be developed among very specialized customers: architects, industrial designers, interior decorators. In such markets you work on a commission, which means that you create a craft work to particular specifications at a predetermined fee.

Market research in a formal way is probably neither necessary nor feasible for most craftspeople. But in an informal way—by discussing the problems with others, by reading the craft publications, by studying different shows, stores, galleries, by keeping your eyes and ears open—you can develop approaches to the market which produce greater selling opportunities at lower selling costs.

(*See also: Architects, Buyers, Customers, Industrial Design, Interior Design, Marketability, Marketing, Marketing Plan, Product Line, Product Research*)

Markup

Markup is the term used to describe the difference between the cost of merchandise and its selling price. It is usually expressed in percentages. A great deal of confusion exists in the use of this word because markup can be calculated either from the cost price or the selling price. The percentage results are different, while the dollars remain the same.

For example, you sell a ring to a jewelry store for $10. The store puts a $20 price tag on it. If the store figures the markup on its cost price, then it is 100 percent (double the $10 cost price). If the markup is figured on the basis of the retail selling price, then it is 50 percent (half the $20 retail price).

There's a logical reason for the two different methods. One or the other figure must always serve as a starting point, either the product cost or its retail price. If a store wants to put in a line of rings to sell for $20 at a 50 percent markup, then it must find a source of rings at $10 each. On the other hand, if the store is out shopping for rings with no specific retail price in mind, then it knows that a $10 ring must be retailed for $20 in order to take a 100 percent markup.

The same principle is used by many craftspeople in pricing their own craft objects. If you know you can't sell a belt for more than $10 and you want to mark it up 50 percent, then you must find a way to produce that belt for $5. If your production cost is the first figure you know, you arrive at the retail price by adding the appropriate markup to the cost. In this example, the $5 belt must sell for $10 if it is marked up 100 percent.

If you know you can't sell belts for more than $8, you either have to find a less expensive way to produce them, or take a smaller markup.

You may tell another craftsperson that you work on a 100 percent markup, and he thinks you're making money hand over fist. After all, he's working on only a 60 percent markup. But then you discover that he's talking about 60 percent of the retail price, which means he spends only 40 percent on the cost of producing or buying the merchandise. You're talking about 100 percent added to the cost of the product, which means you're spending 50 percent of the selling price on the cost of the merchandise. So it turns out that he's actually making more money than you are.

Markup is critical because it has to cover all operating costs plus profit, except the cost of the merchandise itself. Every store and every craft producer should know how much markup is needed in order to remain solvent and operate profitably.

(*See also: Margin, Markdown, Pricing, Profit*)

Mass Production

This term applies to factory procedures in which a great many identical copies of the same product are produced by machines, usually on an assembly line basis.

When craftspeople produce a number of copies from the same design it is called multiple production rather than mass production as long as each piece is handmade, even if machinery is used at some points in the process. Being handmade, no two pieces are ever identical. Each has its own individual characteristics, which is what distinguishes such work from mass production. The fact that a mass produced item may be made in various sizes and colors does not invest it with sufficient distinction to be called handcrafted, since the basic design is stamped out by machines from a blueprint.

(*See also: Multiple Production, One-of-a-Kind*)

Materials

(*See: Suppliers*)

Media

(*See: Advertising*)

Medicaid

Medicaid is a state-run medical assistance program which came into existence after passage of the federal Medicare law in 1965. Through Medicaid, the federal government provides financial assistance to the individual states which, in turn, provide five basic health care services for the "medically needy":

1) In-patient hospital services;
2) Out-patient hospital services;
3) Lab tests and X-rays;
4) Doctor's services;
5) Skilled nursing home services for people over 21.

All the states and territories of the United States have a Medicaid program which covers everyone on public assistance (welfare), and others who are medically needy. The determination of who is medically needy is left to each state. In New York, for example, that includes anyone whose annual income is under $2,500 and who has not more than $1,750 in "allowable reserves," such as the cash value of a life insurance policy. New York State also has a "catastrophic illness" clause which covers people between 21 and 64 years old who might not otherwise qualify. Under that provision, a person can receive in-hospital benefits if his or her hospital expenses exceed 25 percent of net annual income.

Under some circumstances, Medicaid also helps cover the medical bills of people 65 or older who already receive federal Medicare benefits which may, however, be insufficient to pay their medical bills. Thus some senior citizens are eligible for both health protection programs.

Certain states have expanded their Medicaid benefits to include dentistry, podiatry, optometry, prescriptions, eyeglasses, and sickroom supplies.

(*See also: Medicare*)

Medicare

Medicare is a federal health insurance program which covers hospital and medical needs of people 65 years and older, and some who are under 65 and disabled. It is run by the Social Security Administration. Medicare payments are handled by private insurance companies under contract with the federal government.

Medicare covers only those services that are "reasonable and necessary" for the treatment of an illness or an injury, and only if the services are rendered by a person or institution approved for Medicare payments. It does not, for example, cover custodial care such as helping someone get in and out of bed, except when that is related to the treatment of a specific illness or injury.

Medicare is divided into two parts: hospital insurance (called Part A), and medical insurance (Part B).

The hospital insurance helps pay for three kinds of care: 1) in-patient hospital care; 2) in-patient care in a skilled nursing facility; 3) home health care.

The words "helps pay for" are important here, because Medicare does not pay for all costs. For example, a patient is responsible for the first $92 in each benefit period (there are four benefit periods in a year). Medicare pays for all other covered services for the next sixty days during that period. For the days from sixty-one to ninety, Medicare pays all costs except $23 a day, which the patient pays.

Among the services included in the medical insurance are 1) doctor services; 2) out-patient hospital services; 3) medical services, supplies, lab work; 4) home health services.

Here again the patient pays part of the costs. Generally, after the patient has spent $60 for covered medical expenses in a calendar year, Medicare pays 80 percent of the reasonable charges for covered services during the rest of that year. That $60 deductible applies only once during a year.

Among the services not covered by Medicare are such items as routine physical examinations, eye examinations for fitting glasses, dentistry, routine foot care, cosmetic surgery, drugs for home use, private rooms and private duty nurses, chiropractic services, and a number of others.

One service available to all insured workers and their dependents regardless of age is dialysis treatment or kidney transplants because of chronic kidney disease.

It is not required that people covered by Medicare have both the hospital and the medical program. People who have medical insurance pay a monthly premium of $6.70. The rest is paid for by federal funds. Some people who are not eligible for the hospital coverage also pay a monthly premium for that insurance, somewhere around $40 a month.

In cases where patients are unable to pay their own portions of the medical expenses, they may be able to get assistance from the Medicaid programs in their own states.

This is necessarily a very abbreviated explanation of a very extensive program. Complete information is available in a 64-page "Medicare Handbook" which explains the details clearly and concisely, and provides the latest rates, which change occasionally. The booklet is available without charge from any Social Security Office (see telephone white pages: "U.S. Government, Health, Education, and Welfare Dept., Social Security Administration").

(*See also: Medicaid*)

Memo

Shipping "on memo" is one way of avoiding what metal and jewelry craftsman Ron Pearson of Maine calls the "consignment quagmire."

Shipping on memo means that work is sent on an invoice with a 30- or 60-day return privilege. It is, in effect, on loan. The unsold work is returned after that period, along with payment for work that is sold. The paperwork is much simpler than it is in consignment selling. The invoice states that the unsold work can be returned after the specified period, and that the merchandise which is sold, or which the store wants to retain for future sales, is paid for at the stated price.

Mr. Pearson does this only with established customers and only on specific occasions. "If an outlet is featuring our work and perhaps advertising the event," Mr. Pearson explains, "it can help them to produce sales if they have a broader range of pieces that includes higher-priced work."

With the 30- or 60-day return privilege, a retail outlet will be more inclined to take such higher-priced work, and stock more than it usually would, to produce more sales and more profits for both the craftsperson and the retailer. While the net effect may not be much different from consignment selling, such matters as ownership, insurance, bookkeeping hassles and other consignment problems are avoided.

A variation of this method is to send samples of new items to established retail outlets "on approval" with a 10-day return privilege. For many craftspeople this can be an inexpensive way of introducing a customer to a new item. Mr. Pearson does this almost daily (shipping the approval item along with a customer's order), and says that "it has proved to be a remarkably good method for generating sales."

(*See also: Consignment, Retailing, Salesmanship, Wholesaling*)

Merchandising

(*See: Marketability, Marketing, Marketing Plan*)

Metric System

The way we measure things is a language all its own. Everything in this world (and outside it) is measured in terms of time, distance, weight, mass, etc. Indeed, there are many people who are quite adept at pounds, inches, dollars, and hours even though they can barely read and write.

The measuring system most common in the world today is the metric system, based on units of ten. The United States is the only major industrial nation still using the difficult fractions of ounces and pounds, inches and feet, pints and quarts. Most of the rest of the world, including every industrial nation, uses the metric system not only because it is easier and more efficient, but because it requires no translation across national boundaries.

It may seem like unfamiliar territory at first glance, but we already use many metric measurements in our daily lives. Our money (100 cents to the dollar) is the best example. Others in common use are the 35mm camera, the 100-meter dash, kilowatt hours of electricity, the dosages of most medicines.

The United States Congress, whose Constitutional duty it is to set standards of weights and measures, determined after lengthy investigation and study that the United States should change over to the metric system, just as Great Britain, Canada, and other holdovers of the old system did recently. A ten-year changeover period was proposed, and it is hoped that by the 1980s the U.S. will be completely metric.

Many trades and professions, especially the sciences, already use the international metric language. Packages have begun to appear on supermarket shelves marked in both the old weights and their metric equivalents. Weather forecasters have started to announce the day's temperature in both the familiar Fahrenheit and the less familiar Celsius (centigrade). The United States is slowly beginning to think metric.

For craftspeople this will require some rethinking of familiar terms, and even some retooling of familiar sizes.

A potter will no longer make a one-pint mug, but a mug that holds half a liter. A weaver won't measure by square feet, but by square meters. Instead of buying an ounce of silver, a jeweler will buy twenty-eight grams.

It may seem strange at first, but other countries have found that the initial difficulties of conversion were worth the eventual convenience of the much easier metric system.

The following table indicates the method by which approximate conversions can be calculated to metric and vice versa:

	When you know:	You can find:	If you multiply by:
LENGTH	inches	millimeters	25
	feet	centimeters	30
	yards	meters	0.9
	miles	kilometers	1.6
	millimeters	inches	0.04
	centimeters	inches	0.4
	meters	yards	1.1
	kilometers	miles	0.6
AREA	square inches	square centimeters	6.5
	square feet	square meters	0.09
	square yards	square meters	0.8
	square miles	square kilometers	2.6
	acres	square hectometers (hectares)	0.4

AREA	square centimeters	square inches	0.16
	square meters	square yards	1.2
	square kilometers	square miles	0.4
	square hectometers (hectares)	acres	2.5
MASS	ounces	grams	28
	pounds	kilograms	0.45
	short tons	megagrams (metric tons)	0.9
	grams	ounces	0.035
	kilograms	pounds	2.2
	megagrams (metric tons)	short tons	1.1
LIQUID VOLUME	ounces	milliliters	30
	pints	liters	0.47
	quarts	liters	0.95
	gallons	liters	3.8
	milliliters	ounces	0.034
	liters	pints	2.1
	liters	quarts	1.06
	liters	gallons	0.26

Converting temperatures takes a slightly different road:

When you know Fahrenheit you can find Celsius as follows: subtract 32, divide by 9, multiply by 5.

When you know Celsius you can find Fahrenheit as follows: divide by 5, multiply by 9, add 32.

Minimum Orders

A certain amount of cost is involved in filling an order, no matter how big or how small the order is. There is a point at which it doesn't pay to ship an order; indeed, it may be a losing proposition.

If you are confronted with many small orders that have to be shipped, it is worthwhile to calculate exactly how much it costs in time and materials for billing, packing, shipping, running to the post office, and all the other steps needed to fill an order. If you find that it costs an average of $2 per order to do all this, then a $2 order is a total loss. You haven't even been paid for the cost of materials and your work in making the item, not to speak of a profit.

161

Establishing a minimum order policy can therefore be an important influence on your profits.

There is no magic formula, but you might start by finding out exactly what it costs you to fill an average order. Keep careful records on the next forty or fifty orders, both the time you spend as well as the costs of the shipping materials.

Now see where the break-even point comes by finding the amount at which your costs of filling an order are the same as your profits. For example, if your rate of profit is 20 percent of the sales price, and it costs $2 to ship an average order, then you need a $10 order to break even.

The minimum order should be at least double the break-even point. In the example given above, therefore, the sales price should be not lower than $20, and preferably $25 or $30.

Be sure to indicate the minimum order requirement in all sales literature, catalogues, and conversations with customers.

Another solution to this problem is to add a service charge to all orders that fall below a certain minimum. That way you can fill such orders and still keep your costs covered. Such a charge may also induce customers to increase their orders to meet the minimum requirement.

There are always exceptions, of course. We can't be hidebound. If a very good customer who usually buys in large amounts needs one particular item, ship it, even if it's below the minimum. Count it as an investment in good will and customer satisfaction.

(*See also: Break Even, Orders, Pricing*)

Minimum Wage

The Federal Minimum Wage Law, known as the Fair Labor Standards Act, was established in the 1930s for a number of reasons:

1) To create a floor below which wages cannot fall;
2) To raise the buying power of the lowest-paid workers;
3) To create a higher standard of living;
4) To protect employers who pay a fair wage from unfair competition by employers who would not voluntarily pay such a wage.

The law was last amended in 1974 and covers the entire country. Many states also have their own minimum wage laws which apply in some areas of work not included in the federal law, such as working papers for minors. In states where both state and federal minimum wage laws exist, the higher rates and standards apply.

The minimum hourly wage has been raised several times in recent years. As of 1976 it stood at $2.40. With some exceptions specifically stated in the law, no one can be employed for less than that.

Overtime must be paid at a rate of 1½ times the employee's regular hourly rate for all hours beyond forty hours per week. Overtime cannot be averaged over more than one week; in other words, if an employee works thirty-eight hours one week and forty-four hours the next, he is entitled to four hours of overtime pay for the second week. Furthermore the work week cannot be capriciously changed from week to week (to avoid overtime obligations). A change can be made only if it is intended to be permanent.

There are several important exceptions to the Minimum Wage Law which could affect craftspeople.

1) The spouse, or children under age 21, of an individual owner of a crafts business need not be paid the minimum wage or overtime.

2) Employees of an individual retail store are not covered by the minimum wage or overtime requirements when all three of the following conditions exist: a) the total sales volume is less than $250,000 a year; b) at least half the annual sales volume is made within the state where the store is located; and c) 75 percent of the annual dollar sales volume is for goods that are sold directly to the ultimate consumer and are not sold for resale.

3) Executive, administrative, and professional personnel are exempt from being paid minimum wages or overtime. The law specifically includes in the category of professional employees those whose work is original and creative in the artistic field. Thus, an employee who helps load the kiln is not a professional employee, since the work is not original or creative. A potter who is expected to create his or her own designs and execute them could very well be considered professional within the meaning of the law. The important thing is not by what title the employee is known, but what the employee actually does. When there is a question of qualifying for exemptions in this category, the basis on which the Labor Department determines eligibility is outlined in the Secretary of Labor's Regulations, 29 CFR part 541.

4) Salespeople who work away from the employer's premises on a commission basis are also exempt from both the minimum wage and overtime provisions. But this exemption applies only to people who sell, not those who do other work off the employer's premises.

5) Under certain circumstances, and with special certificates from the Department of Labor, students can be employed at wage rates below the minimum on a part-time basis or during school vacations. This also applies to learners in vocational education programs, or handicapped persons.

Where piecework rates exist, they must be so constructed that an employee can, under reasonable circumstances, earn the equivalent of the minimum hourly wage.

The federal law also requires that no differentials in wages are allowed if they are based on the employee's sex, color, or other extraneous reason.

Wage differentials are permitted when they are based on seniority, merit, or any other job-related factor.

The Labor Department is quite strict in the enforcement of this law. Failure to pay minimum wages or overtime is a federal offense. Not only can the Secretary of Labor or the employees themselves go to court to recover unpaid wages, but serious violations may also be subject to civil or criminal prosecution.

The law requires employers to keep accurate records on wages, hours, and other information. Such records must be kept for at least three years (two years for time cards, piecework tickets, etc.).

Questions on wages, overtime, hours, sex discrimination, and other subjects covered by the Fair Labor Standards Act can be directed by both employers and employees to any of the 350 offices maintained throughout the country by the Wage and Hour Division of the U.S. Labor Department. The telephone book white pages list them under "U.S. Government, Department of Labor, Employment Standards Administration."

(*See also: Apprentice, Employees*)

Model Release

(*See: Photography*)

Money Order

If you have a checking account you can write your own checks. If you have a savings account you can receive cashier's checks. If you have no bank connections at all, you can buy money orders when you need to send money to a distant point.

Money orders are available from a variety of agencies such as banks, the U.S. Post Office, American Express, and others. They are written in specific amounts and are sold to anyone with the cash to buy them. A fee is charged based on the amount of the money order.

Money orders can be cashed, upon proper identification, at any office of the agency which issued them (e.g., any post office in the case of postal money orders), or they can be deposited like checks in a bank account.

Mortgage

A mortgage is a special type of loan in which the borrower puts up property as security for the repayment of the loan. In effect, he signs a conditional transfer of title (ownership) to the property, even though he is still in possession of it and can pretty much do as he pleases with it, including selling it. In the case of a sale, of course, the mortgage has to be transferred to the new owner or paid off from the proceeds, or the sale cannot be consummated.

Mortgages are usually paid off in monthly installments over a period of years, as many as thirty years in many cases, plus interest charges. If the borrower fails to make his payments, the entire balance is due. If he fails to pay that, the lender can exercise his conditional right to the title. This is known as a foreclosure. The lender then sells the property for as much as he can. If he sells it for more than the balance on the mortgage, the borrower gets the difference.

Mortgages, even more so than most financial transactions, require careful consideration and examination of all the details. Most important among these is the rate of interest. While the differences between various lending institutions may seem small, the dollars can be significant. Suppose one bank charges 8.5 percent interest, while another charges 9.25 percent. That three-quarters of one percent may not seem like much of a difference, but look at the end result: a twenty-year, $20,000 mortgage will cost a whopping $2,306.40 more in interest at 9.25 percent than at 8.5 percent.

A few other questions: does the bank allow the mortgage to be taken over by a buyer if you sell the property? That's important because an assumable mortgage makes it easier to sell a property.

What (if any) are the penalties if you are late with a payment or want to prepay the balance of the mortgage before it is due? Are you required to pay into an escrow account at the bank from which the bank pays your annual or semiannual real estate taxes, water bills, etc. (but on which it pays you no interest), or can you put the money in your savings account, earn interest, and pay the taxes and other bills yourself? Are you permitted to take a second mortgage?

A second mortgage is an additional loan when the down payment and the first mortgage don't add up to the total purchase price. For example: suppose the total price of the property you want to buy is $30,000. You make a down payment of $5,000 and obtain a first mortgage of $20,000. That leaves a gap of $5,000 which a second mortgage can fill. A second mortgage can also be used to raise cash on a piece of property you already own if you have an old first mortgage at a low rate of interest which you don't want to disturb by refinancing that first mortgage at a higher interest rate.

First mortgages are generally obtained from a bank or some other institution; second mortgages usually come from private lenders. In the event of a foreclosure, the first mortgage has a claim ahead of the second mortgage if there are not sufficient funds to pay off both. Since the risk is greater, the interest rate on a second mortgage is almost always higher than on a first, and the term is shorter, usually not more than five years.

Lending institutions such as banks and insurance companies normally require that the property be insured against loss from fire and the like. Prudent real estate owners also carry mortgage insurance which pays off the mortgage in case the owner dies or is otherwise incapacitated and cannot make the payments. The premiums on such insurance go down as the mortgage payments reduce the balance due.

A loan on a major piece of property other than real estate, such as an automobile, is often called a chattel mortgage. The basic principles of payment, interest, insurance, and foreclosure apply in such mortgages as well.

(See also: Interest, Lien, Loan)

Multiple Production

This term defines craft objects of which more than one piece is made from the same basic design. Since all the pieces are crafted by hand, each differs in some detail, however slightly, from the others. It is distinguished from mass production, in which large numbers of absolutely identical pieces are turned out by machines, even though the original design may have been created by a skilled craft artist.

Most craftspeople work in multiple production, since this is the most effective way to survive economically without becoming a mass production factory, or without having to rely on the occasional sale of expensive one-of-a-kind pieces.

Multiple production provides a number of advantages:

1) Economies in the purchase of raw materials and supplies, since they can be bought in larger quantities.

2) More effective use of production time.

3) The development of a line of craft products which increases sales potential.

4) Ability of retail stores to reorder items that sell well, based on the knowledge that you are in a position to furnish more of the same item.

(See also: Inventory, Job Ticket, Mass Production, One-of-a-kind, Overhead, Pricing, Production, Wages)

Museum

Museums have traditionally been scholarly institutions, collecting works of historic or artistic significance, often displaying such work for public viewing, but generally interested more in acquisition than education or participation.

This approach has changed significantly in recent years with the advent of museums that not only mount a great many exhibitions and change them frequently, but also conduct lectures, tours, demonstrations, concerts, and other activities for the public. An even more recent innovation is the actual participation of the public in museum activities, such as art classes and workshops. Many museums also operate shops in which craft objects and fine reproductions of paintings can be purchased.

The possibility of having craftwork purchased by a museum is comparatively rare. It is certainly not a major market for most craftspeople, though museum shops may be. But participation in temporary exhibitions and invitational museum shows can provide important exposure to the public. There may be little money in it (except for prizes and purchase awards in a number of instances), but the prestige of having been shown in a reputable museum adds considerably to a craft artist's future selling potential.

When you lend your work to a museum for exhibition purposes, a written form should clearly outline the length of time involved, who is responsible for shipping and insurance, an accurate description of the object(s) you are lending, and the conditions under which your work will be exhibited. Be sure that each object is properly identified as your property so that it can be returned to you.

Such a written form should also safeguard all your rights in the work in case the museum wants to reproduce it in some form for sale in its shop, even if that reproduction is only pictorial.

Museums will occasionally ask for donations of craftwork of unusual interest or quality to their permanent collections. Since most craftspeople are not rich patrons of the arts, this is not generally recommended, especially if the museum has funds with which it buys other works. Unlike donations from collectors or other sources, who can count their contribution as a tax deduction, the tax laws do not permit the artist who created the work to enjoy this same tax advantage.

Contributions of craftwork to a museum, therefore, make sense only if you have a special feeling for the particular museum and that museum is really strapped for funds, or if the fact that your work is in a museum's permanent collection is a feather in your cap which you feel is important on your resumé.

If you make such a contribution, be sure that the conditions are specified in writing, especially whether the museum has the right to put the piece in storage or to sell it, or whether it must be returned to you if there is no further interest in exhibiting it.

National Endowment for the Arts

The National Endowment for the Arts is an independent agency of the federal government, funded by Congress, which makes financial grants to individuals and organizations concerned with the arts throughout the United States.

The endowment describes its major goals thus: "To make the arts more widely available to millions of Americans, to preserve our rich cultural heritage for present and future generations, to strengthen cultural organizations, and to encourage the creative development of our nation's finest talent."

Craft activities are an important ingredient of the endowment's visual arts program. Grants are available in fifteen categories that involve crafts as well as other art projects, and in six specific craft programs: craftsmen in residence, craftsmen's services, crafts exhibition aid, crafts workshops, master craftsmen apprenticeship, and fellowships for craftsmen. Some of the grants are made to nonprofit organizations on a matching fund basis (ranging to $10,000), some are made directly to individual craftspeople (ranging to $5,000).

Deadlines for grant applications occur once a year, on different dates for different grants. Specific details about each grant are spelled out in the Endowment's "Guide to Programs," published every August. Information and details about grants in the crafts field are available from the Crafts Coordinator, Visual Arts Program, National Endowment for the Arts, Washington, DC 20506.

(*See also: Government Activities, Grants*)

Net

When this word precedes another word, such as price, profit, income, worth, or weight, it means that specified deductions have been taken and that the described subject is free and clear.

When used as a verb, it usually indicates the final, true income or profit, after all expenses and taxes have been deducted from the selling price, as in "I should net $10 on each of these leather bags."

The opposite of net is gross.

(*See also: Gross*)

Net Price

The price after allowing for discounts; if an item retails for $100 and wholesales at 50 percent off, the net price to the retailer is $50.

Net Profit

The profit that remains after deducting taxes.

(*See also: Profit*)

Net Weight

The weight of a shipment after the weight of the packing materials has been deducted; that is, the actual weight of the product being shipped.

This can become a cost factor because shipping charges are based on gross weight, the content as well as the packing materials. The development of new, lightweight packing materials has been an important influence in keeping shipping costs in line even while the per pound rates have gone steadily upward.

If you ship a two-pound glass object in a five-pound crate, you wind up paying more for sending wood than for sending glass. Craftspeople who do any sizable amount of shipping of craft products may find that a study of the various packing materials can save them quite a bit of money.

(*See also: Shipping, Packing, Post Office, United Parcel Service*)

Net Worth

The equity held by the owner(s) of a business on a specific date after all liabilities have been deducted from all assets. It could be said that this is the true book value of the business on that date, although that is not related to the market value, which would take into account such intangibles as good will, future potential, and other factors.

(*See also: Balance Sheet, Equity*)

One-of-a-Kind

One-of-a-kind means exactly that! There is no other craft object like it, not even a second copy by the same craft artist. Concentrating exclusively on this kind of production is viable only for the most successful craft artists, who can command the generally high prices for their distinctive one-of-a-kind work.

However, many craftspeople create one-of-a-kind pieces in addition to their multiple production for several reasons. First, there is the need for creative expression which can occasionally be satisfied only by creating a large or unusual piece in which the possibility of sale does not determine the investment of time, labor, and materials.

But there is another reason, one which can directly influence sales. An elaborate one-of-a-kind object can serve as a centerpiece for the display of the craft artist's line of multiple production items. It can thus help sell the line even if the big piece itself is not sold.

An elaborate glass chandelier, for example, can create an aura of prestige and artistry for the display of smaller glass objects made by the same craftsperson. This can happen in a store or gallery setting, or in the presentation of a line to a retail store buyer. In either case, it serves to create a dramatic impression on the potential customer.

One-of-a-kind pieces are also very suitable for publicity purposes, particularly if they incorporate some innovative or unusual design features. This is especially true for exhibitions or gallery shows which might attract press coverage.

(*See also: Multiple Production*)

Orders

The next best thing to actual money is an order.

The order can be translated into money, but not until you've satisfied the customer. To avoid hassles and disputes, it is important that all orders specify at least three basic conditions very clearly:

1) Exactly what is ordered (by catalogue number or description, size, color, material, quantity, etc.);

2) The price per piece, the total price, payment terms, and sales tax exemptions where applicable;

3) When the merchandise is to be delivered, where it is to be shipped, and who pays the shipping charges.

Depending on the nature of the object and the relationship with the customer, various other specifications may be necessary. In some instances, especially where a heavy investment in materials is needed, it may be advisable to specify a partial payment with the order if you don't know the customer well. You should certainly check credit references.

An order can take many forms. It can be as simple as a letter from a customer. Whenever you get a verbal order, be sure to acknowledge it in writing with all the details mentioned so that there can be no misunderstanding later.

You can enter orders on your own order forms, printed either specifically for you, or on a stock form on which you can rubber stamp your name and address. Such stock forms are available from suppliers in most major cities (look under "Business Forms" in the Yellow Pages).

Many institutions and stores have preprinted purchase order forms that include a lot of fine-print conditions. Read them carefully. You'll often find very specific billing addresses which differ from shipping addresses. Note also such requirements as confirming the order (very important), sending duplicate copies of invoices, etc.

When an order has been accepted, it is implied between you and the customer that all the conditions are acceptable. To violate a condition and then plead ignorance because you didn't read it won't stand up in court if your customer won't accept shipment or refuses to pay for the merchandise.

Turn the tables for a moment. If you order blue yarn and the shipment is green, or you want delivery by March 15 and don't get it until May 1, you have every right to return the yarn and refuse to pay.

If you receive an order with unacceptable terms and conditions, notify the customer at once. Holding on to the order implies acceptance. In most cases, an unacceptable condition—a delivery date you can't meet, for example—can be negotiated if you discuss it with the customer immediately. Don't wait three months until the day before you're due to ship the items. If the customer then tells you not to bother, you've not only lost a customer, but you've spent a lot of time and money producing objects which you now have to try to sell elsewhere.

(*See also: Business Forms, Credit, Collection Problems*)

Organizations

Organizations of craftspeople exist on a national, regional, state, and local level. Some have full-time professional staffs and permanent headquarters, while others operate strictly through volunteer officers, and a few are merely paper organizations. There are also a great many organizations in the various craft media, such as weaving, glass, pottery, embroidery, jewelry, metal, and woodworking.

Activities vary considerably. Some groups confine themselves to periodic meetings and perhaps an annual craft show or exhibition. Some are also extensively involved in marketing programs, and a number operate their own shops where members' craftwork is sold, such as the League of New Hampshire Craftsmen, Piedmont Craftsmen, The Kentucky Guild of Artists & Craftsmen, Southern Highland Handicraft Guild, and others. Most organizations publish newsletters or magazines of various degrees of regularity, ranging in competence from dismal to superb.

Among other services which some organizations offer their members are help with collection problems, hospital and medical insurance, publication of directories, extensive educational programs, special prices on craft books, and business advice. Quite a few craft organizations, especially those which conduct marketing activities, admit members only after a screening process to determine technical and design proficiency.

The one common denominator of all such organizations is that they provide their members with opportunities to share information and ideas, improve their professional competence, and upgrade their selling potential.

An extensive list of craft organizations in all fifty states appears in *Contemporary Crafts Marketplace,* compiled by the American Crafts

Council and available for $13.95 (plus 40¢ postage) from Bowker Publishing Co., PO Box 1807, Ann Arbor, MI 49481. This book, which is updated every other year, is also available in many libraries.

(*See also: American Crafts Council, Southern Highland Handicraft Guild, World Crafts Council*)

Outstanding Check

Any check which you have written but which has not yet been paid by your bank is an outstanding check. Outstanding checks have to be calculated in the monthly reconciliation with the bank statement, and should be closely monitored. If a check is outstanding for an unusually long time, it is wise to find out why it has not been cashed. Perhaps it was lost or stolen, in which case a stop payment order should be issued and a new check written.

(*See also: Bank Statement, Stop Payment*)

Overdrawn

Overdrawn means you wrote more checks than you have money in the bank. When such a check arrives at your bank for payment from your account it is usually returned to the person or company to whom you issued it with the notation "sufficient funds." This can be embarrassing. It sometimes happens when you think you have enough money in the bank to write a check because you recently made a deposit. However, a check you deposit is only a piece of paper until it has actually been collected by your bank. That takes between three and ten days, depending on the distance of the bank where the check was issued.

If your bank knows you very well, it will sometimes honor the overdrawn check and add a service charge, especially if it happens rarely and they note that you have a deposit waiting to clear. That saves you embarrassment, but don't depend on it. Much better to keep the checkbook in good order to avoid this difficulty.

Writing a check when you know full well there's not enough money in the bank to pay it is illegal in many states. In addition you could run into problems of fraud or theft if the check was in payment for goods or services you've already used.

(*See also: Balance, Checking Account, Cleared Check, Deposit, Insufficient Funds*)

Overhead

A crafts business has three major areas of cost: raw materials, labor, and overhead. That's true whether the activity is conducted by a craftsperson all alone in a basement workshop, or whether it's an extensive operation with employees, elaborate equipment, and a store.

Overhead consists of all the operating costs that are not directly related to the production of specific craftwork. The cost of raw materials and labor (including your own) change in direct proportion to how much is produced. Overhead does not. It remains fairly constant, even if nothing is produced. That's why overhead is also known as general or fixed expense.

Rent, insurance premiums, telephone bills, and utilities have to be paid every month, whether you are away at a craft show or burning the midnight oil to complete an order.

Overhead can be the drain down which flow many profits if it isn't figured carefully into your pricing. Accountants have devised a great many ways to do this, but two seem most practical for a small crafts operation: 1) assign a certain dollar amount of overhead to each hour of production; or 2) increase each dollar of production cost (materials and labor) by a specific percentage to account for overhead.

Before we develop some formulas to do this, let's examine exactly what ingredients go into overhead. If your craft activities and your personal affairs are completely separate, that's not too difficult. All your bills and all your payments appear either on your personal account or on your business account.

However, if you work at home, have one telephone bill, one electric bill and so forth, it is essential that you maintain very careful records to be able to know exactly how much of the rent, how much of the telephone, how much of your car expense, how much of the electric bill can be charged to your craft activity, and how much is a personal expense. It is all too easy to overlook overhead items in such a situation. But overlooking them eats into your profits two ways: 1) if you don't list a cost item as a business expense you cannot use it as a tax deduction; and 2) if you overlook a business expense you cannot include it in your pricing.

Here are some of the major items to include in a list of overhead expenses:

>Rent
>Insurance premiums
>Payroll taxes
>Transportation (car or van)
>Utilities (electric, gas)
>Heat and hot water
>Telephone
>Maintenance and cleaning
>Repairs
>Shipping and packing materials

> Freight and other delivery costs
> (unless charged separately to customer)
> Office equipment and supplies
> Show and sales costs
> Nonproductive service time
> Miscellaneous

There are some obvious items missing from this list: mortgage payments, loan payments, taxes. Since these are not related to the day-to-day operation of the business but to investment and profitability, they have to be calculated into profit, not overhead. A sizable craft business with extensive sales costs may want to list those as a separate category, but for many craftspeople it is probably more practical to include them in overhead, especially when they are primarily for show and fair expenses.

One essential overhead ingredient that is all too often overlooked is the service time you spend on nonproduction work such as billing, shipping, bookkeeping, cleaning up, running to the post office, and so on. It can amount to a pretty penny and has to be included in overhead. Service time is described more fully in the section on wages.

Now to the formula. It will take a little time and thought to put this together, but once it is done it need not be done again for at least a year, unless major items change significantly.

First, make a list of all your major overhead items. Use the list above, and add other categories you consider important in your operation. Next to each item indicate the total amount you spend (or expect to spend) for that item in one year.

Certain amounts are easy to identify, such as rent and insurance premiums. Others have to be estimated, based on previous experience or some specific plans you have made. If you went to only two craft shows last year, for example, but plan an extensive tour this year, that item should be increased proportionately.

Although we ultimately want to wind up with a monthly figure, we start with an annual total because many items (insurance premiums, show and fair expenses, repairs) don't occur every month.

If the list you've made up has been calculated carefully, taking into account price increases for utilities and supplies, additional insurance, etc., you now have a total of your annual overhead expense. For purposes of developing a pricing formula, let us create an example in which the total overhead amounts to $3,816.60. Divide that by twelve to come up with a monthly figure: $318.05 in this example.

Two methods now present themselves for figuring that overhead cost into the price of a specific craftwork.

1) *Assign a certain dollar amount of overhead to each hour of production.*

For this method you have to determine how many hours you spend in actual production of your craftwork, not counting the hours spent on such activities as billing, shipping, and selling. Let us assume that you average 140 hours a month actual work on your craft objects.

Dividing the 140 monthly hours into the $318.05 monthly overhead gives us an hourly overhead figure of $2.27. That means a craft object which takes an hour to produce must have $2.27 included in its price to account for overhead. If the object takes twenty minutes (one third of an hour) to make, 76¢ should be added to its price for overhead. And if it takes ten hours then overhead of $22.70 must be included.

2) *Increase each dollar of production cost (materials and labor) by a specific percentage to account for overhead.*

Let us assume that the total cost of materials and labor in your craft operation is expected to be around $13,600 this year, based on previous experience and future plans.

Now divide that production cost figure into the overhead figure from the previous example ($3,816), and you find that overhead costs are equivalent to 28 percent of production costs.

All you need do from now on is to add 28¢ for overhead to every dollar of production cost. If labor and materials for a specific item total $8, you add $2.24 (8 x 28¢) for overhead. To find the percentage on odd amounts, just move the decimal point two notches to the left and multiply by 28. For example, if labor and materials costs are $12.46, you find the percentage this way:

$$
\begin{array}{r}
.1246 \\
\times \quad 28 \\
\hline
\$\ 3.49
\end{array}
$$

If you want to simplify this and avoid the long division every time you try to calculate the cost, make up a chart that shows the overhead cost in relation to specific dollars of production. Taking the same 28 percent example, we would have a chart like this:

Production Cost	Overhead
0.25	.07
0.50	.14
1.00	.28
2.00	.56
3.00	.84
4.00	1.12
5.00	1.40
6.00	1.68
7.00	1.96
8.00	2.24
9.00	2.52
10.00	2.80

Let's calculate the overhead costs with this chart now, again on the example of $12.46 in production costs. In our head we can break down $12.46 into three units: $10, $2, and 50¢. We add up the amounts next to each of those figures on the chart ($2.80, 56¢, and 14¢) and come up with a total of $3.50, only a penny off the true amount ($3.49) which we found through long division.

All of this may seem like an awful lot of trouble to go through, but once you've got it down on paper, you can save a lot of time when you price your craftwork, and know that you've priced it accurately to reflect all your costs.

The figures we've discussed here are used primarily for pricing. For tax purposes, your accountant will determine the actual overhead costs. That figure can be important to you in two ways: 1) to compare with the estimates you used, and 2) as a basis for next year's estimates.

(See also: Expenses, Pricing, Profit, Wages)

Packing

More is probably lost through improper packing for shipment than any other single cause; lost not only in terms of actual cash in broken objects, but in terms of tarnished customer relations as well. The customer has to write a letter, you have to write a letter, damage claims have to be filed, and if the item was destined as a gift, or to be sold at a special event, the occasion may have passed before the situation is straightened out.

The American Craft Council's very valuable guide to packing and shipping puts the whole problem into focus: "Since shipments are inevitably subjected to shock and stress, the main concern is to pack in such a way that the container, rather than the object, will absorb the shocks inherent in transit. If the object inside the container moves, if the inner cushioning material shifts and the object hits the side of the container, or if one object hits another, shocks and damage result."

Fortunately, modern technology has provided a great variety of excellent packaging materials that overcome precisely the problems outlined above.

Bubble paper is one of the most economical and most versatile for protection against shock. Shredded or crumpled paper, and various types of paper or plastic padding, are also readily available. Test the different materials by making several typical packages, exactly as you would ship them, and give them a good workout, exactly as though they were being handled under the roughest conditions. Then unpack them and see what works best.

But breakage is not the only concern. Some objects must be protected against moisture, others from extremes in temperature. The construction of the outer package should be related to the weight of the content, so that a very heavy pot is not shipped in a light corrugated container.

It is best to wrap small breakable objects securely, fill the insides of cups, glasses, and vases with crumpled paper, wrap all pieces (lids, etc.) separately, protect exterior protuberances such as spouts and handles, and pack in small boxes which are then packed into a larger shipping carton.

Items that need protection against moisture, such as jewelry or fiber work, should be wrapped in tarnish-proof paper and then placed inside sealed plastic bags. It is also advisable to line the carton with waterproof paper.

If you ship a number of breakable items in one carton, observing a few simple rules will go a long way in reducing breakage:

1) Wrap all items individually in paper at least two layers thick.

2) Place at least three inches of crumpled paper on the bottom of the box or carton.

3) Place larger or heavier items on the bottom of the carton.

4) Cushion well between layers. Use about two inches of paper or cushioning material between layers. If the pieces are fairly heavy and have to be packed in the same carton, corrugated dividers are advisable between the pieces, in addition to cushioning material.

5) Start packing from the outside edge of the box and continue filling toward the center.

6) Place bowls, plates, platters on edge. Never place them flat.

7) If only one item is being packed, place it in the center of the box with cushioning under, over, and around it.

8) Fill the box to within three inches of the top, then fill the last few inches with paper or cushioning material.

9) Mark the outside of all boxes or cartons containing breakables with the word "FRAGILE," and if necessary, "This Side Up" and "Other Side Up."

Every package should contain a packing slip. This is usually a carbon copy of the invoice, often with the prices blocked out. It enables the recipient to check the contents against the packing slip. This is especially important in shipments to stores where the receiving department verifies receipt of the shipment in good order and sends the packing slip on to the bookkeeping department to be paid.

The packing slip can be enclosed inside the package, or better yet, fastened securely to the outside in a separate envelope prominently marked "Packing Slip Enclosed."

It doesn't pay to cut corners on packaging of craftwork that can break or be otherwise damaged in transit. The few pennies saved may become very expensive if breakage occurs. But there is a way to save if you can afford the investment: buying packaging materials in quantity from a wholesaler who specializes in such items may not be a small initial outlay, but saves money in the long run. Buying 100 cartons at a time is a lot less expensive than buying five cartons twenty times.

A good packing materials wholesaler can also be very useful in helping you determine what kind of packing materials to buy for your specific needs. Since he keeps up with the latest developments in the field, and is aware of the experiences other shippers have and how they solve their problems, his advice can be very useful.

Finally, any craftsperson who ships craft objects which need protection (and almost all craftwork does) would do well to get a copy of the publication "Packing/Shipping of Crafts," published by the American Crafts Council, 44 West 53rd Street, New York, NY 10019. The cost is $3, and the booklet not only contains many practical suggestions for packing and shipping specific kinds of craft objects, but also includes names and addresses of professional packers and shippers, firms that specialize in packing supplies, shipping agents, insurance advice, and other practical information.

(*See also: Shipping*)

Partnership

When two or more people own a business it can be organized as a partnership. This requires an agreement between the parties. It should be written, but can be oral or even implied by their dealings. It also requires the filing of a partnership certificate. Your county clerk can tell you what and where to file.

The big danger in a partnership is that each partner has full power to contract debts for the partnership, and each partner is personally liable for those debts, regardless of which partner incurred them. If the business goes under, the creditors can collect not only from the assets of the business, but also from each partner's personal income and assets such as savings, homes, cars, etc.

The one exception is a limited partnership. This is never a do-it-yourself project, and even a regular partnership should have legal guidance.

It is important to avoid the danger of becoming partners by accident. The laws of many states often interpret a close business relationship in which two or several people agree to work together in the same legal terms as a partnership. The absence of a written agreement doesn't make it any less binding. Any ongoing relationship of this nature should be specifically described in writing so that an unintentional partnership does not occur.

When a partnership is established, it is best to have an agreement describing each partner's participation—for example, how much of a share each partner has, whether they are active or inactive (silent) partners, and what happens if one partner leaves. If one partner dies, for example, the law provides that the partnership is dissolved and the business liquidated, unless provisions are made in the contract for the remaining partner(s) to carry on by buying the deceased partner's share from his or her heirs. Since that may involve a sizable sum of money which often is not readily available, partners can take out insurance on each others' lives, specifying that the proceeds are to be used to pay the heirs for the deceased partner's share.

Unlike the Gettysburg Address, this is not something to be written on the back of an envelope. Legal advice is essential to protect the interests of all the partners.

(*See also: Contract, Corporation, Joint Venture, Sole Proprietorship*)

Part Time

(*See: Expenses*)

Patents

A patent is a government document which certifies an inventor's claim to his or her invention, and protects the rights in his or her discovery. Patents cover inventions of a mechanical or utilitarian nature, as distinguished from copyrights, which protect artistic creativity, or trade marks, which protect brand names.

But what exactly is an invention?

Raymond Lee, a former U.S. Patent Examiner and one of the nation's foremost authorities on patents, puts it this way: "Suppose that while preparing a batch of dye, you accidentally dropped part of your breakfast into the vat and discovered, much to your surprise, that it improved the color coverage considerably. Would that make you an inventor? Absolutely—provided you remember what it was you dropped in."

A wide variety of inventions may be eligible for patent protection. The four which are probably of most concern to craftspeople are: mechanical patents, process or method patents, composition of materials patents, and design patents.

A *mechanical patent* is granted for any object whose mechanical construction is new and different. A totally new device for firing ceramics, for example, would be eligible for a mechanical patent.

A *process or method patent* is granted for new ways of producing an object. A new method of glazing, for example, could be eligible for a process or method patent.

A *composition of materials patent* is granted for a method by which existing materials are mixed or compounded to create new and different materials. This generally applies to such products as medicines, plastics, and other chemical formulations. It could also apply to a totally new mixture for ceramic glazes.

A *design patent* protects new and original designs or ornamentations for functional objects, not the way those objects are constructed. The design patent covers how an object looks, while the mechanical patent covers what the object does. If the object has no function at all but is purely decorative, then copyright laws apply.

For an imaginative example, we turn again to Mr. Lee: "If you invented a new kind of radio, you would apply for a mechanical patent. If that radio, in addition to being new inside, also looked like a grapefruit, you would need both a mechanical patent *and* a design patent. If you made a conventional radio look like a grapefruit, just a design patent would suffice. If you created a grapefruit sculpture with no radio inside, it would fall under copyright."

Unlike copyright protection, for which you simply submit two samples of the work with a fee, patent protection is much harder to come by. It requires careful documentation of your invention. Specific sketches and notes at the earliest stages of discovery, dated and witnessed, help to document when you first dreamed of your great idea.

A preliminary patent search will usually determine whether someone else already holds a patent on a discovery which is the same or similar to yours. This can cost as little as $100 or as much as several hundred, depending on problems encountered in the preliminary search.

Once your patent application has been filed, you are entitled to claim "patent pending" on the product of your invention. This affords a certain amount of protection and establishes a prior claim in case someone else comes up with a similar idea later on.

Filing such applications, and the subsequent legal work that is usually required, is best done through a patent attorney. The applicant is permitted to do it himself but the complications are monumental. If you seek legal assistance, it must be from a lawyer who is registered to practice before the patent bar. At this point, extensive patent searches have to be conducted, drawings and specifications have to be prepared, forms have to be filled out, and filing fees have to be paid.

It is important to do this properly and speedily. Someone else may be thinking the same great thoughts at this very moment, and your rights may be lost through delay or improper handling of the application procedure.

The costs for such legal services are rarely below $1,000, and can run into much higher figures. It's worth the effort and expense if your invention is likely to produce a sizable amount of money for you. Before you sign up with a patent attorney, ask about fees and what he or she will do for you.

The address of the U.S. Patent Office is Washington, DC 20231. A detailed booklet of "General Information Concerning Patents" is available for 75¢ from the Superintendent of Documents, U.S. Government Printing Office, Washington, DC 20402.

(*See also: Copyright, Trademark*)

Payroll Tax

(*See: Withholding Tax*)

Pensions

Self-employed craftspeople, and those who are employed by firms without pension plans, can set up their own retirement funds at considerable tax advantages.

1) If you are self-employed, or an owner or partner in an unincorporated business, you can each year deposit up to 15 percent (but no more than $7,500) of your self-employed income in a Keogh Plan for your later years.

2) If you are employed by a firm which does not have a pension plan you can start your own Individual Retirement Account (IRA) with up to 15 percent (maximum $1,500) of your annual salary.

3) Dividends, rents, interest, etc. are not eligible for inclusion under either the Keogh or IRA plans.

4) The money you put into your Keogh or IRA plan is not taxable in the year you earned it. The deposits, as well as the interest they earn, are taxable when you withdraw them. The assumption is that you will be in a lower tax bracket when you are of retirement age, and can also take advantage of special retirement tax benefits then. For example, if your self-employed income this year is $10,000, and you put $1,000 into your Keogh Plan, you pay taxes on only $9,000. You are, in effect, postponing your tax obligation on the other $1,000 until you are in a lower tax bracket. If you are in a 25 percent bracket now, you save $250 this year.

5) You must leave the money in your Keogh Plan until you are at least 59½. If you withdraw it earlier you not only have to pay back taxes based on your tax rate in the year that you earned it, but you'll also face stiff penalties.

6) If you die before 59½, your beneficiaries receive immediate payment. If you are permanently disabled before 59½, you receive your full amount at once, with no penalties.

7) If you have employees who work for you at least twenty hours a week and five months per year for three years you *must* include them in your Keogh Plan and contribute the same percentage of their earnings as you contribute for yourself. Employees have full vested rights to all contributions made in their behalf.

How to Invest

There are a variety of ways to invest your Keogh Plan: mutual funds, annuities, bank accounts, certificates of deposit, etc. Whatever plan you choose, it must be one that is approved by the Internal Revenue Service.

If the amount each year is not substantial, our suggestion is to put the funds into certificates of deposit at your bank. They earn good interest and are protected by the FDIC. The banks act as trustees and generally charge no fee.

Talk to your lawyer, accountant, or bank. They can give you the best advice on starting a Keogh Plan that suits your particular circumstances, or whether to start one at all.

Remember, a Keogh Plan means that you tie up your money for a number of years in exchange for significant tax benefits. Only you can decide whether that's worthwhile for you. You may never plan to retire, but hopefully you'll be 59½ some day.

Periodicals

Since crafts are a creative process, a craft artist's education never really stops. New ideas, new designs, new techniques are as constant as the morning's sunrise.

A great deal of information can be found in the plentiful supply of craft periodicals which are published throughout the world. Some of these are elaborate magazines with full-color illustrations, others are newspapers, some are simple but informative organizational newsletters.

Some deal with the whole gamut of crafts, others concentrate on only one craft. Some are published monthly, many every other month, quite a few only four times a year.

But whatever the source, most craftspeople who intend to stay abreast of developments and ideas in their craft read at least one or two publications regularly.

(*See also: Books*)

Petty Cash

Proper bookkeeping and accounting methods require that all expenses be paid by check and entered on the books under the proper category.

There are always small expenses, such as local carfare or delivery tips, which are too petty to warrant the check-writing procedure. A petty cash fund is established for this purpose. The petty cash fund is usually very small, perhaps $10 to $25, depending on the size of the operation. To start the petty cash fund, a check is drawn and cashed. The cash is kept separate from all other monies. Whenever a small payment is made from the petty cash fund, a slip of paper (petty cash voucher) is placed in the box or envelope along with the remaining petty cash money. The combination of cash on hand and vouchers should always total the original amount of the fund.

When the fund is almost depleted, all the vouchers are added up, and a new check is written in the amount of the vouchers. That brings the petty cash fund back up to its original amount.

Where elaborate bookkeeping systems are used, the accountant will want to break down the petty cash vouchers into various types of expenditures to apportion them into the proper expense categories. For very small craft operations this is rarely done.

One warning about the petty cash fund: even though you may be the boss and it's your own money, be sure to put an IOU into the box or the envelope whenever you borrow a buck or two for personal use. Redeem the IOU as soon as you can. To take out the money without leaving a note, hoping you'll remember to put it back, can cause untold havoc.

(*See also: Bookkeeping, Expenses*)

Photographs

Almost every photograph has one or more of these three purposes:

1) to record an event (vacation snapshots, wedding pictures, news photographs, etc.);

2) to serve as a sales tool (advertising or catalogue illustration, publicity stills, slides of craftwork, etc.);

3) as an art form in itself.

This section concerns itself only with the use of photographs to help sell or publicize craftwork. The technical aspects of photography could fill a whole other book, which indeed has been done in *Photographing Your Product* by Norbert Nelson (Van Nostrand-Reinhold), *Photographing Crafts* by John C. Barsness (American Crafts Council), and *Photography for Artists and Craftsmen* by Claus-Peter Schmid (Van Nostrand-Reinhold). These three books concentrate on the technical aspects of craft photography and assume a basic understanding of photography on the part of the reader. Numerous other books and manuals on photographic techniques and the use of equipment, both elementary and advanced, are available in libraries, bookshops, and photographic supply stores.

Almost everyone has handled a camera at one time or another, but there is a big difference between snapshots and photographs of craft objects. Norbert Nelson describes the difference as one of *taking* a picture or *making* a picture.

In snapshots, the amateur photographer has comparatively little control, except perhaps in the adjustment of the camera's timing and exposure. When you take a picture of the happy couple running down the church steps in a shower of rice you can't tell them to turn this way or stand that way. You shoot away with whatever light the sun provides, and let the shadows fall where they may. That's *taking* a picture.

But when you photograph a craft object you have complete control. You can arrange all sorts of lights, backgrounds, reflectors, positions, and other fancy footwork, and you can shoot the same subject over and over again with various exposures, shutter speeds, lighting arrangements, etc., until you feel fairly secure that you have just the shot you want. That's *making* a picture.

This very control scares a lot of craftspeople. It seems awfully complicated at first. But try to remember, if you are a potter, the first time you centered a glob of clay on the wheel. It probably went every which way until you learned how to control your medium. That's true of every other craft medium as well.

Photography itself is a craft, and requires a certain minimum amount of equipment: a fairly good camera and a tripod at the very least. Flash equipment is not very useful for craft photography since you need better light control. But sunshine will do fine if you can't afford elaborate lighting equipment. Craft photography presents special problems, such as capturing textures in pottery and weaving, avoiding reflection in jewelry and metalwork, and so forth.

Some reading, some practice, and some experimentation will provide most craftspeople with the basic skills to photograph their craftwork. But whether you take the pictures yourself or hire a professional photographer to do it for you (for a sales presentation or a juried show, for example), there are some basic principles.

For craft objects, the most common photographs are 35mm color slides. They are comparatively inexpensive, they can be mailed easily, they can be projected so that more than one person can see them simultaneously (such as a jury), and they provide faithful color reproduction. Slides are also very useful when you are asked to give a talk about your craft at a school or before a local club. A well-organized slide presentation contributes immensely to making your presentation lively and dramatic.

Slides which are used for selling or jurying purposes should be as simple in composition as possible so that nothing detracts from the craft object. Backgrounds should be neutral (white, gray, or black) and uncluttered. Extraneous subjects should be used only if they play a key role, such as providing a comparison frame of reference. The size of a huge wall hanging may be put into proper perspective by placing a simple chair next to it.

The same basic rules apply to black-and-white photographs to be used for advertising or catalogue illustration. Remember that you are selling craftwork, not fancy photographs. The illustration serves to give visual support to the selling text and the specific details which are provided through words. You want the reader to see the craft object, not the photograph.

Publicity Photos

The rules change a little bit with publicity pictures which you hope to have printed as news (without charge) in newspapers or magazines. Now a little human interest becomes important. Put some flowers in the vase and place it on a table. Put the rings on a finger or the belt around a waist. But don't let the human interest overshadow your craftwork. Again, you're not publicizing fingers and waists, but rings and belts.

Another form of publicity photograph is a picture of yourself doing your craftwork, getting an award, exhibiting at an important show, giving a lecture-demonstration, or participating in some other newsworthy event. You'd be surprised what editors consider newsworthy. If the photograph shows someone doing something visually interesting, it has a good chance of appearing in print. The law of averages is at work here, too. You can't expect to see yourself in the papers every week, but if you submit photographs to editors periodically, you're bound to increase your opportunities for having something used. This is especially true of small-town newspapers which may not have their own staff photographer and are always on the lookout for interesting pictures to spruce up their pages.

Competition being very keen among editors, it is best not to send the same photograph to several newspapers in the same town at the same time. If you've taken several pictures, you can submit different ones to each editor, even if the subject matter is similar. Otherwise they'll both be sore at you.

If you hope to have your publicity photographs published, don't make them Polaroid snapshots. Avoid slides or color prints too; they lose a lot when they are converted to black-and-white. Editors almost universally prefer 8″-x-10″ black-and-white glossies, and it is wise to give editors what they want. These glossies are also relatively inexpensive to reproduce in quantity if you have a commercial processing laboratory in your area.

Identification

Be certain that all photographs are properly identified. Write your name and address on the cardboard frame of every slide and on the back of every print. Use a soft pencil on the back of prints; ball-point pens press through to spoil the image.

Slides that are submitted for selling purposes should be coded to the price list or whatever other information you send along.

Publicity photographs *must* have a caption securely attached. The best way to do this is to type the caption on a piece of paper with two or three inches of blank space at the top. Then tape the top of the sheet to the back of the photograph so that the caption sticks out below the photo. For mailing purposes you fold the part that sticks out over the front of the picture. When the editor opens it, he or she doesn't have to turn the picture over to see what it's all about. Be sure the caption also includes your name and address or phone number so that it can be easily identified with the accompanying press release.

Mailing

Having spent all that money on photography, a little protection is in order when you send the photos through the mail.

For slides, the best method is to wrap them securely and mail them in a padded envelope (available at most major stationery supply stores). If that's not possible, surround them with corrugated or chipboard protection. If it's only a few slides, two pieces of chipboard in an envelope will usually do the trick, but mark the envelope "Hand Cancel" so that it doesn't go through the cancelling machines at the post office.

Prints should always be sent in an envelope large enough to hold them without folding, and backed with a piece of chipboard. Mark the front of the envelope "Do Not Bend." Address the envelope before you insert the photos to avoid possible damage from the pressure of a ball-point pen.

If you want your slides or prints returned, be sure to enclose self-addressed stamped envelope of the proper size and with the proper postage.

Model Release

If an individual is recognizable in any photograph that is used for commercial purposes, it is necessary to obtain a model release, even if it's your best friend or someone who works for you. If the model is a child, get a release signed by the parent or guardian. The best time to have a release signed is at the time the picture is taken. True, this can get ticklish at times, but you can always say that your lawyer or your printer told you to get a release. If someone refuses to sign a release, don't use the picture under any circumstances. You'd only be inviting trouble.

The model release (a form available at major photographic supply stores) is the legal means by which an individual whose likeness appears in a photograph gives permission to use that photograph for advertising or other commercial purposes. Such releases are not necessary for non-commercial use such as publicity photos, but most photographers consider it advisable to obtain a model release for all purposes. You never know when you might want to use the picture for a brochure or some other commercial promotion piece.

(*See also: Portfolio, Press Release, Publicity*)

Politics

Many craftspeople pride themselves on being individualists by nature. The self-sufficiency that's built into crafts sometimes extends to the artist's view of himself or herself as separate from the rest of the community. The difficulty of gaining recognition as an artist further sets craftspeople apart from the rest of the world. We have our studios, our workshops, our clients, our families, our friends—and that's that.

The reasons for noninvolvement are many, but the results are always the same. The voice of the craft artist is rarely heard in public, so the economic interests of working craftspeople are overlooked. Laws are passed, programs planned, grants and commissions awarded, all with little or no input from the crafts community.

Political clout is an unacceptable phrase to many craftspeople, but it is a concept whose time has come. Only by participating in (or at least influencing) the legislative and planning processes can craftspeople hope to get a fair share of the action or the proper protection of their interests.

The very least that craftspeople can do is to write a letter to a legislator or public official (local, state, or national) when a matter of direct concern to craftspeople is on the agenda.

Involvement might seem like an unattractive distraction from the creative life, but lack of involvement costs the crafts community too much in the long run.

Portfolio

A portfolio is *you* reduced to two dimensions. A good portfolio plus your best foot forward in terms of your craftwork, what you've done, where you've sold, exhibited, studied, and what others say about your work.

The portfolio consists essentially of three ingredients: 1) your resumé; 2) clippings or reviews; 3) slides or photos of your craftwork.

The preparation of a resumé is discussed under that heading. To show clippings to best advantage, cut them carefully out of the newspaper or magazine and mount them flat under two-sided acetate sheets, available in most good stationery supply stores. Do the same thing with gallery programs or other prestige documents in which your name is listed.

Black-and-white or color prints can also be mounted under two-sided acetate sheets. For 8"-x-10" prints, 10"-x-12" sheets are most suitable since they allow you to show prints either vertically or horizontally without turning the portfolio binder around.

For color slides, photo supply stores have plastic sheets which are clear on one side and frosted on the other to diffuse light. They can accommodate a dozen 2¼"-x-2¼" transparencies, or twenty 35mm slides which can be easily removed for showing in a slide projector.

Arrange the slides or prints in some logical sequence, if possible, so that the person who loks at them doesn't have to jump from one idea to another.

If you plan to make a sizable number of presentations to galleries and store buyers, have a few of your best slides converted into color prints. It's much easier to examine them, especially if a slide projector or viewer is not readily available. But be sure it's a good shot to begin with; every defect is magnified when a poor slide or negative is blown up.

The portfolio itself can be one or more ordinary looseleaf binders carried around in a case, or a zippered case which has the three-ring binder feature built in. Don't skimp on this. It's the first impression a prospect gets of your work and your attitude.

Another suggestion, this one from craft photographer Doug Long: "Please assign a safe, cool place for your portfolio. I cringe every time I see one lying next to a kiln, on the corner of a worktable, or some other imminently disastrous spot. Slides and prints get dirty and warped easily, so unless that's the way you feel about your work, protect your investment."

Long also observes that "showing pictures is a sadly lacking level away from handling the real thing, but it doesn't have to be a necessary evil. There is room for your own expression in a portfolio. There are no rules, no limits. Just the reaches of our imaginations."

(*See also: Photographs, Resumé*)

Post Office

The government activity that touches most of us on a daily basis is the post office—officially the United States Postal Service. A great deal of cynicism exists with regard to the efficiency and the cost of postal service, but since it's the only post office we have (except for parcel post), we might as well make the best of it by understanding the variety of services it offers.

Mail is transported in four basic categories (Postal rates quoted are 1976 figures):

First Class

All handwritten or typewritten matter, bills, and other individualized material *must* be sent via first class mail, although almost anything else *may* be sent first class. First class mail is completely private and may not be opened for postal inspection.

If you move, the post office will forward first class mail to your new address at no extra charge for one year, provided you notify your old post office of your new address before you move. First class mail for which no new address is available is returned to the sender as undeliverable.

First class mail under twelve ounces generally receives air mail delivery. Over twelve ounces it is called "priority mail" and, according to the post office, receives "the fastest transportation service available."

The maximum weight for first class mail is seventy pounds; the maximum size is 100 inches in length and girth combined. First class mail should be marked "First Class" whenever it is not of normal letter size.

First class mail weighing less than thirteen ounces costs 13¢ for the first ounce, 11¢ for each additional ounce. Post cards, which are handled as first class mail, cost 9¢ each. Rates for first class mail weighing thirteen ounces or more (priority mail) are based on weight and distance by zone. A six-pound priority mail package from New York to Philadelphia, for example, costs $3.37, to California $4.72.

Second Class

This is a special category for newspapers and periodicals, and is of little importance to craftspeople. Second class mail is never forwarded.

Third Class

This category may be used for single pieces of printed matter or merchandise weighing less than a pound, or for large mailings of identical pieces sent under a special bulk rate.

Delivery time for third class mail is unpredictable. It has been known to take as long as three weeks to reach distant parts of the country, especially during heavy mail-volume periods such as Christmas. It usually waits until everything else moves.

Third class mail is not forwarded, nor is it returned to the sender, unless it is marked "Return Postage Guaranteed" or "Forwarding and Return Postage Guaranteed." That means the sender guarantees to pay the extra postage for the extra handling. "Return Postage Guaranteed" is often used by senders of third class mail to get the undeliverable pieces back and clean up their mailing list to remove the names of people who have moved. Such mail can also be marked "Address Correction Requested," in which case the post office will provide the new address (if it has one) and you can determine whether to retain the name on your list at the new address. The charge for this service is 10¢ per piece.

The single piece rate for third class mail is 14¢ for the first two ounces. If a piece weighs less than one ounce, therefore, it is pointless to send it third class since it gets much faster delivery for 13¢ via first class mail. The rate increments for heavier third class pieces are as follows:

2 to	4	ozs.	28¢
4 to	6	ozs.	39¢
6 to	8	ozs.	50¢
8 to	10	ozs.	61¢
10 to	12	ozs.	72¢
12 to	14	ozs.	83¢
14 to	15.9	ozs.	94¢

For bulk mailings, an annual permit fee of $40 is required, in addition to a one-time application fee of $20. The postal rates vary according to the nature of the material that is mailed, in some instances according to zone distance, and whether the mailer is a nonprofit organization or a commercial enterprise. However, third class bulk rate is the least expensive way of mailing large quantities of identical material.

For example, if you mail 5,000 announcements to your customers twice a year, the minimum per piece charge is 7.5¢. The annual bulk fee of $40, spread over the total 10,000 pieces, brings the per-piece postage to 7.9¢, which saves you more than a nickel on each piece, or over $500 in this example, as compared to first class mail.

Third class bulk rate mail is governed by very specific rules and regulations. If you plan to make such mailings and take advantage of the lower rate, consult your post office before you have anything printed.

Fourth Class

This is also known as parcel post, and here's where the post office has some competition from such organizations as United Parcel Service.

Parcels mailed between first class post offices, mostly in larger cities, are limited to forty pounds and eighty-four inches in length and girth combined. Larger packages can be mailed to and from smaller post offices.

Rates depend on weight and distance. Special rates apply to books and some other materials. Packages sent over long distances get faster delivery by the use of priority mail or express mail, since those move by air. The cost, of course, is higher. The six-pound package mailed from New York to California costs $2.52 via fourth class mail against $4.72 via priority mail.

Fourth class mail will be forwarded (if a new address is available) if additional postage is paid by the recipient. Fourth class mail that is undeliverable will be returned to the sender if the sender pays the additional postage. This extra postage is computed on the basis of the applicable fourth class rates.

Express Mail

This is a new service being tested by the post office, which guarantees overnight delivery for letters and packages. As of mid-1976 it was available at fewer than 400 post offices in major cities throughout the country. The post office makes full postage refund if overnight delivery is not performed. Also included is $500 free merchandise insurance.

Express mail service is available in two forms: 1) From one post office to another post office where the customer can pick it up; or 2) from one post office directly to the addressee. Express mail must be deposited at the sending post office by 5 P.M.; it is available at the receiving post office by 10 A.M. the following morning, or is delivered to the addressee by 3 P.M. the following afternoon, 365 days a year, holidays included.

Rates for this service are quite high, and are useful only for the most urgent and critical mail.

The same six-pound New York to California package would cost $12 from post office to post office, and $16 from post office to addressee. The minimum charge to mail even a letter anywhere in the country is $1.50 from post office to post office, $5.50 from post office to addressee.

Business Reply Mail

Mailing pieces which ask for an order or for payment of a bill often enclose a self-addressed envelope in which the recipient can send the order or the check. Experience has shown that such an envelope encourages recipients to respond. For many years, those envelopes almost always had the return postage included in the form of a business reply permit number in the upper right corner.

With the rapid increases in postage rates in recent years, more and more such reply envelopes no longer include reply postage. The envelopes are simply self-addressed, and the recipient is expected to use his or her own stamps, especially on bill payments.

However, business reply mail with return postage is still used when a mailer wants to produce a large number of replies and is willing to pay the postage to get them. The post office will supply the exact form and wording in which this permit must be shown on the reply envelope. The actual postage is paid when the mailman returns the reply envelopes, or through an account established at the delivering post office if the volume is large enough.

The postage for Business Reply Mail is calculated in one of two ways. If a mailer pays an annual account maintenance fee of $75, the cost per piece is 3½¢ in addition to first class postage, or 16½¢ for a letter, 12½¢ for a post card. In the absence of this fee, the cost is 12¢ per piece in addition to first class postage, or 25¢ for the regular letter. Anyone who expects to receive at least 900 pieces of business reply mail a year is ahead of the game by paying the $75 fee. This would obviously be an advantage for the large mailer who sends out millions of pieces on which he formerly paid 5¢ and now pays only 3½¢ plus first class postage. In both cases, an annual fee of $30 must be paid for the use of a business reply permit number.

The post office performs various services for its clients in connection with the delivery of mail. Among these are:

Registered Mail. This provides insurance protection for domestic first class mail and is handled with special precautions. Rates vary according to value. The minimum $100 of insurance costs $2.10, $1000 costs $3.50, $10,000 is $6.20, and so on into the millions.

Insured Mail. This provides insurance up to $200 for third class, fourth class and priority mail containing printed matter or merchandise. Rates range from a minimum of 40¢ for value up to $15, to $1.20 for value between $150 and $200.

Certified Mail. This provides only a receipt and record of delivery at the post office. It travels no faster than first class and provides no extra security. The fee is 60¢ in addition to the postage.

Return Receipt. A receipt showing when, where, and to whom the mail was delivered is available for registered, insured, or certified mail. When requested at the time of mailing it can show when and to whom it was delivered (25¢), plus the address where it was delivered (45¢). If the return receipt is requested after mailing, it costs 45¢ and will show only when it was delivered and who signed for it.

C.O.D. Mail. Payment for merchandise ordered by the addressee will be collected by the post office and remitted to the sender by postal money order. The maximum amount is $300. The fees for C.O.D. service range from 85¢ to $1.85 and include collection of the postage and money order fee from the addressee. C.O.D. fees include insurance protection against loss or damage. C.O.D. may also be sent as registered mail.

Special Delivery. This service assures prompt delivery of mail when it arrives at the delivering post office, including Sundays and holidays. Costs range from $1.25 to $2.15, depending on weight and class. The normal special delivery charge for a letter is $1.25 in addition to the postage.

Special Handling. This service is available only for third and fourth class mail. It is difficult to determine exactly what special handling means, except that perhaps the post office won't run over the package with a truck. The fees in addition to postage are 50¢ for the first two pounds, 70¢ for two to ten pounds, and $1.00 over ten pounds.

Money Order. If you can't send a check, you can buy a postal money order for a maximum amount of $300, which the recipient with proper identification can cash at any post office or deposit in his or her bank like a check. Fees are 50¢ up to $10, 70¢ from $10 to $50, and 90¢ for $50 to $300.

Five important points should be observed to speed your mail through the laborious machinery of the Postal Service:

Zip Code. This identifies the precise post office to which your mail is destined. It is *required* for all but first class mail, and strongly recommended for first class mail as well. Every post office has a zip code directory which you can consult. Be sure your own zip code is included wherever your address is printed: on stationery, envelopes, labels, advertising, catalogues, and so forth.

Stampless Mail. Mail without stamps is no longer being delivered with postage due paid by the recipient. If you don't put stamps on the mail, it is returned to you. If your mail goes out without stamps or a return address, it winds up in the dead letter office.

Proper Packing. Improper packing, especially of packages, is a major problem for the post office. Wrap all parcels carefully, and place the name and address of the recipient inside the package for extra precaution in case the wrapping comes undone.

Clear Handwriting. Names and addresses which cannot be deciphered cause delays in the post office. Some scrawls require the expertise of a hieroglyphics decoder, and wind up in the dead letter office.

Change of Address. If you move, the post office provides post card forms on which you can notify publishers of newspapers or magazines to which you subscribe of your new address. Most publications require thirty to sixty days to change their records, and they generally request that you send the mailing label with your new address for better identification on their computerized mailing lists.

The change-of-address forms are free, except for postage. You can also use them to notify friends, relatives, department stores, insurance companies, and others who have occasion to write to you. It will get the mail to you more quickly. Unfortunately it will get the bills to you more quickly, too.

(See also: Delivery, Freight, Shipping, United Parcel Service)

Press Release

A press release is a very particular means by which you get information to newspapers, magazines, radio stations, and television news programs with the hope of having it made public. The content is different for every release, but the format is quite fixed.

A few basic rules:

1) A press release should always be typed, double spaced, on one side of the sheet only. If the release runs to more than one page, type "more" at the bottom of each page except the last, where you type "end."

2) The press release should be typed on 8½"-x-11" letter-size white paper, with plenty of margin space on all sides so that the editor can make notations, corrections, or changes.

3) If the press release is not typed on stationery, the name and address of the sender should be typed at the top, centered on the page. Skip a few spaces and at left type the date the release is sent, and immediately below it type the earliest date it is to be used. If it can be used

---

THE VILLAGE SMITHY
138 E. MAIN STREET
Penfield, MO 27359

September 5, 1977   Contact: John Hammer
For Immediate Release   (627) 355-0846

EXHIBIT TO CELEBRATE
WELDED SCULPTURE WEEK

An exhibition of welded sculpture by John Hammer will open on Sunday, September 16th, at the Louisville Gallery, 617 Main Street, in observance of National Welded Sculpture Week.

Hammer's unusual work has received national acclaim, and has been shown in many major museums and galleries. The Louisville exhibit will be open from 10 A.M. to 4 P.M. daily until September 29. Admission is free.

Welded sculpture is one of the newest art forms based on one of the oldest crafts: blacksmithing. The Hammer exhibit will be the first public view of this unusual new technique in the Louisville area, according to Gallery Director Simon Simple.

John Hammer, now 72, began to work on the anvil at age 13, when he apprenticed in his uncle's blacksmith's shop in Fairfax County, Missouri. Horses were still being shod then, Hammer explained, and it was a busy shop. But with the appearance of the automobile, blacksmithing became a dying art. Hammer estimates

(more)

---

any time, type "For Immediate Release." Otherwise type: "For release on. . . ."

Lined up with the date lines, but far to the right, type the name of the individual who can be contacted for further information, and immediately below it that person's telephone number (include area code).

When you write the press release, remember a few basic rules of newspaper writing. First of all, get all of the important information into the first paragraph. Those are the five Ws of journalism: when, where, who, what, and why, plus how. Not all six apply to every story, but where they do they should lead off the release.

Look how it's done in the sample press release: "An exhibition of welded sculpture (*what*) by John Hammer (*who*) will open on Sunday, September 16 (*when*) at the Louisville Gallery, 617 Main Street (*where*) in observance of National Welded Sculpture Week (*why*)."

The subsequent paragraphs should be written in descending order of importance, so that the least important information comes at the end. When an editor makes up a newspaper page, he cuts from the end if he can't fit everything in. If the important information appears at the end of the release, it is more likely to disappear when the newspaper is printed.

What will tickle an editor's fancy and what will wind up in the waste basket is unpredictable. But one type of press release is almost sure to be ignored: a release which sounds like nothing more than an ill-disguised sales pitch. Editors are interested in news and features; sales messages belong in the advertising columns.

Study newspaper writing style by reading the papers from that point of view. Sentences are short. So are paragraphs. Good stories are written to appeal to readers, not the egos of writers. Fancy words with obscure meanings may impress your inlaws, but they'll turn most readers (and most editors) off. The simpler and more direct the press release, the better its chance of being printed.

If the editor thinks there may be a feature story in the activity announced in the press release, he'll assign a reporter to contact you. If he's never heard of National Welded Sculpture Week, he may want to know more about it for a possible feature. Anything in your release that might intrigue an editor is a bonus.

If you send the sample release to the weekly in sculptor Hammer's home town as well as the big city dailies, you might want to add a p.s. to alert the hometown editor that Hammer lives in the neighborhood. That may produce interest or even a feature story in the weekly.

Timing is an extremely important factor. A daily newspaper can process a release for print overnight if it wants to. A weekly newspaper often has deadlines a week ahead of publication date. Monthly magazines usually require information two and even three months ahead of time to get it into print.

Most newspapers and magazines, even small weeklies, have special editors for special departments. A general news release can go to the city editor. A release on a gallery opening could also go to the arts editor. A release on a new line of earrings should go to the woman's page editor. Since editors are busy people, sending a release to the wrong department could be a total waste. The few phone calls to determine the name of the appropriate editor are usually worth the time.

Finally: photos. Don't bother with Polaroid shots, fuzzy candids, or color slides. Most editors want 8"-x-10" black-and-white glossies, with the picture caption and your name and address securely taped to the back. Some papers will take 5"-x-7" shots, but the bigger size stands a better chance. Getting a picture into the papers is worth the investment to have a good one taken. If it's a picture of a craft object, be sure to mark which end is the top.

Two small tips on mailing photos:

1) Never fold the picture. Get a large enough envelope and use a piece of cardboard for protection.

2) Address the envelope before you enclose the picture. Addressing the envelope later may find the ball-point pen pressing through and defacing the photograph. For that same reason, never write on the back of a photo, except very lightly with a soft pencil or crayon.

(*See also: Advertising, Photographs, Publicity, Public Relations*)

Price

(*See: Pricing*)

Price Cutting

Reducing prices under competitive pressure or because of customer insistence is a temptation which may produce a few dollars immediately, but can be costly in the long run.

There are some very obvious dangers. Suppose a customer finds out that another customer bought the identical item under the same circumstances but at a lower price. You've earned nothing but bad will.

Price cutting also undermines the confidence your customers can have in the real value of your work. If the price tag was $50 yesterday and $25 today, there had better be a very good reason.

Cutting the price may seem the easiest way of overcoming competition, but it may prevent a serious examination of the real reason why you're not selling more. Price may have nothing to do with it. Having cut the price may not solve the problem, but only create new ones.

Price cutting is not to be confused with normal and accepted price reductions such as clearance sales of incomplete sets, limited selections of discontinued items, seconds, and so forth. Nor are pricing procedures such as wholesaling or quantity discounts to be confused with price cutting. In all of these cases there are legitimate reasons why the price has been reduced.

If the original price for a given craft object has been reasonably determined, taking into account the costs of production, the market conditions, and the profit, then it is both dangerous and costly to engage in random price cutting.

Another situation arises in which craftspeople may not even consider that they are cutting the price. This happens when you take a booth at a craft show and sell your work at prices below those that are charged by nearby retail stores which stock your craft objects. Undermining the retailer's established price for your work when you are, in effect, in direct competition with him, is ill advised. You're in town for only a few days. The retail store (you hope) will sell your work all year long and reorder from you in the future. Here again the temptation for a quick dollar can undermine your profitability if you do any substantial volume through retail stores. Once you get a reputation for undercutting your own retail store customers (they do talk to each other), it will be much more difficult to sell to retail outlets in the future.

(*See also: Pricing*)

Pricing

You are now in what may well be the most important part of this book, and of your economic success in crafts.

Pricing can make you or break you. If your price is wrong, it hardly matters whether you do everything else right. The old joke that "we lose a nickel on every sale, but we make it up in volume" doesn't work here.

Before we get down to methods for determining the price you charge for your craftwork, it is useful to discuss the various ingredients which enter into the determination of price.

There are four major elements to be considered:
1) How much does it cost to produce the product?
2) How much does it cost to operate the business which creates the product?
3) How much profit do you want to make?
4) Will the customer buy it at the price?

These four are all interrelated. None can stand alone, and none can stand without all the others.

The cost of production, the cost of overhead and sales, and your profit margin can all be determined with a fair amount of accuracy.

To simplify things (we'll get more detailed later): suppose an object costs $5 in labor and materials to produce, the overhead apportioned to that object is $3, and you want to make a 25 percent profit ($2 on $8); you charge $10. That takes care of the first three considerations.

Number four is the tricky one. It doesn't matter how rational you think the price is: if there are no customers who'll buy it at that price, forget it!

Customer acceptance of a price is based on both economic and psychological reasons. First, of course, there's the question of want or need. It is unlikely, for example, that many people would buy this book if it were priced at $100 a copy. There simply aren't many craftspeople who see the need for so expensive a book. Conversely, if this book were priced at 39¢, many craftspeople might ask: "If it's so cheap, can it be any good?"

The customer's perception of the value of a product to fill a need, then, affects price.

The customer's desire for prestige and recognition also affects the price. Some people will pay ten times the amount for a Dior original than they will for a mass-produced imitation. They pay the price so that they can be the first (or the only) people wearing that particular garment.

The same principle applies to one-of-a-kind objects created by a craft artist. A vase created by a well-known potter will fetch a better price at a gallery than a vase created by an unknown potter will get at a craft fair, even though the cost of the clay is the same and the vases may both be beautiful. This has been true in the field of fine art for many years. It is beginning to be a factor in the field of crafts.

There's also the customer's pocketbook to be considered. If you can only afford a Plymouth, it doesn't matter how rational the price of a Cadillac is; you simply can't buy it. Translated into crafts, this means that a $1,000 tapestry won't sell at the average craft fair—not because it isn't worth every penny, but because the customers simply don't bring that kind of money.

Finally, there's the competitive situation. If you offer a line of jewelry at one price, and a very similar line is offered at a lower price, you must have some very good reasons why your price is higher, or lose customers to the competitor. That doesn't mean your price should be based solely on what the competition charges, but the marketplace is such that this factor must be included in your calculations if you're both after the same customer. The fact that you pay a much higher rent or want to make a better profit couldn't interest your customer less. If you use better materials, or your craftsmanship is obviously superior, then you have a reasonable claim to a higher price. If, on the other hand, your competitor is simply more efficient and can therefore charge less for the same product, then he or she is going to make the sale.

Price, in the last analysis, is simply a way of expressing the value of a product in terms of money. And as we've seen, there are a great many elements which determine the value of a product.

Now let's get down to actual pricing procedures. There are two basic ways to go about this: 1) determine the ultimate selling price and then work backward to establish materials costs, production procedures, and other steps necessary to meet that price; or 2) find out how much everything costs and set a price on the basis of those figures.

Experienced craftspeople probably know by instinct in what general price range a particular craft object should fall, and proceed accordingly. In actual practice, however, the pricing procedure usually starts from the other end: calculating the cost of production, materials, labor, overhead, and profit to arrive at a price, and perhaps making adjustments if the price is not right. We'll concentrate on that approach, although the principles can work in either direction.

To begin with, every business activity involves two types of cost: fixed costs and variable costs.

Fixed costs are those that remain constant, regardless of how much you produce. These are almost always included in overhead. Your rent, for example, goes on month after month, even when you go on vacation and produce nothing.

Variable costs are those which relate directly to production. Making 100 belts require ten times as much leather as making ten belts. If you reduce production and let a helper go, you also reduce your labor cost.

In both cases, there may be slight variations. The telephone bill, generally a fixed cost, is likely to be somewhat lower when you're on vacation, although there's still a monthly minimum.

Increasing production may enable you to achieve a slightly lower cost per unit for raw materials if you get a better deal for buying a larger quantity.

Determining price requires a certain amount of record keeping during the course of production. Craft artists who produce one-of-a-kind objects find this much simpler than production craftspeople. They need to maintain cost records only for the one object they're working on at a given time.

Craft producers, however, must be much more careful. Following are some of the major categories of expense; many of these are discussed in more detail under their own subject headings. In all cases the dollar amounts for each expense item must be apportioned to the individual craft objects that are produced, either by fixing the actual cost of time or materials related to the item, or by converting expenses into hourly averages and then applying them to the time it took to produce a given item.

Production Costs
  1) Raw Materials
  2) Wages (your own included)

Selling Costs
  1) Advertising
  2) Shows and fairs
  3) Operating a store or showroom
  4) Commissions to outside sales staff
  5) Wages (your own included)
  6) Photography
  7) Samples

Overhead
  1) Rent
  2) Utilities
  3) Water
  4) Telephone
  5) Stationery and supplies
  6) Packaging materials
  7) Maintenance
  8) Repairs
  9) Transportation
  10) Taxes
  11) Insurance
  12) Bad debts
  13) Loss through breakage and theft

Financial
  1) Profit
  2) Loan payments
  3) Depreciation
  4) Value of inventory

Not every craftsperson itemizes every one of these expense factors. Selling costs are often included in overhead, for example. On the other hand a potter, being a heavy user of fuel to fire the kiln, may want to apportion some of his fuel bill directly to production costs.

Overhead is most easily totaled into a weekly or monthly figure, reduced to a per-hour overhead cost, and then applied to the cost of the various items according to the time it takes to make them. Thus, if your overhead is $3 per hour, and you produce five stained-glass owls per hour, the price for each owl must include 60¢ for overhead.

With experience, some craftspeople have even arrived at a pricing formula based on some specific element of the production process. If you discover, after several years of careful record keeping, that the ultimate wholesale price always turns out to be ten times the cost of raw materials used in making the item, then it becomes a simple matter of keeping track of the cost of materials and multiplying by ten. But that's risky unless you're on sure ground, and even then it has to be constantly examined and reexamined to determine whether other factors have changed sufficiently in cost to affect the formula. If your rent doubles, for example, it could throw the whole calculation out of whack.

By and large—especially for craftspeople just getting started—it is safest to pin down every last expense item and add it into the total. How to do this is discussed under the appropriate subject headings such as Overhead, Wages, etc.

Revising the Price

Suppose you've done all your calculations, and you discover to your chagrin that the price comes out too high. You aimed for $20 and it came out $22. If your calculations are based on a prototype, a first piece, you'll undoubtedly find savings in the production process when you begin to make a dozen at a time.

The normal tendency, unfortunately, is to simply cut $2 off the price and let it go at that. So you've simply cut into your profit, perhaps even demolished it. Much better to go over all of your expenses to see where you can save.

Let's use a hypothetical example where the arithmetic is simple: suppose you've designed a belt that's two inches wide. The leather for the belt represents 25 percent of the ultimate wholesale price. If you can make the belt 1¾″ wide without affecting its esthetic quality, you have saved 12½ percent of the raw materials cost, or just over 3 percent of the total wholesale cost. At the same time you're talking to several suppliers, and find one who will sell leather to you at 12 percent less than you've been paying. That's another 3 percent on the wholesale price. You've now saved 6 percent. Not much, you say? Well, if your net profit was 10 percent before the savings, you've just increased it by 6 points or 60 percent. Nothing to sneeze at. On top of that you've found a way to make six belts an hour instead of five, so your labor cost per belt has gone down approximately 20 percent.

Multiply this careful examination into a dozen different areas of your craft activity, and you will find that you can either produce at a better price or realize a bigger profit at the same price.

Odd Pricing

It is a common retail practice to price products at a fraction below the next highest round-number price. Thus a pound of bananas is 19¢ instead of 20¢, a radio is $49.95 instead of $50, and a car costs $3995 instead of $4000.

This is known as odd pricing, and is done on the assumption that customers think the price is much lower than it actually is. Marketing experts have questioned whether that's true, and many marketers agree that it has little bearing on such products as craftwork where prestige, originality, creativity, and similar attributes are as much a part of the product as the material of which it is made or the use to which it is put.

Odd pricing, therefore, seems to be of little or no consequence in determining what price you can put on your craftwork. Indeed, it may have an undesirable effect by creating a bargain basement atmosphere around your price tag.

Trading Up

A basic objective in selling is to build up the ticket, to have each retail customer spend more. That is often based on prices which establish an advantage in buying a larger quantity. We're not speaking here of wholesales prices, but of establishing prices for sets which are slightly lower than the prices would be for a similar number of single pieces. Not all craftwork leads itself to this kind of pricing, but it's worth considering.

For example, if the price tag on a pillow is $9, sell three of them for $25. In addition to selling mugs at a dollar each, offer them at $10 a dozen. It may appear at first that you're cutting into your profit, but many of the basic costs (rent, telephone, the booth at a craft show) remain constant, whether your sales are $100 or $1,000. It may therefore turn out to be more profitable to induce customers to buy in logical quantities at special prices, and thus build up your total dollar volume.

Pricing for Profit

As long as your costs are covered, you can set prices according to the biggest profit return you can get. Sometimes a lower price will bring a bigger profit: if you price an item at $10 which includes a $2 profit, you will earn $400 if 200 of those items are sold. If you reduce the price to $9, your profit will be only $1 per piece. But suppose now you can sell 500 pieces at the lower price. You've earned $500 in profits. Indeed, the larger volume may bring even greater returns because you can buy the raw materials more economically in large quantities.

This is not to suggest that if the price is lower, the volume will necessarily be larger. You may not even want to produce a larger volume. But it is a consideration that should be included in your calculations.

Finally, if you've figured your wholesale price properly, it will include a decent wage for your production time, and a decent profit for your creativity, management skills, capital investment, etc. No need to cry over the store's selling your work to the consumer at double what you got for it. The store is performing a legitimate function for you, unless you already have more customers than you can handle.

When you are both a craft producer and a craft retailer—opening your own shop or selling at a craft fair—your retail price should be established exactly as any other retailer establishes his. In effect, you are buying from yourself at wholesale and adding a markup to cover your operating expenses, wages, and profits. The temptation may be great to go into retailing whole hog, but don't do it before you've calculated whether your time is spent more profitably producing the craftwork or selling it. If you can price for a profit margin of 25 percent at wholesale, and a profit margin of 10 percent at retail, stick to producing the craftwork. You'll make more money.

(*See also: Advertising, Bad Debts, Cost Accounting, Insurance, Inventory, Loss Leader, Margin, Markup, Overhead, Profit, Raw Materials, Rent, Retailing, Samples, Shipping, Shows and Fairs, Taxes, Telephone, Wages*)

Printed Materials

Letterheads, envelopes, business cards, order forms, brochures, catalogues, tags, labels, invoices—the list of printed materials that is needed by even the smallest business with the simplest procedures seems endless.

While your craftwork is your most important medium of communication, your printed material often precedes it. What you send to customers or prospects in the form of letters or sales literature is often their first introduction to you, and helps to establish the initial impression, positive or negative.

It costs no more to have something printed that is well-designed and expresses your individual style or personality than to print a jumble of pedestrian type. A basic design for your name or your company name, carried through all of your printed materials, gives each item greater impact and value as an extension of your craft business.

A friend in the advertising business, or a helpful printer, can often provide valuable suggestions on how to produce your printed materials at the lowest possible cost, how to print several different pieces at the same time to get more for your printing dollar, or how to take advantage of special colors or papers to make your printed material uniquely yours.

(*See also: Advertising, Business Forms, Catalogues, Direct Mail, Portfolio*)

Production

Production is the general term given to all the steps involved in making a craft object, from the first contact with the raw material to the finished product ready for packing and shipping.

In the crafts field, the term production craftsman distinguishes the craftsperson who makes a number of copies (or multiples) of the same design from the craftsperson who makes one-of-a-kind pieces. Each of these multiple pieces is, of course, a fully handcrafted item with its own unique characteristics. It is is not, as in factory production, stamped from the same mold.

The production process influences both the amount of satisfaction crafts producers get from their time at the bench or wheel or loom, and the amount of money they make from their work. No two craftspeople will use the same production procedures. Individuality, after all, is the hallmark of craftwork. There are, however, a few basic considerations which can help make the work more satisfying and more profitable.

1) Get organized! Keep raw materials in one place, properly identified and easily accessible, so that you don't spend useless and frustrating time looking for things. Shelving for storing raw materials, pegboards for tools, jars or cans for small bits and pieces, make life much easier. Raw materials that can spoil or soil easily should be properly protected so that time need not be wasted in getting them back into shape, nor money wasted in throwing them away because they're unusable.

2) You've got to have rhythm! The secret of the well-organized craft producer is that the production steps follow in logical sequence. The very nature of the craft dictates much of this. A piece of pottery, obviously, can't go into the kiln until it's been glazed, and it can't be glazed until it comes off the wheel. But in production crafts, the important question becomes one of how many steps should be performed at the same time. Who would dream, for example, of making a single mug, glazing it, and then firing it? That would be a clear waste of time and money. But if we refine that example, it would also seem to be laborious to make a mug and attach a handle, make a mug and attach a handle, make a mug and attach a handle. Getting two dozen mugs off the wheel and then attaching two dozen handles expedites the process, reduces the production time, and thereby increases the profit.

Care must be taken, of course, to avoid the boredom and thereby the potential decline in craftsmanship that can result from repeating the same step too many times before going on to something else. Achieving the right combination is a matter of individual style and experience.

(*See also: Inventory, Job Ticket, Multiple Production, One-of-a-kind, Overhead, Pricing, Turnover, Wages, Work Area*)

Product Liability Insurance

You make a beautiful chair and find an enthusiastic customer. And then you get a call to tell you that the chair collapsed when the customer sat down in it and she sprained her back. She threatens to sue.

If she can prove that the chair collapsed because of defective workmanship, she might win her lawsuit.

Product liability insurance is available to protect you in case of a lawsuit based on some defect in the product for which you are responsible, or some characteristic about which you should have warned the customer. It doesn't matter whether you sold the item directly to the customer or whether it was sold through a retail store: the maker of the product can be held responsible.

The best product liability insurance, of course, is to make the product as safe as possible, and to alert the customer if special precautions have to be taken. If you inform the customer not to put the glassware in a dishwasher, and he or she cuts two fingers taking the broken glass out of the dishwasher, you have met your responsibility. But if the glass breaks and spills hot liquid on someone because you were careless in the production of the item, watch out.

Most craftspeople find that product liability insurance is too expensive in view of the relative safety of their craftwork. But for those who make objects which could cause accidents or injuries due to product defects, such liability coverage is worth a discussion with an insurance broker.

Product Line

An essential truth in merchandising is that a line of products tends to increase the sale of each item in the line. If Campbell's Soups, for example, made only tomato soup, it would not be nearly as successful (even with its tomato soup) as it is with a line that includes chowder, vegetable soup, onion soup, and a variety of other soups.

Similarly, a potter who makes only drinking mugs will most likely find that sales go up if plates, platters, and other related items are added to the line. A jeweler who makes only pins often increases sales when earrings and other related items are added to the line and the whole line is displayed together.

A line is also enhanced if the same craft object is produced in a variety of colors, shapes, or sizes. A group of pillows, all of which are red and square, will not sell nearly as well as a group of pillows which offers the customer a selection of colors and shapes.

A product line, then, is a group of related items, easily identifiable as coming from the same source and having similar characteristics. Related does not mean that they look alike, but simply that they have something in common with each other.

A product line succeeds when it accomplishes one or both of two purposes:

1) *Offers the customer a choice.* If the customer doesn't like the red pillow, he or she can buy one in blue or green or yellow. Or three pillows in three different colors. If you have only red pillows, he or she may not buy any.

205

2) *Increases the sale.* If the customer likes the mugs, sell him or her the plates as well. If you carry only mugs, he or she will either buy plates elsewhere, or won't buy from you at all if matching mugs and plates can be bought from another potter.

Developing a product line is an important activity in successful crafts merchandising. It requires a bit of experimentation; items are added, others are dropped, based on the experience in the marketplace.

Customers themselves are often the best source of inspiration for a new item in your line. Listen carefully to what they ask for. Big business calls this market research; you can call it keeping your ears open. If you detect a trend for a particular item your customers want in your particular style or design, make a few and test them. If they sell, add them to your line on a regular basis.

(*See also: Product Research*)

Product Research

Product research is something most craftspeople do automatically, even if they don't call it that. The decision to make a particular craft object is the end result of having made others, having made mistakes, having learned from experience, having sold (or not been able to sell) particular craft objects, and so on.

A craft object must, of course, satisfy your own creative needs. But it must also satisfy a customer's needs or it won't sell. Those needs may be functional, emotional, psychological, esthetic, or whatever.

To state the obvious: a batik blouse, in addition to being beautiful, must also meet some specific human proportions or it won't satisfy the customer's need for a blouse. A batik wall hanging with the identical design, on the other hand, can be of any shape or size, and still satisfy the customer's need for something pleasing to hang on the wall.

Once you've determined that your craft product can satisfy a need, the question is whether a large enough market exists to make it worthwhile. Making eighty-inch belts may fill a need for men who weigh more than 300 pounds, but how many such men are there, and where do you find them? But wait, a "big men's" shop or a specialty magazine may be just right to reach such a very specialized market.

Next comes the question of uniqueness. Making a craft object which is being made by everyone else will inevitably reduce your share of the market. Can you make it different enough to stand out among the competition? Is there something unique in the design or the material which you can point out to a customer to make it more salable?

Variety, or a line, is another consideration. How many different sizes should you produce? How many colors? And which colors? Does it make sense to produce only mugs, or can you increase your sales by having plates of the same design?

If you produce a wide range of craftwork, you may decide to make certain items because they will sell best at craft shows, while others are more suited to exclusive shops in major cities. That doesn't make one better than the other, just different. Each serves a different need.

The end result of product research, by whatever name or means you conduct it, is to determine what you should produce that can be sold to sufficient numbers of customers who want it and can pay the price you ask for it. That applies even to one-of-a-kind craftwork. True, you need only one customer, but if that customer doesn't exist or cannot be found, then there's no sale.

(*See also: Buyers, Customers, Marketability, Product Line*)

Profit

If making a profit were only as simple as defining it: what's left over after all expenses are deducted from all income.

For accounting purposes, there is a whole variety of profits: *gross profit* (the sale of merchandise less the cost of that merchandise); *net profit* (total income less the cost of production and other expenses in running the business); *paper profits* (profits not yet realized, as represented, for example, by craft items in unsold inventory); and a number of others.

From the viewpoint of most craftspeople, the only significant profit is net profit. Some people call it the bottom line—the last line in the financial statement which indicates what's ultimately left over for the owner of the enterprise. Even that profit is subject to taxation.

It is a common misconception that "the more you sell, the more profit you'll make." To sell $300 worth of craftwork that costs $100 to produce is usually more profitable than to sell $400 worth of craftwork that costs $250 to produce. In the first case you have $200 above the cost of production; in the second only $150, even though sales dollars were higher.

Since profits are so directly tied to both sales and costs, any change in either of those factors affects the profit. To increase sales can increase profits, as long as costs don't rise out of proportion. Profits can also be increased if costs are cut, even though sales don't go up. The ideal situation, of course, is to increase sales while decreasing costs; that really makes the profit picture sparkle.

How to do all of this is the underlying reason for this book, and is present in almost every section, especially the discussions of pricing, selling, and overhead.

Unless you're independently wealthy and money is of little consequence, a constant analysis of all your operations is essential for maintaining a healthy net profit. Keep asking yourself questions: Are some items less profitable than others, and can they be discontinued? Can some operations be modified to reduce expenses? Can I increase my profit by increasing production and reducing the price, or vice versa? Am I attending a particular craft show out of habit or because I know it is profitable for me? Where can I find more economical sources of raw materials? Are some of my orders so small that it costs more to pack than I make from the sale? Does a promotion mailing in October bring better results than one in June?

The list is endless, the questions without limit. Take nothing for granted. Profits are found not in always having a ready answer, but in always asking questions. And in keeping careful records which help you answer those questions.

(See also: Accounting, Expenses, Income, Minimum Orders, Overhead Pricing, Selling, Wages)

Profit and Loss Statement

This statement, prepared by an accountant once a year, is also known as an income statement. Essentially it lists the total income from sales and the total cost of producing the product. The difference is known as gross profit (or deficit if there is a loss).

Operating expenses, sales costs, and taxes are deducted from the gross profit to determine the net profit.

(See also: Income Statement, Financial Statement)

Promotion

(See: Advertising, Catalogues, Direct Mail, Mail Order, Printed Materials, Publicity, Public Relations)

Property

(See: Assets, Equity, Mortgage, Property Insurance, Property Tax)

Property Insurance

A wide range of insurance coverage is available to protect you against loss by fire, damage, or property destruction.

The most common of these is known as comprehensive insurance, which covers a number of related risks at a premium rate lower than that covering those risks separately. Typical of such policies is a homeowners insurance policy, which is available in most states and includes protection against loss from fire, wind damage, vandalism, theft, personal liability, and so forth. Similar types of policies are available for business purposes.

Costs of property insurance policies can vary widely, depending on the potential risk. A frame building, for example, generally costs more to insure than a brick building. Hurricane insurance is almost impossible to get at any price in areas subject to frequent hurricane damage.

Specific policies to protect against theft, burglary, or damage can also be obtained. This is especially important to craftspeople who put their work out on consignment to galleries. Although galleries should, by rights, provide insurance protection for work that is on their premises, they often don't. The only protection a craft artist can have, then, is to provide his or her own insurance coverage. This may be done by adding a fine arts floater to another policy, or through an inland marine policy with a personal property floater.

Theft and burglary insurance also varies in cost, depending on the crime rate in the insured's area, and the nature of the coverage. Premiums may be higher for a goldsmith, for example, than for a sculptor, simply because gold is more tempting and easier to steal.

Each individual's property insurance coverage should be tailor-made by the insurance agent or broker to suit the specific needs for coverage, the potential size of the loss, and the cost of the premiums.

(*See also: Fine Arts Floater, Insurance*)

Property Tax

Except for income tax, property tax is probably the most common form of taxation. Most towns, cities, and states use the property tax as the most important source of revenue for operating their governments.

Property taxes fall into two categories: real estate and personal property. All real estate (with some exceptions such as religious buildings) is taxed locally. A specific tax rate per dollar of value is determined, and each piece of property is then assessed according to its dollar value. The assessed valuation is not necessarily the same as the market value of the property. Thus taxes can be increased in two ways: either by raising the tax rate, or by reassessing the property at a higher value. In the worst of combinations there's a third way: increase both the tax rate and the assessment.

Another form of property tax is the automobile license plate, which is a state property tax. An inventory tax, which exists in some states, is also a form of property tax.

Craftspeople in states where an inventory tax exists would do well, therefore, to plan their production schedules even more carefully in order to keep inventory at the lowest workable minimum.

(*See also: Estimated Tax, Income Tax, Sales Tax, Withholding Tax*)

Prospect List

(*See: Mailing List*)

Publicity

There are two ways to get your name in the papers. One is to pay good money for advertising space, the other is to come up with a good story idea for free editorial space. ("Getting your name in the papers" is an old colloquialism which today includes magazines, radio, television, and any other medium for reaching the public in large numbers.)

Any mention you get in the public media without paying for it is publicity, and good publicity is usually the result of an effort on the part of the person being publicized.

You may think that what you do is not particularly newsworthy. After all, you're so familiar with it that you can hardly imagine why anyone else should give a damn.

But editors do! If you read your local papers carefully, you'll notice that news is made not only by presidents, baseball players, movie stars, and criminals, but by hundreds upon hundreds of people who are newsworthy simply because they do things that are not done by everyone else.

The fact that you drive a car is not newsworthy. Lots of folks do that. But if you drive a 1926 Model T, you can be sure the local papers would be interested. And if you're ready to drive the mayor around in your Model T in the next St. Patrick's Day parade, even the television cameras may show up.

The same principle applies to crafts. You are unique since you are able to create things most people cannot. Someone who can hardly shape dough into a loaf of bread is sure to marvel at the skilled hands of a potter.

The first step toward getting publicity, then, is to get over the modesty, shyness, and concern that nobody else is really interested.

The second step is to realize that editors without stories are like weavers without yarn. In newspaper jargon, your story is human interest, and editors are always on the lookout for human interest stories to relieve the tedium of politics, wars, crime, and economic troubles.

From your point of view, publicity has two values. One, of course, is to rub your ego the right way. It never hurts to see something nice about yourself in print. But the other, even more important, is that publicity is a sales tool. It does not sell as directly as advertising. People know that advertising is bought, but publicity is earned. If a reporter or an editor or a television newscaster—all of them exercising their independent judgment—say that your craftwork is worth a story, then the viewing and reading public is much more likely to listen.

To get the most out of publicity, a few basic principles should be observed:

1) *Timing.* Obviously, a Christmas item is not publicized in March, and you don't send out an announcement about your new line of lawn chairs in January if you're in a cold climate.

Also, don't waste valuable publicity to announce that you are planning to design a new line of jewelry. If a reader is interested, how can he or she buy it? Announce it when it's ready. Always keep the sales potential in mind.

2) *Directness.* Make your presentation to an editor as simple and as straightforward as possible. Editors can (and often do) rewrite and cut to suit their style. If the editor thinks there's more to the story than your announcement, he or she may assign a reporter to interview you. Accommodate yourself to the reporter's needs and deadlines. The story may be worth its price in gold.

3) *Angle.* Provide the editor with a news peg if possible. A new product line, a gallery opening, an award, moving into a new shop, a trip to Arizona to see the work of the Hopi Indians as inspiration for your own weaving—those are all news pegs. The possibilities are limited only by your imagination.

4) *Press list.* Most of your publicity will be with newspapers and radio or television stations in your area, and not to the national magazines. Occasionally your local emphasis may change if you are at a craft fair in some other area, or participate in an exhibition at a gallery or museum in a large city. In either case, compile a list of press contacts on 3"-x-5" cards. If there is more than one contact at a given newspaper (city editor, arts editor, women's page editor, etc.), make up a separate card for each. Keep a record on each card of the contacts you've made, and the results. If you don't succeed on the first contact, it is good to know when to make another, and you can time it according to the dates shown on that card. Make a note of the reaction: were they favorably impressed, polite or curt, enthusiastic or disinterested? Did they tell you to call again in May? Do they want photos?

All of this is useful because the more you can tailor your publicity to the particular editor's need, the better your chance of getting it into print.

Which brings up another important point: unless the subject is a general news announcement, such as a gallery opening, it is best not to give the same story to more than one editor at a time. Give the editor a few days or a week to make a decision on a feature story. If the first one isn't interested, then take it to the next. The worst thing that can happen is two editors running the same feature story. Both of them will put you on their thumbs down list for the future.

5) *Approach.* Editors are not as difficult to approach as you might imagine. Most of us have a movie-version impression of editors as some sort of demigod. Most of them are hard-working, shirtsleeve journalists. They may be a little harried when they're working against a deadline, but

they are always interested in a good story. A simple telephone call is often all that's necessary to make an introduction. If the story sounds mildly interesting, the editor may ask you to send a brief outline. Don't write a story; that's his or her job. And if the presentation sounds exciting enough on the telephone, a reporter may be assigned.

Generally, however, most craftspeople find that the best approach is a press release with a suitable photo. The form and nature of a press release is discussed under that heading.

Aside from the print and electronic media, there are numerous other publicity opportunities for craftspeople. An unusual interest has been shown recently by banks all over the country in crafts. Numerous banks have invited craftspeople to display their work in the bank's lobby (where security is good). Some new office buildings and hotels also have display cases in their lobbies. A guest appearance on a radio or television talk show is another good opportunity to reach large numbers of people. If you can demonstrate your craftwork on the air, your chances are much improved.

Finally, there is an afterglow to much of this publicity. Use it in your own promotion materials. Reprint some of the articles that have appeared about you in the newspapers or magazines. Make a list of the radio or television stations on which you've been mentioned or have appeared. Arrange all this neatly on an 8½"-x-11" sheet of paper. Don't make a montage of all the headlines, one pasted over the other; people have difficulty reading such jumbled arrangements. Have the whole sheet reproduced. The new, inexpensive offset printing processes available in most cities can do it for $3 to $5 for 100 sheets. Use the reprints on every occasion: with promotion mailings, as enclosures with bills, at shows and fairs, and anywhere else where you're trying to make a sale or impress a customer. What others have said about you is more convincing than what you say about yourself. And remember to list your name and address somewhere on the reprint.

(*See also: Photography, Press Release, Public Relations*)

Public Relations

Public relations means exactly what those two words say: relations with the public. But that's easier said than done.

Public relations covers every aspect of your contact with the outside world: salesmanship, price, publicity, advertising, community involvement, display, even your own appearance and conduct when you encounter your public at shows and fairs, or when you see a buyer for a department store.

The various ingredients mentioned above are described in more detail under their appropriate headings. However, they all add up to one thing: your image. What other people think of you and your work.

The image of a Cadillac, for example, is quite different from the image of a Volkswagen. That doesn't make one better than the other, but they each have their own personality which represents not only the inherent nature or quality of the product, but how it is presented to the outside world.

If your pottery sells only in the gift shops of high fashion stores, it will obviously have a different image than if the very same pottery were sold only at flea markets.

How do you go about creating your image as a craftsperson? Well, pretty much the same way you have created an image of yourself as an individual. People have certain impressions of you: stingy or generous, soft-spoken or blunt, calm or excitable, talkative or quiet. There is no one trait and no one time when images take hold. They are the cumulative experience people have with you.

Let's look at an example in crafts. Suppose you make a very fine product, but then you pack it in a slapdash, helter-skelter manner and ship it off to a customer who just sent you a check for $200. The piece may not break in transit, but the customer may well say: "If he thinks so little of his own craftwork to pack it this way, how much good can it be?" Do that a few times and your image in that customer's eyes will decline perceptibly.

Neatness counts. So does reliability. If you get a reputation for always missing delivery dates, or for great variations in the craftsmanship of your items, your reputation for reliability will suffer.

Price is another factor. The higher the price, the greater the public's perception of quality (and vice versa). The story is told of a supermarket which installed carpeting. The public stayed away in droves. Carpeting was associated in the public's mind with high priced stores. Not a single price had been changed in the supermarket, but the image had changed.

Nobody's perfect. Everyone has debits and credits. It's when the debits outweigh the credits that your public relations begin to suffer. If you keep an ear tuned, you'll know soon enough where the debits are. If many customers complain, for example, that you don't ship on time, you know you have a weak spot that needs correcting and it had better be done before those customers find a more reliable craftsperson. Analyze your activities constantly to find the defects, and then plan carefully how to change them.

One side of the public relations coin, then, is how you conduct yourself as a craftsperson, as a professional, as the owner of a craft business.

The other side involves the many things you can do to bring your name before the public. This need not always be related directly to sales, although you would hope that your public relations ultimately produces more sales.

Demonstrating your craft on a local television program, or discussing the history of weaving on a radio talk show, or being interviewed by the local newspaper, or participating in a community activity that brings your name to the attention of the public are all good public relations activities. None of these will produce an immediate dollar-and-cents return, but when you show the clipping of the interview to a prospective store buyer, or quote from it in an advertising brochure, a good impression will be made.

Many craftspeople are shy about making such public relations contacts. "What's the big deal," they might say. Since they are so thoroughly familiar with their own work, they can't possibly conceive that others would find it interesting. But if you read the papers carefully, you'll find that the personal items which interest you because you find them new or novel are probably very ordinary to the people who were being interviewed. "A Day in the Life of a Fireman" might make interesting reading for you, although when approached, the fireman probably said "what's the big deal."

Don't be shy. Go out and tell the world about your work and your skill and your art. And don't be discouraged if you don't succeed on every try at PR. If you keep at it, sooner or later you'll find an opening.

(*See also: Advertising, Display, Photographs, Press Release, Publicity, Salesmanship*)

Quality Control

Production craftspeople have to meet two objectives: quantity and quality. The question is not how many or how good, but whether the objectives, whatever they may be, are fulfilled.

It is essential to establish definite quality standards in production crafts, especially if some of the work is done by others. Defective or substandard craftwork is a waste of money and effort because it cannot be sold, or if it is sold it produces complaints, demands for replacements, lengthy paperwork, and tarnished reputations.

Crafts produced to fill a specific order require particularly careful inspection. To avoid rejection of all or part of the order, and to maintain a reliable reputation, multiple items must meet the same standards as the sample from which they were ordered, and should be inspected before shipment.

Quality control begins at the beginning, when you purchase your raw materials. You can't bake a first-rate cake with second-rate ingredients. Quality-control steps should also be taken at various points along the production process. A whole batch of superbly-shaped pots, for example, can be wasted if the glaze formula is defective.

There can be no prescribed method. The particular quality control procedure must be suited to each individual's craft medium, work process, and quality standards.

Work that does not meet the standard established by the craftsperson need not always be a total waste. Some types of work can be sold as seconds to outlets which specialize in that type of merchandise, but it is usually best for the craftsperson not to identify his or her name with such products.

(*See also: Seconds*)

Record Keeping

Keeping good and accurate records serves two purposes:

1) Many records are required by the government for tax purposes and other reasons. These generally fall into the category of bookkeeping.

2) Records which contain useful information can produce useful information.

Keeping records is the best way you can control your business, rather than the business controlling you. Inventory records, for example, should indicate at a glance what's selling and what isn't. This in turn points to proper production planning.

Records of advertising results can help pinpoint where your promotional dollars are being spent wisely, and where they are being wasted.

Keeping records of show income and expenses can avoid costly errors. Judging a show strictly on sales performance can be an illusion. Balanced against those sales dollars must be the expense dollars for booth space, travel, motels, etc. The net result is the true picture. Only a careful recording of all factors will produce a realistic picture, as well as providing the necessary documentation of business expenses for tax purposes.

Financial records must be maintained for tax purposes, and are also necessary if you need a financial statement in order to apply for a bank loan.

Craft producers who sell to retail stores and other regular customers find it very useful to keep accurate records on each customer: what was ordered, when the last sale was made, what the terms of the sale were, and so forth. This information, in turn, can provide important direction for the next sales approach to the same customer. Including payment performance on such records will also indicate how promptly the customer pays and how much credit you can afford to extend. A card index serves a very useful purpose in putting all information about each customer in one place; the whole history is then available at a glance.

The law requires that some records be maintained for a specified period of time. Documentation for income tax forms, for example, must be retained for at least three years beyond the filing date in case of tax examination. Some payroll records have to be kept for as long as seven years.

But aside from the legal requirements, it is good business practice to maintain files of correspondence, checks, accounts receivable, bills payable, orders, contracts, and most other records of business activities and transactions so they can be easily located.

Memory plays all sorts of tricks. Record keeping is the only reliable way of providing the facts about your business which can keep you on the right track by avoiding past mistakes and planning for the future.

(*See also: Accounting, Advertising, Bookkeeping, Budgets, Collection Problems, Inventory, Loans, Systems*)

Refunds

(*See: Returns*)

Release

(*See: Photography*)

Rented Crafts

When a corporation buys equipment or other property, the tax laws allow depreciation as a tax deduction. This allowance, however, does not apply to works of art purchased by a corporation. Tax deductions, however, are often available to the corporation if the art or craftwork is rented rather than purchased. This approach can provide a good source of income for some craftspeople.

Various rental plans are currently being used, the most popular being rental with option to buy and lease-finance agreement.

Rental with option to buy is normally a short-term arrangement, sometimes for only a few months, after which the work is returned to the artist. The monthly fees are fairly modest, normally between 5 and 10 percent of the retail price. The firm which rented the piece can usually take the rental fee as a tax deduction. If the piece is not returned in good condition, the firm is required to buy it, which gives it no tax advantage.

A lease-finance contract often runs for several years and is renewed automatically. The artist sets an annual rental fee, which is tax deductible to the renter. The concept here is that the annual fees will have paid the equivalent of the retail price by the time the initial contract period is up. Thereafter the contract is automatically extended at a fairly low annual rental, which continues to produce income for the craft artist beyond the original retail price.

For example: you have a $1,000 wall hanging. Under rental with option to buy you might rent that hanging for six months at $60 per month. At the end of the period you have $360 plus your wall hanging back.

Under the lease-finance arrangement, you might sign a four-year contract at $250 a year. At the end of the four years the entire price has been paid, but the wall hanging remains in the custody of the renting firm; you now receive $100 a year for as long as the firm wants to keep your work.

Contracts like this should have a lawyer's advice; they offer good financial advantages to the craft artists and tax benefits for the renting firm.

Renting

(*See: Lease, Retail Outlets*)

Repossess

(*See: Installment, Mortgage*)

Résumé

You résumé is your biography, without the novelist's frills. As Sergeant Friday used to say, "just the facts, please."

A résumé consists of several clearly defined sections, each of which should be identified and separated from the others:

1) *Personal statistics.* Name, address, telephone number, craft media in which you work.

2) *Work experience, including teaching positions.* Start with the most recent one and work backwards. Indicate what your job function was and include dates of employment and names of supervisors.

3) *Professional experience.* Exhibitions, gallery shows, awards, honors, workshops you've conducted, lectures you've given, articles you've had published, membership in craft organizations, etc.

4) *Educational background related to crafts.* (Complete educational background is needed if you're applying for a teaching position.)

5) *References.* Two personal references and two professional references from people not related to you are normally sufficient.

Résumés are used as a way of introducing yourself for a wide variety of purposes: when you approach a gallery, when you seek a job or teaching position, when you want to furnish background material for a newspaper interview.

R É S U M É

FIBER ARTIST   Suzanne Smith
1529 East 19th Street
Middletown, SC 28764
(308-479-0218)

WORK EXPERIENCE

10/73 to date   Freelance fiber artist

6/70 to 9/73   Textile Designer
Burlingame Mills
272 East Street, Charleston, SC 28167
John Peterson, Design Director

8/65 to 4/70   Weaving Instructor
The Shuttle School
226 Raleign Road, Fairfield, NC 19862
Margaret Taylor, owner

PROFESSIONAL EXPERIENCE

Second Award, National Weaving Design Competition, 1971; Permanent Collection, Tapestry Gallery, Atlanta Museum of Art; Guest Lecturer, Art Department, University of South Carolina; Articles on Appalachian Design published in The Crafts Report, 1974
Member: American Crafts Council, Southern Highland Handicraft Guild, Association of Master Weavers

EDUCATION

BFA in Textile Design, University of Georgia, 1962
Studied privately with Henry Jones, The Weaver's Loft, 1963

REFERENCES

Personal: Rev. Sam Smith   Dr. Frank Hamill
8633 Third Street   179 West Broadway
Middletown, SC 28745 Charleston, SC 27693

Professional: Terry Witherspoon
President, Association of Master Weavers
229 Lenox Road, St. Louis, MO 44598

Robin Robinson, Boutique Buyer
Kneeman Markers
Dallas, TX 67219

If your professional and work experience is very extensive and you've been showered with numerous awards, written numerous articles, and had numerous exhibitions, it may be wise to prepare two résumés. One is a single page and lists only the most important accomplishments; another can go on and on to list all of your accomplishments and activities. Busy gallery owners or personnel people may not have the time or interest to read through several pages of biographical material on the first go-around.

A résumé should be neatly typed on one side of the sheet only. Most offset printers can type and reproduce your résumé at fairly low cost. Major cities have specialty printers who can print them for you within an hour at less than $5 for 100 copies.

A résumé should almost always be accompanied by a covering letter which explains why you are sending the résumé, even if you are sending it in response to a specific request (in which case you should mention the request in the letter to remind the recipient).

False modesty has no place in the preparation of a résumé. If you've won an award, or are in a museum's permanent collection, don't be shy about it. No need to brag, of course, but let the facts speak for themselves—and for you.

Retail Buyers

(*See: Buyers*)

Retailing

Retailing means selling to the consumer in small quantities. Most craftspeople become involved in retailing at one time or another, generally by renting a booth at a craft show. Others are more extensively involved by operating their own stores or galleries.

It is not the intention of this book to discuss how to operate your own retail store; that would require another book. Besides, the vast majority of craftspeople probably have neither the time, the inclination, the location, the money, or the interest to run a retail store. That doesn't mean you can't sell at retail out of your own shop or studio; but an examination of what a retail store offers will quickly make clear the many pitfalls which await a craftsperson who plans to open a full-fledged retail craft outlet.

Nonetheless, many craftspeople become upset when they see that the work they sell to a store is resold for double the amount. They feel that, somehow, they are entitled to the higher retail price. After all, it's their work on which someone else is making a profit.

But retail stores perform numerous legitimate functions:

1) They find customers which the craftsperson might not otherwise find.
2) They offer a wide variety of merchandise which itself attracts customers.
3) They advertise.
4) They display the merchandise attractively.
5) They extend credit to their customers.
6) They are located in areas convenient to shoppers and furnish parking space.

It has been estimated that the cost of performing these functions costs the average retail store approximately 45¢ of every retail sales dollar. When a store buys craft products at 50¢ of the retail sales dollar, that leaves about a nickel for profit.

On the assumption that an effective retail sales operation conducted by a craftsperson would also cost approximately 45¢ of every retail sales dollar, the question of a retailer's markup takes on a new perspective. The craftsperson's understandable concern that a retail store doubles the price and makes a pile of money on the craftsperson's labors becomes a question of whether the services provided by the retailer as a craftwork outlet warrant a 5 percent profit for the retailer.

The question really is whether it is more productive and profitable for you to work for the 5 percent retail profit or spend the same amount of time in your shop or studio producing craftwork at a better rate of profit. The problem is not the total retail sales dollar at which your craftwork sells, but how you can spend your time and talent most productively and profitably, and which gives you the greatest satisfaction.

If the craftsperson has figured the wholesale price properly, it should reflect a decent wage for his actual labor, and a decent profit for his craftsmanship, management skills, and investment return.

The assumption has to be made that you work in crafts because that's what you like to do and it's what you do best. If your creative and production time is more profitable than your retail selling time, there's nothing wrong with having someone else make a profit selling your work at retail. When that someone else is you, as at a craft show, all the better. But when it's not, consider that you're making more money and enjoying it more when you're making things than when you're selling them.

Good relations with your retail outlets are a prime ingredient for continued success. The first sale is always the hardest. Once you have a store signed up to buy your work, do everything you can to keep that store satisfied. It brings reorders.

Here's a brief check list of good retailer relations:

1) *Maintain quality*. Every item you ship should be as good as the sample you showed.

2) *Maintain price*. The same item should never be sold to different stores at different prices, except when the quantities are different. Aside from the fact that it's illegal under the Robinson-Patman Act, it's also poor business practice. A store won't stick with you long if it finds another store across town selling your work at a lower price because you cut your wholesale price.

3) *Maintain delivery schedules*. There's nothing worse than receiving a Christmas shipment on December 26. Make certain that delivery schedules are clearly stated when you get the written order. Many stores work on very short deadlines. Be sure you can meet them, or discuss the problem with the store before you accept the order.

4) *Pick the right outlet*. Every store has its own personality. The public image of Saks Fifth Avenue is certainly different from that of a roadside discount store. Your quality, your price range, and the stores in which your work is sold have to be mutually compatible. A $1,000 wall hanging can go to Saks, and a dozen mugs that fired imperfectly can go to the discount store. But never the twain shall meet. Check the various stores in your own area. Examine the kind of craftwork they sell, the quality, the price ranges. You'll soon get an idea of what type of retail outlet is best suited to sell your work, and will therefore be most interested in buying your work.

Your own retail operations at a craft show are discussed under "Shows and Fairs," but there is one important area of concern here, and that affects price competition with your normal retail outlets.

It is very poor practice to undercut your usual wholesale customers by selling cheaper at shows, especially when the show is in the vicinity of a store which sells your work. If customers get wise to the fact that they can buy your work cheaper from you than from a store, your store outlets will dry up. Why should they be in price competition with you? There are plenty of other craftspeople from whom they can buy.

The proper way to handle show pricing is as though you buy from yourself at wholesale prices, add your markup, and then sell at what should be near the usual retail price. After all, you are entitled to be paid for the time and expense you spend selling at shows, just as the store in town is entitled to be paid for its time and expense.

(*See also: Consignment, Contracts, Memo, Orders, Salesmanship, Shipping, Wholesaling*)

Return on Sales

(*See: Sales Cost*)

Returns

Your policy on returns must strike a delicate balance between two objectives:

1) It must be fair enough to allow customers to return damaged or defective merchandise and thus maintain your reputation for integrity in your work;

2) It must be stringent enough not to allow returns for unsupported reasons or after lengthy use, because returns are expensive both in terms of actual cost and in terms of objects that cannot be resold.

For example, if a retail store wants to return a broken pot three months after it was shipped, you can be fairly certain it wasn't broken when it arrived, but was knocked off the shelf last week. The most common policy on a time period for the return of damaged goods is within five days after receipt. That should give even a busy store an opportunity to examine the merchandise.

The possibility also exists that a store may want to return goods it cannot sell. You should spell out clearly under what conditions, if any, you will accept such returns; in what time period (perhaps thirty days at most); that nothing will be accepted without prior written authorization, and who pays for the return shipment.

Returns (or refunds) based on damage claims should never be made unless the recipient has made such claims to the proper party, which is usually the agency or freight company which handled the goods in transit. Don't be too free and easy with refunds—it's your money you're giving away. If the claim is legitimate, the carrier's insurance company will cover it if it was damaged in transit.

As in most other business practices, you have to be flexible with your returns policy. If a very good customer wants to return something, even if you think the reasons are not entirely legitimate, your good will and future sales are enhanced, even if your wallet is a few dollars shorter. If a customer does this consistently, perhaps it's time to say goodbye and find someone else who is more reasonable.

To condense all of this into a single sentence, your returns policy might be stated thus: All claims must be made within five days after receipt of merchandise. No returns will be accepted more than thirty days after delivery and without prior written authorization.

This policy should be clearly stated on your price list and invoice forms.

(*See also: Quality Control, Sales Terms and Conditions*)

Revolving Credit

When a bank, a supplier, or a store make credit available to you up to a certain maximum, the money can be withdrawn or purchases made up to the credit limit without negotiating each loan or purchase separately. The credit is replenished every time a payment is made. This is called revolving credit.

This is most common with credit cards and department store charge accounts, and more recently with special types of bank accounts.

If your credit line is $500, and you make a $100 purchase, the credit line has been reduced to $400. When you make a $50 payment, the credit line is back up to $450. There is always a minimum payment due on the total monthly withdrawals or purchases, generally in the neighborhood of 10 percent of the outstanding balance.

Since revolving retail credit accounts usually charge high interest rates, as much as 18 percent in some states, it is wise to pay off the total outstanding balance each month, even if the money to do that has to be borrowed from a bank at a lower interest rate. There is no charge for having a revolving credit line, only for using it. Interest generally applies only to the balance that is more than a month old. Thus, if you always pay off your total monthly balance, you can enjoy the benefit of having credit always available, and you have the use of the money interest-free, sometimes for sixty days or more (from the date of the purchase to the date the payment is due). My Master Charge card, for example, has a billing date the twelfth of the month, and a payment due date the seventh of the following month. If I make a purchase on May 13, it shows up on my bill dated June 12 and is due for payment July 7. Thus I have used their money for sixty-two days without paying a penny of interest. All of this takes some self-control, of course, because it is all too easy to fall into the trap of paying only some of the balance due and then being charged a high interest rate on the unpaid balance.

(*See also: Installment, Loans*)

Robinson-Patman Act

This federal law was enacted by Congress in 1936 to prohibit any practice which would tend to stifle free competition in the marketplace. Among the law's major prohibitions is price discrimination between customers, and other special concessions which are not justified by cost. Thus it is unlawful to sell a dozen items to one store at a lower price than the identical items are sold to another store. However, differences in price based on quantity are legal; a price based on an order for 100 pieces can be lower than a price based on ten pieces. Special concessions which affect the price are also illegal; you cannot charge one customer for shipping costs and pay the costs for an identical order to another customer. The shipping charges themselves can vary, of course, depending on the actual costs involved. You can also differentiate among various groups of customers, say, by making local delivery free but adding shipping charges to deliveries beyond 100 miles.

The essential thrust of the Robinson-Patman Act is to protect competitive buyers by making it illegal for one customer to have an unreasonable advantage over another, whether at the wholesale or retail level.

The law also protects craftspeople when they buy raw materials and supplies. It is illegal for your supplier to charge you one price for 100 pounds of clay and charge another potter in your area a lower price for the same quantity.

None of this prohibits special sales or other price reductions, as long as all customers buying the product under the special conditions are treated equally.

Royalty

Royalty is a per-unit method of payment for the use of a particular piece of property. The term originally described the amount of payment a king would receive for granting rights to the use of his lands, hence the expression royalty. It is still used to determine payment for such land use as oil drilling, whereby the owner of the land is paid a specific amount per barrel of oil extracted from the land. It is also very common in payment for the use of patented or copyrighted work.

For artists, craftspeople, writers, performers, and other creative talents, the royalty is generally a specified percentage of the per-unit sale of the person's creative work. This arrangement is most common in agreements between writers and publishers.

If you design a pendant which is then manufactured in quantity by a costume jewelry house, you can either sell the design outright for one lump sum, or you can agree on a royalty based on a specific amount of each pendant sold.

The determination has to be based on an estimate of the potential income of an outright sale versus a royalty arrangement. A royalty arrangement obviously entails a certain amount of risk, and if you're short of cash, a bird in hand (outright sale) may well be worth more than two in the bush (royalties).

If the manufacturer who wants to buy your design pushes hard for an outright purchase, you can assume that he expects a good sale and considers royalties a more expensive road for himself than paying you one lump sum. But he's also taking all the risks in case the thing flops. On the other hand, if the manufacturer insists on a royalty arrangement, you can assume that he's not so sure of the sales potential and wants you to share the risk, at least as far as your own income is concerned.

Royalties generally range anywhere from 5 to 15 percent. Royalty agreements often provide for a step-up in percentages as the number of units sold increases, e.g., 6 percent on the first 5,000, 8 percent on the next 5,000, 10 percent on everything over 10,000. If the sums are potentially high, it is wise to consult a lawyer before signing a royalty agreement.

Safety

Some safety precautions are obvious: we don't let young children play with sharp knives, we don't smoke when we work with gasoline, we don't drink liquids clearly marked poison.

But in craftwork there are many dangers that lurk in unexpected places. A major problem erupted in early 1976 when it was discovered that certain imported yarns used by weavers contained fatally toxic substances.

Several basic precautions can be undertaken to reduce the dangers of illness or injury:

1) All machinery should have proper protective guards. Don't remove such protective devices because it seems more convenient to work without them. They are there not to protect the machine, but to protect you.

2) All work areas should be properly ventilated, especially where chemical substances, solvents, etc. are used. Almost anything that is heated gives off dangerous fumes—wax and acids used in batik or dyeing, molten metal, ceramic glazes in the kiln, even combinations of chemicals which create their own heat. Kilns and furnaces should be properly vented.

3) Read all labels carefully to be familiar with any warnings the manufacturer may provide.

4) Any product which is labeled as being toxic or hazardous should be used carefully and sparingly.

5) Since chemicals can enter the body through the mouth, nose, or skin, the finer the particles are, the greater the danger. Sprays are more hazardous than liquids, and liquids more hazardous than solids. Dust is particularly hazardous when inhaled.

6) All dangerous materials should be properly stored. Flammable liquids should always be kept in sealed containers.

7) When working with machinery that produces dust or chips, wear safety goggles to keep foreign objects out of your eyes.

8) Don't eat in the workshop, and don't work in the kitchen.

9) If you notice any change in your general health—headaches, nausea, skin discoloration, coughing, dizziness, etc.—see your doctor. Keep careful track of any new products you use in your craftwork.

It is important to remember that many effects of dust or chemicals are cumulative. You may not feel any ill effect after the first use, but the impact can build up. This has been found particularly true among people who use aerosol sprays continuously, or who inhale dust particles for long periods of time.

These are only a few guidelines to staying healthy in the face of potential hazards in craftwork. Several researchers and organizations have recently begun to concentrate on this long-overlooked subject. Most active has been Hazards in the Arts, 5340 North Magnolia, Chicago, IL 60640, a nonprofit information exchange directed by Gail Barazani, who has written extensively on the subject and has reprints available. Among its most comprehensive publications is a study of "Health Hazards in the Arts and Crafts" by Dr. Bertram W. Carnow, Professor of Occupational and Environmental Medicine at the University of Illinois, which is available for $1.50 plus 35¢ postage. A "Health Hazards Manual for Artists" by Michael McCann is available for $2 from The Foundation for the Community of Artists, 220 Fifth Ave., New York, NY 10001.

(*See also: Fire Prevention*)

Sale

A sale is not a sale until one basic condition has been met: the goods have to be delivered, or at least shipped. The fact that someone ordered a dozen pots, or sent you money for a wall hanging, does not constitute a sale.

The sale is complete if you've shipped or delivered the goods, even if you haven't been paid. What the customer owes you becomes an account receivable.

When you have an order and haven't shipped the merchandise, even if you've already been paid, it's not a sale; it's simply an order.

If you ship only part of an order, the undelivered part is called a back order and doesn't become a sale until it is shipped.

All this may sound like a silly semantic game, but it becomes a matter of concern if a sale or an order becomes a subject of dispute.

(*See also: Accounts Receivable, Orders, Sales Terms and Conditions*)

Sales Agents

(*See: Sales Representatives*)

Sales Cost

Since time is money, the time you spend selling, or the money you pay for someone else's time to sell your work, should be calculated carefully so that it doesn't eat into the profits you make in the production of craftwork.

For craftspeople, the costs of selling fall into four major categories:

1) Selling to retail outlets, whether you do that yourself, hire someone to do it for you, or do it by mail.
2) Selling at craft shows and fairs.
3) Operating your own retail store.
4) General sales expenses, advertising, etc.

Some of these selling expenses are very easily identifiable. If you print a brochure, or make a set of slides, or pay a sales representative a commission, or rent a booth at a show, you know exactly how much you've spent for those purposes.

Opening your own retail store opens a whole Pandora's box of cost factors and selling problems. If you already have an established reputation, and if you can sell from your shop or studio or home without the necessity of hiring sales help, paying extra rent, or committing yourself to expensive advertising campaigns, the problems are substantially reduced. But if you're thinking of opening a full-fledged retail operation, selling not only your own craftwork but others' as well, a little experience under the belt provides a better chance of money in the pocket. Doing a good job at retail store operation requires some solid background and study in business skills, just as doing a good job at craftwork requires some solid background and study in craft skills. Retailing may seem easy from the customer's point of view, but many a danger lies in wait for the uninitiated.

Mail-order selling, like retailing, can be an expensive proposition. But in mail order, at least, it is easier to pull in your horns if you find that the results don't justify the costs. The biggest cost here, and the one that must be most closely monitored, is advertising. It's not so much how expensive a particular ad is, but how much it produces. An ad which costs $200 and brings in $2,000 is more productive (and hence less expensive) than one which costs $50 and brings in $300.

Anyone who is seriously contemplating opening a retail store or going into mail-order selling would do well to read a book or two on the subject (there are many good ones at the nearest library), perhaps take a course or two at a local college, consult with other retailers and the chamber of commerce, and get hold of some of the publications issued by the Small Business Administration. A list of their publications can be had from any of the SBA offices in the major cities (see telephone white pages under "U.S. Government, Small Business Administration"), or by writing to the SBA, Washington, DC 20416.

The biggest problem most craftspeople face is in the hidden sales costs. Take a craft fair, for example. The cost of the booth, the cost of transportation, and the cost of a motel and meals away from home are clearly defined sales expenses. But what about your time? Not only the time you actually spend at the show, but the time spent packing up the craftwork the day before, loading the car, unloading and unpacking when you get back. What about breakage or theft, display materials, business cards or other printed material you hand out at your booth— all of these are selling costs that must be included in your final accounting of a craft fair to know whether it has been worth the effort.

The actual costs of selling to retail outlets must become part of the wholesale price. It doesn't matter whether you do it yourself and use your own car, whether you hire your own salespeople and pay salaries or commissions and expenses, or whether you engage the services of an independent sales representative who usually gets approximately 15 percent of the wholesale price but pays all his own expenses.

Sales literature, slides or photographs, order forms, samples, and all the other paraphernalia associated with the selling process must also be included in the sales cost, whether it's done in person or by mail.

The question is often asked: "What percentage of my gross should I spend for selling?" It's a difficult question to answer. If a half-dozen good retail outlets keep you busy with orders and reorders, your selling costs will be quite low. If every order you sell is a new order, the selling costs will increase substantially. The cost of going on the road to attend craft shows and fairs may seem relatively higher, but then you're selling at retail prices which may justify the higher dollar cost.

Without prescribing any rule of thumb, since each situation is different, it would probably be safe to say that sales cost at wholesale should not exceed 10 to 15 percent, and at retail no more than 40 percent. In mail-order selling this may be quite a bit higher, but the assumption is that mail-order selling produces a large volume of business, so that the profit on each transaction can be a little smaller and still show a healthy total.

One important thing to remember: the sales cost is part of the price you charge. The fact that a retail store sells your work for twice the amount it paid you doesn't make the store's markup part of your sales cost. You are selling it at wholesale, not retail. That's why the percentage of sales cost on your own retail selling is so much higher.

(*See also: Advertising, Catalogues, Display, Expense Accounts, Mail Order, Mailing List, Overhead, Photographs, Pricing, Public Relations, Retailing, Salesmanship, Sales Representatives, Sales Records, Sales Terms and Conditions, Samples, Shows and Fairs, Wholesaling*)

Salesmanship

The word salesmanship conjures up in many minds a vision of a huckster on a circus midway, hawking his shoddy wares to an unsuspecting public. But selling, in truth, is nothing more nor less than explaining the benefits of a product to a potential customer so that the customer can make a buying decision.

There are, of course, unethical salesmen, just as there are unethical doctors, lawyers, and craftspeople. But that is a defect in the individual, not in the process. While the seller obviously benefits from making a sale, the buyer also benefits through a better understanding of what he or she is buying.

The first principle of salesmanship, therefore, is a thorough understanding of the craft object being sold, what makes it unique, how it can benefit the buyer, and so forth. In every transaction something is not only sold, something is also bought. The customer is trading money for something which is worth more to him or her than having the money.

In craftwork particularly, the necessity of a sales explanation is an important factor. It's not like buying a pound of apples or a can of soup which sell themselves because the customer is fully aware of the benefits of eating regularly.

The next major concern is to know what motivates each particular customer. No two customers are ever alike. Each brings to the transaction a particular set of needs, wants, perceptions, and expectations based on prior life experience and circumstances. Try selling a pack of cigarettes to a nonsmoker, or a hard-rock record to a Beethoven fan.

Selling a pair of earrings to a man requires quite a different approach from selling the same pair to a woman (unless, of course, the man is wearing earrings himself). Is the man buying the earrings as a Mother's Day gift? Or to be thoughtful? Or to play the big spender? Is the woman buying them for herself to be fashionable? Or different? Or to match a pendant she just bought?

In other words, it is necessary to determine, if possible, the key motivation on which the buying decision will be based in each particular case. Those motivations are as varied as the range of human emotions. Some may satisfy a practical need, others a yearning for prestige, still others the hope to be noticed, or admired, or to keep up with Jones, or to be imitated.

Although it is often believed that price is the first and foremost factor in any sale, that's not always so. Indeed, price does not come into play until some other decisions have been made. The old expression "you can't give away ice in Alaska" expresses this best. If there's more ice than you can ever hope to use, it doesn't matter how cheap it is.

Oh yes, the price becomes a major factor when the buyer has already made a tentative decision to buy. There are always some people who will ask how much without any intention of buying. And there are always products so familiar to the customer that price is the only deciding factor.

But in craft selling, the effectiveness of the sales presentation plays a big part in justifying the price tag. An effective presentation makes the object so desirable to the customer that he or she understands its value and will consider the price a fair one. This doesn't mean every potential customer will buy; there's competition and the pocketbook to be considered. But good salesmanship helps.

These principles apply not only to direct selling, as at craft shows, but also to selling to retail stores or other outlets. The motivations are different, to be sure. The store buyer's concern is whether the craft object can be resold at a profit, whether it suits the store's merchandising policy, whether it is sufficiently different from other products in the store, and whether the price is suitable.

In such situations it is much easier to prepare an effective sales presentation. Look around the store before you make an appointment to see the buyer. See what type of merchandise is being sold, what type of craftwork, in what price ranges. Does your craftwork fit into that store's pattern? Will it give the store a competitive advantage over another store down the street? Can you explain to the store buyer why you feel your particular craftwork will be a profitable addition to the store's inventory?

Selling to a store buyer usually requires a good portfolio in addition to some samples, unless the nature of your craft (jewelry, for example) allows you to carry a large selection with you.

At a show, of course, salesmanship combines with a little bit of showmanship. Demonstrating how your craftwork is made adds some life to your booth and perks up your relationship with your customer. If you're tuned in to what the customer is saying as you show various items, you'll quickly determine in what direction to move.

In both cases, closing the sale is an important crossroads in the process. This is where you actually ask the customer to buy. Experience and sensitivity will tell you at what point to ask for the order; this point is unlikely to be the same for any two customers.

There's also something called a trial close. This comes when the customer may not be quite ready to make a decision, and you have to nudge him or her a little. At some point in the proceedings you may want to ask: "Do you think you'd prefer this in blue or brown?" or "This larger size suits you beautifully." At this point the customer who's simply wasting time will disappear, and the serious customer will move a little closer to the moment of truth.

We come now to two major roadblocks which many craftspeople find difficult to overcome. If you are not by nature an extrovert, the approach to customers may be awkward in the beginning. It is not necessary to be aggressive; indeed, that turns a lot of customers off. But an effective sales approach requires that the seller display some real interest in the customer. Sitting in the back of a booth at a craft show, nose buried in a book, is not likely to produce much activity. The customer must at least get the impression that you are interested in selling something.

A few character traits are sure to interfere with a productive sales presentation: impatience, haughtiness (talking down), sloppiness, distraction. The attitude that comes across when you sell is as important as any of the words you speak, sometimes more so. Being positive and confident always works better than being negative and apologetic.

The other roadblock is rejection. Since your craftwork is so important an extension of your personality, there is a tendency to consider a refusal to buy as a personal affront or rejection. Many aspiring craftspeople have been crushed and emotionally drained when a customer didn't like their work sufficiently to buy. But perhaps they simply didn't need it, or didn't have the cash.

Even Babe Ruth didn't bat a thousand. When a sale is not successfully completed, it doesn't mean the customer has rejected you personally. That probably never entered the customer's mind (unless you were rude or insulting). It is simply that the fundamental balance of needs and wants and money didn't jell.

If you know that you have a good and salable product, and if that knowledge comes across positively and cheerfully, then the little tricks of the trade of salesmanship will come with experience.

(*See also: Buyers, Customers, Display, Marketability, Marketing Plan, Photographs, Portfolio, Publicity, Public Relations, Retailing, Shows and Fairs, Wholesaling*)

Salesmen

(*See: Sales Representatives*)

Sales Promotion

(*See: Advertising Catalogues, Direct Mail, Mail Order, Publicity, Public Relations*)

Sales Records

(*See: Record Keeping, Sales Cost*)

Sales Representatives

The boom in craft marketing is a fairly new phenomenon, and not all the wheels are yet in place in the distribution process. In many established industries, one of the most common links in the chain of getting products from the manufacturer to the ultimate consumer is the sales representative. He or she represents several small, noncompeting manufacturers who have neither the need nor the finances to hire their own sales force.

The vast majority of craftspeople do their own selling, either by contacting retail outlets, or by exhibiting at craft shows and fairs. Very few produce in such quantity that the cost of a full-time salesman or saleswoman can be justified.

More and more craftspeople, however, utilize the services of independent sales representatives (also known as sales agents or manufacturers representatives), especially to develop business in areas away from the craftsperson's immediate area. The rep is the contact between the manufacturer (crafts producer) and the retail outlets.

Sales reps usually carry a line of related but noncompeting products, and cover specific territories. In the case of crafts, for example, a sales rep may handle a potter, a woodworker, a silversmith, and several other craft producers, and call on the stores in his territory, talk to the buyers he knows, and take orders for the products he carries.

Sales representatives work strictly on commission, usually 15 percent of the wholesale price. This is an added selling expense for the craft producer, but it has two distinct advantages: 1) payment is made only on the basis of what is sold; and 2) a good sales representative can keep a craft producer busy making craft objects instead of running around trying to sell.

Of course 15 percent of the wholesale price is only 7½ percent of the retail price. In other words, if an item sells for $10 to the ultimate consumer, the retail store pays $5 for it. The sales representative gets 15 percent of that $5, or 75¢. That commission is a selling expense which has to be figured into the wholesale price when all the costs are calculated.

In addition to taking the order, the sales representative usually performs several other functions. Most important of these is the responsibility to check the customer's credit references. Since the rep normally gets his commission only after the bill is paid, it is in his own self-interest to make sure that the sale he makes is paid for.

The crafts producer who sells through reps is responsible for all the things he would normally do if he sold the merchandise himself: production, packing, shipping, billing, handling complaints, and so forth. It must be remembered that the sales representative is not a customer. He represents you to the retailer, but he never buys anything from you.

You must furnish the rep with price lists, order forms, and samples of the craft objects you want him to sell. And you must have a written understanding of the basis on which you are represented, the territory, the terms of sale, the commission structure, credit policy, and also how the relationship can be dissolved if either party is dissatisfied.

To justify having your own sales force requires a considerable amount of production and money. Your own sales people would normally receive a salary or a draw against commission, they would be entitled to vacation and other benefits, you would have to pay them during a training period, and you would have to pay their expenses. The sales rep works for himself, and if he's good, will give you no management headaches (anyway, very few).

Balanced against the advantages of a rep are several minus points: 1) you do not have complete control over the rep, as you would with your own sales force; 2) if the relationship is ended, the rep may take on a different line that competes with yours and sell it to the same people to whom he previously sold your merchandise.

If you already have more sales than you can handle, there's hardly a need to get someone to sell for you. But if you want to sell in parts of the country you can't reach easily or economically, or if you want to get into retail outlets you haven't been able to sell, then a rep who covers a given territory or is experienced in a particular type of retail market can be of considerable help.

The greatest difficulty is how and where to find a sales rep. There aren't that many in the crafts field. The good reps are already very busy and may not be able to carry another line, and you wouldn't want a lazy rep. Reps would naturally prefer to carry a line by someone who is already well known as a crafts producer, which sometimes works against the newcomer who really needs a rep's help to get into the market effectively.

The best source of finding a rep is by asking questions of other (noncompeting) craftspeople, retail store owners, department store buyers, craft organizations, and so forth. Sooner or later you will probably make a good contact.

The rep's first question, after he has looked over your craftwork and decided that it's salable, is how much of it you can produce. It won't do him any good to sell 100 pieces on which he can earn a decent commission if you can only make ten.

The craft producer's first question, after determining that the rep can do the job, is to determine the minimum volume that the rep will produce. To turn the table, what good is a rep who sells only ten pieces when you can produce 100.

Once you establish a business connection with a sales representative, work closely with him. Let him know promptly when you have a new product or design; let him know equally promptly if you run into a problem with delivery or collection. Let him hear it from you when a delivery is going to be late, not from the retailer to whom he made the sale. That's only common courtesy and good business practice.

Furthermore, unless it's specifically spelled out otherwise, don't invade the rep's territory. A rep usually works hard to make a living, doing what he does best (selling), just as you work hard at what you do best (making fine craft objects). Going after his customers yourself can sour an otherwise beautiful relationship and probably cost more in the long run.

The most important point to remember in selecting a sales representative, whether he or she is on your payroll or working independently, is that this person is you in the eyes of the customer. What the sales reps say, how they present your craftwork, what promises they make, their appearance and conduct, all reflect on you. That does not mean they have to be exactly like you; indeed, as sales specialists their interests and personalities may be quite different from yours. But since they represent you to the customer and are your contact with the buyers, they must reflect your business policies and standards. A good sales rep can be a great help, a bad one a great hindrance.

And if you have a good rep, you'll find that he or she can be an excellent source of information about conditions in the market. Some reps have even come up with design suggestions or product ideas based on the demand they detect as they call on the retail stores. If a rep has a suggestion to make, don't brush it off. His interest is the same as yours: to produce sales for your craftwork so that you can both make money.

(See also: Sales, Sales Cost, Salesmanship)

Sales Tax

Many towns, cities, and states impose a tax on retail sales to consumers. The tax is collected at the point at which the sale is made, and is based on a percentage of the price. The amount of the tax varies from one state or city to another, and so does the type of product or service on which it is collected. In some areas, for example, restaurant meals are taxable, in others they are not. Food bought at retail is almost never subject to sales tax, although nonfood items such as paper towels, matches, soap, and soft drinks are taxable.

Craftspeople who sell at retail in an area where sales taxes apply must get a certificate from the local taxing authorities which authorizes them to collect the sales tax. How, when, and where the sales taxes are then forwarded by the retailer to the taxing authorities varies, but it is always illegal to retain the collected sales tax as personal income. Records have to be kept to relate total sales to sales tax collections. Sales receipts and invoices are usually sufficient for this purpose. The sales tax must always be shown as a separate item from the price.

A sales tax situation peculiar to the crafts field involves selling at craft shows and fairs in areas where a sales tax applies. In some cases, the show management is authorized to obtain one blanket sales tax certificate, and the exhibitors must then report their sales, or handle their sales, through the show management. In other cases, where the authorities do not permit this or where it is impractical, each exhibitor must obtain a temporary sales tax certificate for the period of the show. Where this is necessary, the show management will instruct all exhibitors how to go about it.

(*See also: Sales Tax Exemptions*)

Sales Tax Exemptions

On the principle that a sales tax is paid only once, by the ultimate customer, the sales tax need not be paid on materials bought by a craftsperson for the purpose of making craft objects which will later be resold. Nor do craftspeople have to collect sales taxes on craft products they sell to a retailer who will then sell them to his customers.

In both cases, a resale number or sales tax exemption number is needed. Different places call this document by different names, but it amounts to the same thing. Contact the appropriate sales tax authorities in your area for information on how to get this document.

When you sell your work to a store for resale, the store will furnish you with its own resale number, which authorizes you to make the sale without charging the sales tax. This is important in the event that the tax collector looks at your books and wants to know on what basis you sold your work without collecting the sales tax. If you don't have the store's resale number (which is normally indicated on the store's order form), you will have to pay the sales tax, whether you collected it or not.

Sales and shipments you make to customers outside your sales tax area are normally not subject to the sales tax. A New York craftsperson (where sales taxes apply) who ships merchandise to a state where there are no sales taxes, does not have to collect the New York sales tax. However, if the out-of-state customer comes to the New York craftsperson's studio or store, buys the craft object there and takes it home, the sales tax has to be collected.

Any raw materials or supplies you buy which will become part of a craft object for resale are not usually subject to a sales tax. You have to furnish your resale or exemption number to your supplier as proof that you are entitled to buy the materials without paying a sales tax.

However, other supplies, such as stationery, paper clips, and similar items which do not ultimately become part of your craft product, are subject to the sales tax when you buy them because you are the final consumer of those items.

(*See also: Sales Tax*)

Sales Terms and Conditions

The logistics of making a direct sale to a customer, as at a craft fair, are fairly uncomplicated: you take the money, hand over the merchandise, and the transaction is completed.

Making a sale to a retail store or some other wholesale customer usually requires a more detailed set of specifications which are known as sales terms or conditions of sale.

The two basic ingredients—products and price—are the most important, of course. These are most prominent on your price list. But the fine print, which spells out a variety of conditions under which the craftwork and the money change hands, are also important. Among the more common terms and conditions which should appear on your price lists and invoices are these:

1) *Cash discounts*. This is usually 2 percent if the bill is paid within ten days of invoice date, the total amount being due thirty days after invoice date. This is generally written 2/10–net 30.

2) *Quantity discounts*. These apply either if a total order exceeds a certain dollar minimum, or is based on specific quantities of a specific item.

3) *Shipping*. Who pays the shipping charges; is the shipment made F.O.B.; are there freight allowances and on what basis are they calculated; is shipment made freight prepaid or freight collect; do you make C.O.D. shipments?

4) *Minimum orders*. Do you have a minimum order, and what are the extra charges if the order is below the minimum?

5) *Packing charges*. Are packing costs included in the list price, or what is the extra charge? Does this charge apply to all shipments or only to shipments below a certain dollar minimum?

6) *Returns and claims*. State your policy clearly on damage claims and other returns. To whom should damage claims be made (usually the carrier who moved the shipment), what is the time limit, will you accept returns without prior authorization?

7) *Credit*. To ship on open account to a brand-new customer without checking credit references is inviting trouble. Sales terms should indicate what kind of credit information is required on a first order.

(*See also: Credit, Discounts, F.O.B., Freight, Minimum Order, Orders, Returns, Shipping*)

Samples

In addition to seeing slides or photographs of your craftwork, gallery owners and store buyers often want to see actual samples of your work. If they are interested, they may ask you to leave the samples so they can be discussed with other store personnel before an order is written.

It seems almost superfluous to note that a sample should be a perfect representation of your work, except that craftspeople sometimes grab the nearest craft object on the way downtown and discover that they should have taken a piece that better indicates their technique and design capability.

When it is necessary to ship a sample, take extra precautions that it is properly protected and packed to avoid damage in transit. Valuable samples should be insured. Before you ship a sample or leave it with a store buyer, reach some understanding when and how you will get it back. In the case of fragile or valuable samples, be sure the store understands that it must be properly packed and/or insured. If a sample is damaged or lost while in the store's possession it should, of course, be paid for.

If a sample is unusually valuable, as an expensive piece of jewelry, it is best to have it covered by insurance beyond the ordinary shipping insurance, and the store should be made aware of its value.

It is usually unwise to send a sample if it has not been requested. This is not a real problem with very inexpensive pieces where the loss of one or two does not create a terrible disaster, but sending unsolicited samples of expensive or unusual work only invites trouble.

When you submit a sample on the basis of which you hope to get an order of multiples of that sample, be certain that you are in a position, both in terms of quality and price, to fill the order with craftwork standards equal to the sample.

(*See also: Buyers, Orders, Salesmanship, Sales Representatives*)

S.A.S.E.

These initials mean self-addressed stamped envelope. Jury requirements or other situations in which slides or photos are submitted often specify S.A.S.E. for the return of the slides. Where special packing materials are used, such as cardboard to protect slides, it is best to include such material in the envelope and affix proper postage.

Savings Bank

A bank whose main function is to handle savings accounts on which it pays interest, although it also performs numerous other banking functions, most notably in mortgage lending. In many states, savings banks are not permitted to handle checking accounts.

(*See also: Banking, Commercial Bank*)

Scholarships

(*See: Grants*)

Schools

(*See: Education, Grants*)

Seconds

Any item which is not up to the best standard is considered a second. This is distinguished from secondhand, which means it was previously owned and used by someone else.

Seconds may have slight defects, such as a scratch in the surface of a glass or a poorly fired piece of pottery. Seconds may also be overstocks of discontinued items which are no longer available in a full range of sizes or colors or complete sets.

Seconds need not be thrown away. If you sell seconds in your shop or studio at half the normal retail cost, you still make the wholesale price. And even if you sell them below cost, you recover at least some of the investment in materials and time.

A sale of seconds may bring large numbers of customers to your shop or studio who may even buy your first line of craft items at the full markup if it is properly displayed and clearly set apart from the seconds.

Security

A major expense item in business these days is loss through burglary and shoplifting. Thieves make no distinction between Tiffany's and a small jewelry display at a crafts fair. If the opportunity presents itself, they go to work. In fact, they're less likely to tackle Tiffany's because security there is tighter.

A large store can afford to install sophisticated burglar alarms and two-way mirrors, hire store detectives, use police dogs at night, and even attach electronic price tags to merchandise which emit a telltale shriek if they're not removed by a special device before they leave the store.

Most craftspeople neither need to, want to, nor can afford to engage in such sleuthing. But there are some simple, common-sense steps that can prevent losses of this kind.

Shoplifting

"Shoplifters and magicians have one thing in common," Addison H. Verrill wrote in a Small Business Administration publication on shoplifting. "Both rely on sleight-of-hand. However, amusement turns to anguish when individuals who pretend to be customers prove that the hand is quicker than the eye."

Shoplifting is not confined to retail stores. How many craft artists haven't had something stolen at a craft fair, especially if their craftwork is small and valuable?

It is not likely that someone will make off with a heavy pot or a large wall hanging. But jewelry is a perfect target. Less valuable items are not immune either, because shoplifters are not all professionals who make their living that way and will only steal what they can easily sell for a worthwhile sum. Some people steal for kicks or on a dare. Others steal because they like the item and don't want to pay for it.

You can't keep everything under lock and key. One of the reasons people visit a craft show or fair is because they can examine the craftwork, touch it, feel it, handle it. There are two basic ways to reduce shoplifting losses under those circumstances.

1) Keep displays neat and arrange them so that you can easily keep an eye on everything. Keep very valuable things, like gold jewelry, under glass or behind you. If customers want to see the item, you can hand it to them and stick with them until the item is sold or safely back in its place.

2) Keep an eye on customers. Most are honest. But if someone is carrying an umbrella when it's not raining, or wearing a cape or coat when it's warm, be extra careful. Umbrellas, shopping bags, coats, even baby strollers are devices in which stolen goods can quickly be hidden.

In that connection, be very careful before accusing someone of stealing. If you're wrong you can be in trouble. Ask them to return what they took, if possible. A question such as "Did you pay me for the ring you took?" will often produce an apologetic return of the item, or a denial that anything was taken. Calling the cops or the show's security force is not always feasible for craftspeople, especially at a craft fair, because it takes time away from the booth. On the other hand, leniency only encourages thieves who will continue to rip off others and may even visit you again.

Burglary

Locking the barn door after the horse is gone is too late to keep the horse thieves away. First of all, most burglars are never caught. Some statistics put the rate of unsolved burglaries at 80 percent. And even if they are caught, the only satisfaction (such as it is) you're likely to have is revenge; you're not likely to get the stolen goods back.

Prevention is the better cure. Retail stores are prime targets for burglars, but workshops or storage areas where goods that can be easily sold are kept, are not immune either.

First of all, install a good lock and don't have too many keys floating around. That will deter the spur-of-the-moment burglar who tries doors and enters those that are easy to open.

Second, burglars prefer to work in the dark. Keep a few lights on inside the house or store or workshop, and keep the outside lit up too. Inexpensive automatic devices such as timers or electric eyes will turn on lights automatically when it gets dark. Keeping lights on all day when you're away so that they will also be on after dark is a dead giveaway to a sharp burglar casing his night's work. Outside lighting should include dark areas and alleys.

If you are in an area where burglary is a particularly high risk, ask the local police department for suggestions on other methods for protecting your shop or store or home. And if you're going to be away for the weekend at a craft show, or on a longer trip, alert your neighbors so they can keep an eye on things.

Finally: cash. Money is the prime target for thieves. It is small, easy to hide, nearly impossible to identify, and need not be turned into cash. Don't keep money out in the open. Keep it in your pockets or in a box under the counter or table. Toward the end of a successful craft show you might have a wad of bills. Don't count out change from a roll. Don't cash checks for people you don't know, and don't take check payments without proper identification.

No matter how carefully you protect yourself, it is an unfortunate fact of life that you can still be a victim of burglars or shoplifters. Being suspicious of everyone and everything can drive you into paranoia. But ignoring potential troubles can drive you into bankruptcy. Being alert and taking some common-sense preventive measures seems to be a good middle ground to cut down on such losses.

(See also: Collection Problems, Shows and Fairs)

Selling

(See also: Consignment, Memo, Retailing, Salesmanship, Shows and Fairs, Wholesaling)

Seminars

(See: Education)

Service Charge

(See: Minimum Order)

Service Time

(See also: Pricing, Wages)

Shipping

Shipments of products can be made in many ways: via local truck, post office, United Parcel Service and other private delivery agencies, freight forwarders, bus companies, airlines, and motor carriers (truckers). Each is suited to a particular need. The post office, for example, delivers everywhere in the world, while UPS delivers packages only in the continental United States and Hawaii. The per pound rate of United Parcel Service is lower than the post office rate, and they pick up as well as deliver. But there is a $2–$4 UPS weekly pickup charge which boosts the price considerably if you make only one shipment per week. If you have 100 shipments per week, the $4 charge adds only 4¢ to each shipment, which brings the total cost below the post office's.

Both United Parcel Service and the post office have size and weight limits, and there are some shipments (flammable liquids, for example) which they won't handle.

Shipments that weigh more than the fifty-pound UPS limit or the forty-pound post office limit can go either via motor carriers or freight forwarders (look in the yellow pages under "Freight Forwarders"). Both pick up at your end and deliver at the other end.

The basic difference between the two is that motor carriers use only trucks and generally charge more, but get the shipment to its destination faster. Freight forwarders pick up your shipment, bring it to a central point where it is consolidated with numerous other shipments into a large truck, railroad car, freighter, or cargo plane, and send it off to its destination where it is unloaded onto local trucks for delivery. That takes more time, but generally costs less.

Freight rates themselves are a complicated business, and are subject to government approval through the Interstate Commerce Commission. The rates are divided into numerous classifications based on the type of merchandise being shipped, its density, fragility, gross weight, distance, and other factors. There is usually a minimum charge based on 500 pounds, and insurance coverage is available.

Some companies, for example Emery Air Freight and Federal Express guarantee twenty-four-hour delivery anywhere in the United States, and pick up as well as deliver. Shipping directly via an airline on a specific flight can get a package to its destination even faster, but it has to be delivered to the airport at your end and picked up at the airport at the other end. Since such shipments are always more expensive than normal ground transportation or UPS and postal air service, the time element has to be balanced against the cost. Companies that handle air shipments are found in the yellow pages under "Air Cargo."

Using a bus service for delivery to nearby areas can often be the fastest way to move a package. Again, it has to be delivered to the bus station at your end and picked up at the bus station at the other end, but a package from New York can get to Philadelphia in less than three hours, or just about as long as it takes for the bus to travel the distance. You need only let the recipient know that the package is on Bus #67 which arrives at 4:30, and he can be waiting for it when the bus comes in.

For unusually difficult situations (for example, shipping a very fragile piece overseas), shipping agents will take care of all the details: packing, shipping, customs declarations, and so forth. It's an expense, but one worth taking if there are special circumstances.

The American Crafts Council has published a very informative brochure on "Packing/Shipping of Crafts" available at $3 from the ACC, 44 West 53rd Street, New York, NY 10019. The booklet contains many practical suggestions for packing specific types of craft objects for shipment, and includes names and addresses of shippers, firms that specialize in packing supplies, shipping agents, and other practical information.

(See also: Customs, Freight Allowance, Net Weight, Packing, Post Office, United Parcel Service)

Shows and Fairs

One of the more remarkable phenomena in craft retailing has been the blossoming of craft shows and fairs all over the country. They range from little Sunday afternoon events on the church lawn with perhaps a half-dozen craftspeople as exhibitors, to major events like the week-long Northeast Craft Fair in Rhinebeck, New York, at which 500 craftspeople sell more than one million dollars worth of their work.

Craft shows are held indoors and out, at street fairs and in exhibition halls, in school gyms and shopping malls. Some are open to all comers, including hobbyists, while others require a tough jury process. The Rhinebeck Fair, for example, screened slides submitted by 1600 applicants to choose 500 exhibitors in 1976.

Show organizers run the gamut from craft organizations to commercial promoters to charitable organizations and local chambers of commerce. Among the most successful, from the craftsperson's point of view, have been the shows and fairs organized by craft groups such as the American Crafts Council, Southern Highland Handicraft Guild, Craft Professionals of Vermont, Kentucky Guild of Artists and Craftsmen, Pacific Northwest Arts and Crafts Association, and others. Occasionally, a small group of craftspeople get together to stage their own show, as in China Lake, California, where seven artists and craftspeople conduct an annual Christmas fair over a period of several weekends in a model home provided for the purpose by a local builder.

From the customers' point of view, a craft show is an excellent way to shop among a large variety of craft objects not available anywhere else in one place. It often offers them an opportunity to watch craftspeople at work, and even what they don't buy is worth the experience of seeing and admiring. A good crafts show also raises the level of appreciation among the public so that they will buy more crafts in the future.

From the craftsperson's point of view, a craft show provides an excellent retail outlet for selling craftwork. Since most craft artists work in comparative isolation, their participation at craft shows also provides an opportunity to test new ideas and new designs through direct contact with customers and other craftspeople. This is a valuable experience for anyone who produces craftwork for sale, and especially so for young craftspeople just getting started on a professional career. Even the most successful craft artists exhibit at shows for this experience alone. Many consider it a vacation from their bench or loom or wheel.

Choosing a Show

Since there are excellent craft shows, mediocre ones, and even poor experiences, picking the shows at which you want to sell is an important consideration. An established show, which has been running for some years and enjoys a good reputation and following, is obviously preferred. Other craftspeople can often provide leads to the best shows they've attended. Dig into such questions as attendance figures, admission prices, and promotion.

But be careful. Attendance figures alone don't tell the whole story. A commercial promoter of a shopping mall show, for example, may report attendance of 150,000, but that includes all the people who come to the mall for their normal shopping excursions. Some of those people may stop to buy a leather belt for $8 or $10, but they're not likely to buy a woven wall hanging for $500. Mall shows are a subject of controversy among some craftspeople who feel that their presence there serves primarily to draw crowds for the mall merchants. Many mall shows also restrict the type of craft that can be shown in order not to compete with merchants who sell similar products—jewelry, for example.

An established show in a popular resort area where people are in a spending mood, which is promoted as a cultural event rather than a commercial operation, is an ideal setting for a summer weekend of selling.

While all shows, even the finest, have a fun atmosphere at which both visitors and exhibitors enjoy themselves, flea markets are avoided at all costs by most crafts professionals. The atmosphere at such events cheapens the value of fine crafts, and flea market customers generally look for bargains rather than quality.

A clue to the integrity of a show can be found in the requirements stated by the show management. Most shows insist that the exhibitor be the person who produced the craftwork. In other words, no distributors or importers are allowed. Many shows also specify that nothing made from kits or molds will be permitted. Such requirements are good indicators that it is really a craft show.

How to Find Shows

The best source for listings of forthcoming shows are the craft publications, particularly *Sunshine Artists U.S.A.* (Drawer 836, Fern Park, FL 32730), which emphasizes and evaluates outdoor shows with heavy concentration in the South; *The Crafts Report* (1529 East 19th Street, Brooklyn, NY 11230), which provides considerable detail about major professional shows; *Westart* (PO Box 1396, Auburn, CA 95603), which concentrates on west coast events; *Craft Horizons*, published by the American Crafts Council (44 West 53rd Street, New York, NY 10019) which lists a fairly complete show calendar; and the *National Calendar of Indoor-Outdoor Art Fairs*, published quarterly by Henry Niles (5423 New Haven Avenue, Ft. Wayne, IN 46803). State craft organizations, art commissions and local chambers of commerce can often be helpful in providing lists of nearby craft shows.

What It Costs

Fees to rent space at a craft show are generally modest, ranging between $10 and $50. Only the most successful shows charge higher fees, and are usually worth the price. In addition to the fee, numerous shows also take a commission on sales, normally around 10 percent. This is particularly true when the rental fee is very low. Outdoor shows are almost always less expensive than indoor ones, but they also offer less in terms of facilities. A craft fair in a park, for example, may furnish only an 8'-x-10' plot, with no protection against sun or rain. An indoor show may furnish the same size space, but it is under cover, well-lighted, with rest rooms and other facilities nearby, and therefore costs more.

It is important to determine what is included in the fee. Does the show management provide tables, chairs, overnight security, electric outlets, a printed program that includes your name and address? If it is an indoor show, are there any labor problems or extra costs connected with moving in and setting up your display? What rules and regulations does the show management impose on exhibitors?

A major expense factor in attending shows, often exceeding the cost of the booth itself, is the cost of travel, eating, and staying overnight if the show is some distance from home. Some outdoor shows in warm climates provide camping facilities at reasonable cost. Others are in high-price areas, such as major cities where hotel rooms can run from $25 to $50 a night or more. All of this expense must enter into the determination of whether a particular show can be a profitable selling experience.

All costs associated with show participation are, of course, tax-deductible business expenses. It is necessary, however, to keep accurate records. The Internal Revenue Service requires that receipts must be kept for all lodging, for all meals exceeding $25, and for any other expense for which a receipt can be obtained. Toll booths on turnpikes give receipts. Automobile expenses can be calculated at 15¢ per mile (not counting parking and tolls). When you go on a show trip away from home, it is best to take a little book in which to record all expenses as soon as they are incurred. Don't trust to memory; even the dimes for phone calls add up. Take along a manila envelope and place all receipts in that envelope. At the end of the trip, the little book and the envelope should provide an accurate record of every expense, which is then put away in a safe place until it's time to fill out your tax returns.

Your Display

It is remarkable how many craftspeople—consummate artists in the creation of tasteful design—make a totally cluttered mess of their displays at a craft show. Simplicity is the essence of selling. There is no need to pile everything you've made on the table. Variety is important, but not so much variety that the customer doesn't know what to look at.

1) Keep table coverings and backgrounds simple. Plain colors enhance, fancy prints detract. Table coverings should come neatly down to the floor. It not only looks better, but provides space under the table to store cartons and extra pieces.

2) Try to display your work in its natural habitat: wall hangings should not lie flat on a table but hang from a wall such as a pegboard; pottery should be displayed on a table or a shelf arrangement.

3) If you construct your own display unit, keep it simple so that it can be transported easily, and assembled without elaborate tools. Study what others do—not to imitate, but to learn.

4) If you go to an outdoor show, bring a sun umbrella to protect yourself against the heat, and a waterproof covering you can quickly throw over your display in case of a sudden downpour.

5) Display your work so that small, expensive pieces are not out in front where shoplifters (yes, they visit craft fairs) can get their hands on them. This is particularly important for jewelers.

6) Have some kind of printed material available, even if it is only a business card. An illustrated piece of literature showing your work is even better. It need not be expensive, but your name, address, and telephone number should be included so that customers can find you after the show if they're not ready to buy right then or don't have the money with them. Many craftspeople find that the interest they generate at a show turns into sales afterwards.

7) Demonstrate your work if you can. Nothing attracts attention as much as activity in your booth. If you're weaving or hammering or turning a blob of clay into a pot, the crowd will gather and, hopefully, buy. That way you also use your time to produce. Demonstrating generally requires prior arrangements with the show management, especially if you need electricity or water. But most show managements encourage demonstrations because it brings the show to life. It also requires more than one person in the booth so that one can sell while the other demon-

strates. Having two people at a show is useful under any circumstance, especially at a long show, for rest breaks and other purposes.

8) By all means bring a chair, but don't sit on it too often. Nothing discourages a potential customer more than to see a craftsperson sitting in a chair, reading a book or looking bored. Hard sell is neither necessary nor appropriate, but a pleasant greeting and an offer to help and explain is the first step toward making a sale at a craft show.

Wholesale Days

A prominent feature of some major shows is a day or two that is set aside exclusively for wholesale buyers from department stores, galleries, museums, and the like. Such a day is known as a wholesale day and is becoming more and more prevalent. The crowds may not be large, but the sales volume can be incredible. Charley Gohn, a Pennsylvania metal craftsman, reported that he wrote $19,000 worth of business during the wholesale days at Rhinebeck in 1974, and had to stop writing orders on the morning of the second wholesale day because there was no way he could fill those orders.

Wholesale days at a few major shows can provide the bulk of the annual income for many craftspeople. Orders are written for later delivery date, and production is thus spread throughout the year. As in all other forms of wholesaling, the ability to deliver when promised is as important a consideration as the quality and the price of the craft objects. Wholesale buyers are experienced and careful. They may not buy from a crafts exhibitor the first time around, but after they've seen the same exhibitor at several successive shows, they will gain confidence.

Pricing

Craftspeople who normally sell wholesale at 50 percent of retail are often tempted to cut their retail price at a craft show. After all, they say, whatever they make above wholesale is gravy. But that's a dangerous proposition. First of all, the costs of attending the show must come out of the retail markup, the other 50 percent. Furthermore, the time spent at a show is time spent away from production, and the profit for that time must also come out of the retail markup. Finally, if you've sold your craftwork to retail outlets in the area where the show is held, it is a dangerous practice to undercut the price of those retail outlets by selling your work at a lower price yourself.

It is intelligent merchandising, therefore, to maintain the retail price of your work even at a craft show.

What to Expect from Show Management

In return for paying the necessary fee, a craftsperson has a right to expect certain services from the show management. First, of course, are the things specifically promised in the show brochure: a space of the promised size, setup time when specified, equipment if included, proper promotion to bring a crowd, etc.

Some show managers fall down even in those areas, but most keep their basic promises. Thereafter, however, management ranges from the superb to the abominable. Some show managers walk away as soon as the show has moved in. Others are constantly on the premises, alert to every problem and eager to solve it.

The first Annual Arts and Craft Show at Disney World in Florida, for example, provided hammers and wire for exhibitors who ran into difficulties in setting up their displays, furnished sitters for booths which had to be left temporarily unattended, and even accommodated pets at their kennels.

Admittedly, this sort of service is rare. But show managers do have certain responsibilities above and beyond providing the promised facilities.

Are booths positioned so that the traffic pattern helps to bring visitors past every exhibit? Are aisles wide enough to enable customers to move around without knocking into displays? Are rest room facilities available? Are all instructions clear, and have they been furnished to exhibitors well in advance of the show so they can prepare for it properly?

If the show is juried, do applicants know who the jurors are and what criteria are used? Are rejected applicants given a reasonable explanation? Does the show management interrupt constantly with entertainment or other distractions which draw people away from the booths where craftspeople are trying to sell? Is a show program or catalogue published with names and addresses of exhibitors? Does the management report to exhibitors on the success of the fair afterwards?

Are promised awards actually given? Is the show well publicized? Does the show management listen to complaints or suggestions with some expression of concern? Above all, are craftspeople treated with respect or are they simply moved around like chess pieces on the show floor?

The exhibitor has some responsibilities also. The major one is to comply with all the rules that were provided in writing. Beyond those, to be friendly and courteous, to operate the booth in a professional manner, to be considerate of the exhibitor in the next booth.

If you've never exhibited at a show, it may be useful to attend a number of different shows as a visitor to get a feel of how they're run. Ask questions, both of visitors and exhibitors. Study all the details carefully.

If you're visiting a show you plan to enter next year, ask yourself some questions. How does your work compare with the work of other exhibitors? Is there already an overabundance of your craft so that competition is even keener? Do the prices at the show make your prices seem rational? Can you produce enough work in advance to keep your exhibit well stocked for the entire run of the show?

Even if you answer all these questions affirmatively, there is still no guarantee that the show will be a success for you. Suppose it pours and nobody shows up? But at least you can avoid some serious mistakes which are within your control, and better judge the prospects of a show at which you plan to take a booth.

(*See also: Display, Marketing*)

Single Entry

This term refers to a bookkeeping and accounting method which uses one set of books to record all transactions. This requires only a journal which you maintain on a daily basis for recording receipts and expenditures, and a ledger in which you or your accountant distributes expenditures and receipts under various columns to indicate their purpose or source.

A ledger for a crafts business, for example, may include separate columns to record receipts from cash sales, shows and fairs, wholesale volume, and consignment business. The expenditures columns may be divided to reflect what you spend on rent and utilities, wages, taxes, selling costs, raw materials, etc.

This system is easy for a layman to understand, and helps to analyze where the money is coming from and where it is going. Important changes which may require attention are quickly recognized even by non-accountants. The ledger is generally brought up-to-date once a month, or at least quarterly.

(*See also: Bookkeeping, Double Entry*)

Slides

(*See: Photographs*)

Small Business Administration

The Small Business Administration is a government agency whose interest in crafts is purely economic. The creative aspects have nothing to do with its functions, which are primarily in the field of making loans to small business.

The Small Business Administration funnels money into small business enterprises in three ways:

1) By guaranteeing 90 percent of a loan (up to $350,000) made by a local bank or other lending institution;

2) By direct loans to small business (up to $100,000) where local financing is not available, or to low-income people whose credit might not meet strict local lending policies;

3) Through loans to state and local development companies, profit or nonprofit, which contribute from 10 to 20 percent of the cost of a small business project in their own area.

The SBA also makes loans to businesses which have suffered from natural disasters such as hurricanes, or economic injury caused by such activities as highway construction, or other reasons beyond their control.

In order to obtain a loan, a detailed application must be filed, explaining the purposes of the loan, the prospects of success, the schedule of repayment, as well as specific information about the nature and size of the business, the experience of the owner, and so forth.

Most craftspeople would probably approach their own bank or other lending institution first. The possibility of an SBA guarantee for a bank loan can be discussed with the appropriate bank officials. They will also know when and how to proceed to make application.

The Small Business Administration has literature available which explains its lending and guarantee functions in great detail. This information can be obtained from any of the SBA offices in major cities throughout the country (see telephone white pages under "U.S. Government, Small Business Administration"), or by writing to the Small Business Administration, Washington, DC 20416.

Another significant service rendered by the SBA to small businesses is an extensive and expanding list of publications on a wide range of business subjects, discussed in clear and easy terms. These include such topics as cost control, business life insurance, cash flow, sales agents, budgeting, accounting procedures, and many more. Many of these publications are free; the cost for others is very modest. A complete list is available at any SBA office or from Washington.

There's even a free bibliography entitled "Handicrafts," but it was last revised in 1973 and is somewhat incomplete.

(*See also: Government Activities*)

Social Security

Social Security is a federal program enacted in 1935 which has become the basic method of providing income to people after they retire or become severely disabled, and to their survivors when they die.

Nine out of ten people who work for a living, including the self-employed (such as craftspeople), are paying into the Social Security fund and earning protection. Nearly one out of seven Americans receives a Social Security check each month. This includes not only retirees, but the disabled or the survivors as well, regardless of age.

About twenty-two million people over age sixty-five, and another two million people under sixty-five who are severely disabled, have health protection under Medicare, which is administered by the Social Security Administration.

The basic idea of social security is a simple one. Employees, employers, and self-employed people pay Social Security contributions into special funds during their working years. When the person retires, becomes disabled, or dies, monthly cash benefits are paid to replace part of the earnings that are lost.

Employers and employees pay an equal share of Social Security contributions. If you are self-employed, you pay contributions at a somewhat lower rate than the combined rate for an employee and an employer, but that does not reduce the ultimate benefits.

As long as a person has earnings from employment or self-employment, the contributions have to be paid, regardless of the person's age, and even if they are already receiving Social Security checks.

Through 1977, employees and employers each pay 5.85 percent of the employee's wages to Social Security. The rate for the self-employed is 7.90 percent through 1977. In the following ten years, the rates will go up as follows:

Employed:	1978	6.05 percent
	1981	6.30 percent
	1986	6.45 percent
Self-employed:	1978	8.10 percent
	1981	8.35 percent
	1986	8.50 percent

Those figures do not necessarily mean that the total Social Security paid each year cannot be increased. The rate or percentage is only half the picture. Since there is a maximum annual income on which Social Security payments have to be made, an increase in that maximum means an increase in the total payments (except when you earn below the maximum), even when the rate remains the same.

The rate in both 1975 and 1976, for example, was 5.85 percent. But in 1975 that was 5.85 percent of $14,100, in 1976 it was 5.85 percent of $15,300, a difference of $70.20. For the self-employed, contributing 7.90 percent in both years, the 1976 maximum meant $94.80 more in Social Security payments.

Social Security payments are automatically deducted from wages every payday. The employer matches the employee's payment and sends the combined amount to the Internal Revenue Service, which is the collection agency for the Social Security Administration.

Self-employed people who earn more than $400 a year must include their Social Security obligations when they calculate their estimated tax payments, and pay any difference when they file their individual income tax. This is required even if no income tax is owed.

Wages and self-employed income are entered on each individual's social security record during the working years. This record is used to determine retirement benefits or cash benefits. A fairly complicated formula is used to determine the average annual income earned since 1950. However, the Social Security Administration has prepared some sample benefit tables which indicate, for example, that a worker who retired at age sixty-five in 1975 with average yearly earnings of $5,000 since 1950 would receive $286.10 per month. A worker with the same average who retired at age sixty-two would receive $228.90. Delaying retirement beyond sixty-five earns extra credits and increased monthly checks. There is also a minimum for people who have worked under Social Security at least twenty years, but whose earnings were unusually low.

Social Security benefit checks are increased automatically each July if the cost of living in the previous year has risen by more than 3 percent over the year before. Future benefits will also go up because they are based on the higher payments made into the fund.

People who work for more than one employer in the same year and pay Social Security taxes on both incomes can get a refund on any payments in excess of the required maximum. In 1976, for example, when the maximum was $15,300, an employee who worked for two employers, earning $10,000 with each employer, will have earned a total of $20,000, or $4,700 above the maximum on which he was required to pay Social Security taxes. That entitles him to a refund of $27.26 (5.8 percent of $4,700). The two employers don't get any refund.

For many years it was the practice to reduce Social Security payments to people over age sixty-five who continued having some employment income by the exact amount of that income. That policy was changed recently. Starting in 1976, a taxpayer could earn $2,760 in a year without having any benefits withheld. On annual earnings above $2,760, Social Security withholds $1 in benefits for each $2 in earnings. However, no matter how much you earn in a year, you can get the full benefit for any month in which you do not earn more than $230 in wages and perform no substantial service in self-employment. It is possible, therefore, to earn a huge sum in one month and still receive full benefits for the other eleven months when you earn less than $230. This situation may apply, for example, to a retired craftsperson who has a well-paying but temporary teaching assignment, or who accepts an occasional lucrative commission project.

Income from savings, investments, pensions, or insurance policies are not counted toward the earnings on which Social Security benefits are reduced. And after age seventy-two, you can earn all you want without any reduction in benefits.

Social Security records are maintained by number, and the individual's Social Security number travels with him or her throughout a working life. It is also used for identification on income tax returns and on many other official documents. A Social Security card can be obtained at any Social Security office (there are about 1300 throughout the country), and must be shown to an employer before beginning to work so that the employer can remit the proper amount to your account. The amount withheld from wages for Social Security purposes is also reported to every employee on the W-2 form, which is furnished to all employees once a year for income tax purposes.

Social Security benefits do not start automatically; you have to apply for them. The Social Security Administration lists the following conditions under which you can apply for benefits:

1) If you are unable to work because of an illness or injury that is expected to last a year or longer, no matter what your age is.

2) If you are sixty-two or older and plan to retire.

3) When you are within two or three months of sixty-five, even if you don't plan to retire. You will still be eligible for Medicare, even if you continue to work.

4) If someone in your family dies.

All the information in your Social Security file is confidential, and better still, Social Security benefits are not subject to income taxes.

An excellent booklet on "Your Social Security" is available without charge from any of the 1300 Social Security offices. They are listed in the telephone book white pages under "U.S. Government, Health, Education and Welfare, Social Security Administration."

The most important thing to realize is that Social Security, contrary to popular opinion, is *not* restricted to the elderly or the retired. Many Social Security benefits and Medicare benefits are available to millions of other Americans under specific circumstances.

(*See also: Medicaid, Medicare, Pensions*)

Sole Proprietorship

This is the simplest method for organizing a business. Few formalities are needed. Most states require filing a certificate if you conduct the business under an assumed name instead of your own. Your county clerk can tell you what and where to file.

Even a sole proprietorship is well advised, especially for tax purposes, to have a business checking account and a federal taxpayer identification number. Talk to your banker or accountant about this.

If the business has employees other than the proprietor, it has to pay for workmen's compensation insurance, Social Security taxes, and the like. Avoiding these fringe costs on the owner's earnings is often regarded as a benefit of the sole proprietorship form. On the other hand, the absence of such benefits to the owner when the need for them arises can be one of the disadvantages of this form of organization.

Finally, and importantly, the sole proprietor is personally and fully liable for the debts of the business. If the business fails, its creditors can go after the owner's nonbusiness income and assets such as car, home, and savings.

(*See also: Corporation, Joint Venture, Partnership*)

Southern Highland Handicraft Guild

Although small in number (500 members), the Guild is one of the most influential regional craft organizations in the United States. Founded in 1930, the Guild conducts extensive educational and marketing activities which include two major craft fairs each year and an active publications program. The Guild staff and committees conduct research and provide information on production costs, marketing, sources of supply, management, and other problems concerning crafts. Through its merchandising subsidiary, Crafts of Nine States, the Guild operates four retail shops for the sale of members' work, and a warehouse for wholesale distribution.

The Guild area covers all or part of West Virginia, Maryland, Virginia, Kentucky, Tennessee, North Carolina, South Carolina, Georgia, and Alabama. All membership applicants must submit five examples of recent work to the Guild's standards committee, which judges for quality of design and workmanship. Only the best work is accepted, and rejected applicants are offered help in bringing their work up to Guild standards.

The Guild is actively involved in regional, national and international craft activities. Its headquarters are at 15 Reddick Road, Asheville, NC 28805.

(*See also: Organizations*)

Special Markets

(*See: Architects, Galleries, Interior Designers*)

State Arts Agencies

Every state, as well as the District of Columbia and all U.S. possessions, has its own arts council. So do some major cities. The councils are official or semiofficial government agencies, which go by different names in different states, and are funded in various ways by the various states. Canada has Provincial Arts Councils in each of its eight provinces.

The purpose of these councils or commissions is to provide leadership and funding for the development of the arts in their areas. Most of them have offices in the state capital. A complete list of all state arts agencies, with addresses and telephone numbers, is available for $2 from the Associated Councils of the Arts, 570 Seventh Ave., New York, NY 10018.

(*See also: National Endowment for the Arts*)

Statement

A statement is a recapitulation of a set of financial transactions or conditions, such as bank statements, financial statements, income statements, and others.

When the word statement is used alone, it generally refers to a statement of account. This is a recapitulation sent by a seller to a buyer, usually on a monthly basis, to indicate all purchases and payments made during the period.

The statement lists each purchase according to the invoice number (sales slip reference in department store or credit card statements), and lists each payment received, either by date or by invoice number against which it is credited. The final balance is what is owed by the buyer to the seller on the date the statement is prepared.

The difference between an invoice and a statement is twofold: 1) A statement is not a request for payment, only a recapitulation of what is owed and what's been paid; and 2) a statement does not generally indicate why or for what the money is owed. That's why invoice numbers are used for reference.

(*See also: Accounting, Banks, Checking Account, Financial Statement, Income Statement*)

Stock Control

(*See: Inventory*)

Stop Payment

If you tell your bank not to pay a check which you have already issued, it's known as a stop payment order. There is usually a service charge of a dollar or so which appears on your monthly bank statement.

Proceed with caution. In most states it is against the law to stop payment on a check except for very good reason. Such reasons include a check that was lost in the mail, or where a contract has been cancelled but the check has already been issued as a down payment and not been returned. To stop payment on a check for an otherwise valid transaction is illegal.

A valid stop payment order must, of course, be given before the check has cleared your bank. In commercial transactions, this has to be done before midnight of the day following the day the check was issued. The stop payment order can be telephoned to the bank, but must be issued in writing as soon thereafter as possible.

Be sure to correct your checkbook entry to indicate that a check has been stopped. That affects the balance shown in your checkbook.

(*See also: Checking Account*)

Stores

(*See: Retail Outlets*)

Suppliers

Since the raw materials—clay, yarn, wood, metal, fabrics—and the tools and equipment you use are major expense factors in any craft producer's budget, the suppliers of these items are important sources with whom a wholesome relationship should be developed.

Craftspeople who produce craftwork for sale are usually entitled to purchase their supplies at wholesale prices, or at least at some discount from the regular retail price. A neighborhood craft supply store which buys its stock at wholesale prices for resale to hobbyists can't really be expected to sell at wholesale to professional craft producers. What they offer is convenience and a selection of products from a variety of manufacturers. However, craft producers who buy supplies in large quantities, or who purchase expensive pieces of professional equipment, can often establish a business relationship with manufacturers or wholesale distributors. In states which have a sales tax, the crafts producer is usually required by the manufacturer or distributor to provide his or her resale number in order to qualify for the wholesale price.

The advantage of the lower price is sometimes offset by the fact that the merchandise has to be ordered by mail, and that minimum quantities are often required. With good planning to meet the minimum requirements and to account for the time element, the savings can be considerable.

A continuing relationship with a supplier generally also provides credit to the crafts producer. This means that the craft artist need not pay cash at the time of purchase, but in effect borrows the money for the period of time between the purchase and when the bill has to be paid, which can be as long as sixty days on a monthly billing cycle. Credit is rarely available to new customers until they've established a track record through payment with order or a number of C.O.D. orders. Some suppliers and manufacturers also require a minimum monthly dollar volume in order to qualify for credit purchases.

It is occasionally feasible for several craftspeople to join together to buy supplies in large quantity and thus earn a better price. This is especially true of supplies such as packing materials, office supplies, and other items not specifically related to the craft object being made. Similarly, by planning ahead it is possible for the individual craft producer to save money by making one large purchase instead of three or four small ones. Of course, that involves a somewhat larger initial outlay of money, but if you can afford it the savings may be very much worth the planning.

A reliable supply dealer or manufacturer also keeps his customers informed of new products, new equipment, new colors. A good relationship with a supply dealer also makes it much easier to return a defective product or make exchanges.

Where to find such supply dealers or manufacturers? That's always a touchy question. So much depends on the personalities involved, on the reputation of the supplier, on the craft producer's needs in terms of delivery, selection, and so forth.

A steady reading of craft publications provides information both on what's available and who has it. Other craftspeople, craft schools, and craft organizations can usually be helpful in making suggestions based on experience. Two excellent books are available: *National Guide to Craft Supplies* by Judith Glassman (Van Nostrand-Reinhold, New York, NY; hardcover, $12.95, softcover, $6.95), and *Craft Supplies Supermarket* by Joseph Rosenbloom (Oliver Press, Willits, CA; softcover, $3.95). The latter lists only those suppliers who sell by mail.

Manufacturers and suppliers who sell by mail furnish catalogues, price lists, and other ordering information. They sometimes charge a small fee for the catalogue, which can usually be applied to the first order. In some cases, as with yarns, leather, and textiles, they will also furnish swatches or samples of material.

Finally, it is equally poor business practice to jump from one supplier to the next as it is to stick to only one supplier. If you develop two or three good, reliable sources of supply, you can usually be sure to get the best prices while at the same time protecting yourself against problems one supplier or another may run into. You can never know when flood, fire, or other disasters may strike. If you have only one source and that source is incapacitated, you're in trouble. On the other hand, if you spread your business too thin among too many suppliers, none of them will consider you a really good customer and none will exert themselves on your behalf.

(*See also: Credit, Equipment, Tools, Trade Credit*)

Surplus

In its dictionary definition, surplus is anything that is left over; in accounting, for example, the amount left over after deducting all expenses from all income is a surplus. In inventory control, having more stock on hand than your books show you should have is also a surplus. If you have an order for 100 pieces and you make 110, the extra ten are considered surplus.

The opposite of surplus is deficit.

(*See also: Deficit*)

Systems

At first glance, a system seems like a waste of time. Why do all that paperwork when you could spend your time more profitably at the wheel or the loom or the workbench. Right?

Wrong! A sensible system for keeping track of money, time, supplies, and inventory has as its central purpose precisely to save you time. Such a system really is nothing more than an orderly procedure for getting things done.

Of course, there are people who get so involved with procedures that the system becomes an end in itself, rather than the means toward an end. That is a waste of time.

Particular systems for particular functions are discussed under the appropriate headings throughout this book. What we are concerned with here is the importance of systems: not a particular system necessarily, but systems that keep your affairs in good order and enable you to plan ahead. Such systems save you both time and money.

A simple system for keeping track of orders, for example, helps you to fill the orders properly. Without a system you either have to rummage all over the place to find the order, or trust to memory that you'll ship the right things to the right place at the right time. If you've shipped the wrong stuff to the wrong place at the wrong time, you'll spend a lot of effort and money to set it right. You might even lose a good customer. An order-control system could have avoided all that.

Don't let the word system scare you. Your own telephone number index is a perfect example of a system at work.

There are three ways to keep track of names and telephone numbers.

You could try to remember them, but that's a little risky unless you have total recall. You could jot them down on little slips of paper and throw them into the nearest drawer. That would require quite a search every time you want to make a call. Finally, you can put them all in one place in alphabetical order. That seems by far the best system.

Your checkbook is another example. It doesn't affect your supply of money one way or another; it just keeps track. There's no law that says you must enter all deposits or checks you write on the stub. But how would you ever know what's left in the bank, whether there's enough to cover the next check you write, or whether there's a surplus that should be transferred to a savings account where it can earn interest? Your checkbook is the system that helps you keep track.

The same systems principle applies to all your other management and production procedures. A system need not be complicated to be workable. In fact, the simpler the system the better. But a system is only as good as its execution.

It is important that everyone who is involved with your operation (even if you're the only one) follows whatever system you devise to make things run more smoothly and give you more time for your creative work.

(*See also: Accounting, Bookkeeping, Cost Accounting, Inventory, Orders, Record Keeping*)

Tax

A tax is the compulsory payment of money, established and enforced by law, to a governmental body for purposes of meeting the general expenses of government. Taxes are normally based on a percentage of the value of the taxable subject, e.g., income, property, sales. Taxes are not related to a specific benefit enjoyed by a taxpayer; your tax does not go up because you call the fire department.

Compulsory payments which relate to a specific benefit or service are not generally called taxes, even though they are also established and enforced by law and paid to a governmental body. These costs, including license fees, highway tolls, and sewer assessments, are usually fixed amounts instead of percentages.

(*See also: Accounting, Capital Gains Tax, Estimated Tax, Excise Tax, Expenses, Income Tax, Property Tax, Sales Tax, Social Security, Unemployment Insurance, Withholding Tax*)

Telephone

The telephone has become not only the major mode of modern communication, but also one of the major items in the monthly over-head.

Most of us have used the phone since we were barely able to talk, clutching the receiver in our tight little fist and muttering "hi, Grandma" without really knowing where Grandma's voice came from. As a result, most of us never learned, or have forgotten, how to use the telephone effectively and economically in our social and business activities.

Shop Around for the Best Buy

There may be only one telephone company in town, but there are many kinds of service you can buy. These are the four most common ones, depending on your location and your needs:

1) Individual-line message rate service, with a monthly allowance of message units, usually fifty.

2) Individual-line message rate service with no message unit allowance. This is most economical for telephones which are used primarily to receive incoming calls rather than make outgoing calls. Once the outgoing calls reach thirty or forty a month, this service is no longer economical.

3) Individual-line flat rate service which allows an unlimited number of calls within a specified calling area.

4) Party-line flat rate service. This is the least expensive, but if another party on your line is using the phone, you cannot receive incoming calls or make outgoing calls.

Fancy Extras

Fancy extras can cost plenty. Princess, Trimline, or Touch-Tone in-struments, unlisted numbers, color phones, long cords, bell chimes, jacks, and other devices and accessories can boost the cost of telephone service substantially, sometimes by more than $3 a month.

Message Units

In many parts of the country, especially in metropolitan areas, the message unit is the way telephone usage is measured and billed. One call is not necessarily one message unit. Distance and time both determine how many message units the call will cost. The time of day when the call is made can also determine the cost of each message unit. In New York City, for example, each message unit costs 8.2¢ if the call is made between 9 A.M. and 9 P.M., 6¢ if it is made between 9 P.M. and 9 A.M.

Thus a call in New York that is three-message units in distance can cost almost 25¢ even if you speak for only a minute. If you talk for fifteen minutes, that call can mount up to more than 65¢ (plus tax). The actual charges are different in different parts of the country, but the message-unit principle is the same wherever it applies. Read the front pages of your telephone book carefully to see how it works in your area.

The secret is to make calls as brief and to the point as possible without being abrupt. If a customer calls, be considerate. Don't interrupt yourself to conduct other business while the caller hangs on. Just waiting for you to come back on the line costs the caller money. That's common courtesy, even in areas where message units are not counted.

Long Distance

Place as many calls as you can by direct dialing. Once you use the operator for such services as person-to-person, collect, and credit card calls, the cost goes up substantially.

Charges differ according to the time of day you place your call. Rates between 8 A.M. and 5 P.M. on weekdays are highest. Between 5 P.M. and 11 P.M., and all day Saturday and Sunday, charges go down significantly. From 11 P.M. to 8 A.M. every day the costs are lowest.

The charge for a long distance call is determined by the time at the point where the call originates, so take time differences into account. Placing a call from Los Angeles to New York before 8 A.M. gets the call to New York before 11 A.M. since there's a three-hour time difference. Conversely, placing a call in New York at 6 P.M. can still reach a business office in Los Angeles at 3 P.M. It does not pay, therefore, to make a call at 4:55 when a five-minute wait can cut the cost of that call in half.

In the front pages of your telephone directory you will find the long distance rates to major points from your telephone. It is often worthwhile to dial direct and take a chance on reaching the person you want rather than placing an expensive person-to-person call. You can generally afford several direct station-to-station calls during the bargain hours for the cost of one person-to-person call completed by the operator. And if you connect the first time you're ahead.

On long distance calls you place often, it helps to establish a regular calling time during the bargain hours, say every Tuesday at 6 P.M.

The operator-assistance charges do not apply if you need help because there's trouble on the line when you try to dial the call directly. But be sure to tell the operator about it.

Wrong Numbers

If you reach a wrong number, call the operator, tell him or her you reached a wrong number, and ask for credit. That applies for local calls where message units are counted as well as long distance calls.

Keeping Track

If your business phone and your home phone are one and the same, the business calls are a tax deductible business expense. Long distance calls are easy enough to identify—the telephone bill shows the number you called and the date you called it. For local business calls, keep a small index card taped to the desk or the wall next to your telephone. Every time you make a local call, make a mark on the index card. If you're in a message-rate area, estimate how many message units you used, based on the length of time and distance you talked, and make a check mark for each message unit. At the end of the month it's easy enough to add up the business calls by counting the check marks.

Beep Tone

If you hear a beep tone every fifteen seconds while you're talking it means that your conversation is being recorded.

Debt Collection

The law prohibits making harassing or threatening telephone calls to obtain money that is owed. Don't make such calls. And if you get a call like that, contact your Telephone Company business office.

Fraud

It is illegal for anyone to use a credit card or charge calls to another number without authorization. If you lose your telephone credit card, or if you find calls on your bill that you did not make, contact your Telephone Company business office.

Displaying your Phone Number

It's good business to let your customers know how to get in touch with you. List your telephone number, including the area code, on all letterheads, business cards, invoices, promotional literature, and wherever you put your name in print.

Information Please

More and more telephone companies are charging for information service. The charge is usually 10¢ for each number requested from the information operator. It pays to look up the numbers yourself. Where such information charges are in effect, the telephone company normally makes directories for areas other than your own available upon request. In New York State, for example, where these charges were introduced in 1975, a telephone user is entitled to request each of more than 100 directories published in the state. Information for out-of-state numbers is not charged, though calling the operator to determine the area code for another area is considered an information call. Area codes for the entire country are printed in the front section of all telephone directories.

Courtesy

Some of the nicest people can become monsters on the telephone. The telephone is your most frequent contact with the outside world, including your customers. A cheerful hello works a lot better than a dour yeah, especially if someone is calling with a complaint. It is discourteous to engage in other activity while you're speaking to someone on the phone. If you must turn away to take care of something else, excuse yourself for a minute; that's what you'd do if the caller were sitting across the table from you. And never, never slam the phone down on the hook, even if you're angry. You could break the telephone.

Terms of Sale

(*See: Sales Conditions*)

Textile Fiber Products Identification Act

The Textile Fiber Products Identification Act, a federal law enacted in 1960, is designed to protect consumers by requiring proper labeling of all textile products other than wool (which is covered by the Wool Products Labeling Act).

Enforcement of the act's provisions is a very haphazard affair, but as far as the letter of the law is concerned, craftspeople who work with fibers and textiles are supposed to observe the act's requirements. The major requirements are as follows:

1) Every item made of any textile or fiber (garments, rugs, stuffed toys, quilts, etc.) must carry a tag or label showing the percentage of each type of fiber used in the item.

2) The name of the maker or distributor of the item must appear on the tag, which must remain with it until it has been sold to the ultimate consumer.

3) Imported products must show the country of origin on their tags. This includes the origin of imported yarns which are used in the creating of a piece made in the United States.

The act requires that all natural or man-made fibers must be labeled with their generic names. A generic name is the one given to a family of fibers all having similar chemical composition, for example acrylic, acetate, rayon.

The law also allows the manufacturer to use a trademark or trade name along with the generic name. For example, a tag marked "Orlon acrylic" identifies Orlon as the trade name and acrylic as the generic name. Other well-known combinations are Dacron polyester and Arnel acetate. Once the two appear together, they must always be used together. That way a consumer can begin to learn what to expect from a specifically labeled textile or fiber product.

If more than one fiber is used, the tag or label must show the percentage of each fiber, for example: 80 percent Dacron polyester, 20 percent wool.

(*See also: Wool Products Labeling Act*)

Theft Insurance

(*See: Property Insurance*)

Tools

Do machine processes and power tools change a handcraft design? Should a craftsman use only hand tools?

These questions are debated whenever craftspeople get together. They were effectively discussed by Miriam Davidson Plotnicov, Exhibition Coordinator of the Renwick Gallery at the Smithsonian Institution in Washington, in an essay on "Production Craftsmen Today" which introduced the catalogue of the Crafts Multiples exhibition at the Renwick in 1975.

Ms. Plotnicov quoted woodworker Emil Milan, who said: "Since I believe that each piece I do should be the best that could be done, it doesn't matter what tools I use, whether it's hand tools or power tools. The method shouldn't show."

"Ultimately it comes down to that," Ms. Plotnicov wrote. "The method should not show, and when it does, the craftsman has failed."

The essay continues: "Tools have been with us from the beginning—some for so long that we no longer consider them tools, but think of them as simple implements of handcraft. But a needle is a tool, and if you look back far enough there was a time when even needles made from bone or a thorn did not exist. A spindle is a tool and a shuttle is a tool and a handloom is a tool also. The hammer is a tool and so is an awl or a froe. But what about a sewing machine, or an electric saw, router, sander, or planer?

"The potter's wheel is part of mankind's earliest technical history. Does the addition of an electric motor change its function? Environments for controlled heat such as forges and kilns are equally ancient. Why should it matter if an electric blower is attached or if the primary source of heat is gas or electricity? Is the lost-wax casting technique fundamentally changed because a mold is filled with hot metal in a motor-driven centrifuge?

"The future must be taken into account as well, when materials, tools, and processes that now can only be imagined will be commonplace to craftsmen; but being craftsmen they will make their objects with the same care and skill that are used by craftsmen today.

"It is quibbling to define a craftsman by the tools he uses to produce his work, though the inclination remains to insist that power tools be hand guided. Craftsmen will always adopt new machines as they develop to make work lighter, and will devise new techniques to make new design concepts possible or improve older fabrication methods.

"The unchanging factor is the skill and care that each craftsman brings to his methods and materials. The method should not show. The care and skill invested in any craft object always do show."

(*See also: Equipment*)

Trade Credit

One of the sources of short-term financing of your business is the use of trade credit. This is the money you owe your suppliers until you pay your bill.

Once your credit reliability has been established, you can purchase equipment and supplies without paying cash at the time of purchase. At the end of the month you will get a bill which you usually must pay within thirty days. It is possible, therefore, to borrow that money for as long as sixty days without paying any interest. For example: you make a purchase for $500 on the second of the month. You are billed twenty-eight days later. Payment is due thirty days after that.

That may not be a major factor in your financing if you buy only a few dollars worth of supplies each month. But suppose your monthly purchases total $2,000, and you always have a $2,000 balance billed at the end of the month; you have in effect borrowed $2,000 all year long. At a normal interest rate of 8 to 10 percent, you save around $200 a year in interest charges. And if you pay your bills within ten days after receipt, you often save another 2 percent which many suppliers give as a discount for prompt payment.

What you are doing, in effect, is having your supplier finance part of your operation. The supply dealer benefits from this arrangement because credit terms are extended only to steady, reliable customers. Credit is one of the services he offers to keep you as a good customer.

(*See also: Capital, Credit, Credit Cards, Loans, Revolving Credit*)

Trademarks

A trademark is described in the Trademark Act of 1946 as "any word, name, symbol, or device, or any combination thereof adopted and used by a manufacturer or merchant to identify his goods and distinguish them from those manufactured or sold by others."

A trademark serves not only to indicate who made the product, but often suggests a certain level of quality based on the manufacturer's past performance. Typical trademarks known far and wide are the oval Ford symbol, the distinctive lettering of Coca-Cola, the Telephone Company's bell, and many others.

When a crafts professional uses a unique symbol to mark his work, it is a trademark. While trademarks need not be registered, registration helps to protect the owner's exclusive right to use the trademark.

The difference between trademarks and trade names is that a trademark identifies a product, while a trade name identifies the producer of the product. When a trade name is designed in a unique fashion and is used on the product, it can become a trademark and be registered as such.

Trademarks must appear on the merchandise or its container, and must be used regularly in interstate commerce to remain valid. Certain material may not be used in trademarks, such as the United States flag, the likeness of a living person without his or her permission, and several others.

Trademarks are registered with the U.S. Patent Office, Washington, DC 20231, by furnishing a written application, a drawing of the mark, five specimens or facsimiles of the mark as it is actually used, and a fee of $35. The registration is valid for twenty years and can be renewed for further twenty-year terms. When a trademark is not used regularly on a product or its container, the registration lapses, even if the twenty-year term isn't up.

After a mark has been registered, that information should accompany the trademark wherever it is used. Various means are available to do this, the most common being a capital R enclosed in a circle and placed right next to the mark.

Variations of a trademark are service marks, to identify a service rather than a product; certification marks, which are not related to a specific product or manufacturer, but might indicate regional origin, method of manufacture, or union label; and collective marks, used by members of an association, cooperative, or other organization. All these can be registered in the same fashion as a trademark.

The Patent Office does not give legal advice regarding trademarks, nor can it respond to inquiries whether certain trademarks have been registered. The Patent Office does maintain a file of registered marks which are arranged alphabetically where words are included, or otherwise by symbols according to the classification of the goods or services in which they are used. These files are open to the public in the Search Room of Trademark Operations in Washington, DC, and it is advisable to have the files searched to determine whether the same or a similar trademark has already been registered.

A detailed booklet, "General Information Concerning Trademarks," is available for 50¢ from the Superintendent of Documents, U.S. Government Printing Office, Washington, DC 20402.

(*See also: Copyright, Patent, Trade Name*)

Trade Name

Many businesses use a name for public identification which differs from the name of the owner. You may be Sam Jones, but the sign on your door reads Pot Luck Pottery. That's a trade name.

Since trade names can't be held legally responsible for anything, it is almost universally required that a trade name be filed with some governmental authority, often the county clerk.

The initials *d/b/a* (doing business as) appears on such documents as legal papers and credit reports to tie the trade name to the owner, as in: "Sam Jones *d/b/a* Pot Luck Pottery."

To protect a trade name from unauthorized use by others, it can be registered with the federal government as a trademark if certain conditions are met. This is usually a complicated and costly affair, and is rarely of value to craftspeople.

(See also: Trademark)

Transportation

(See: Freight Allowance, Post Office, Shipping, United Parcel Service)

Travel

(See: Business Trips)

Traveler's Checks

Craftspeople who spend quite a bit of time selling at craft shows and fairs, especially in tourist areas, have encountered traveler's checks. Such checks are sold in units of $10, $20, $50, and $100 by most banks and some other financial firms such as American Express.

Traveler's checks are extremely popular because they are very safe to carry, and are recognized almost everywhere in the world. The safety factor exists because purchasers sign their checks once in the upper left hand corner when they buy them, and then again in the lower left corner when they use them.

Two precautions: 1) Do not accept a traveler's check unless the person who offers it signs it in your presence. Compare the signatures and accept the check only if they match; and 2) a traveler's check with *both* signatures but no endorsement is as good as cash if it is lost or stolen. Don't let the hustle and bustle of a busy booth distract you. Immediately upon receiving a traveler's check as payment, endorse it with your name, the words "for deposit only," and your checking account number. Then handle it like any other check on your bank deposit slip.

266

Turnover

In all forms of merchandising and selling, turnover is one of the most critical elements of success or failure. It means, essentially, how often your investment turns into cash and is reinvested, or turned over.

Let's start with a simple example: suppose you invest $1,000 to produce a certain number of craft objects on which you make a 10 percent profit. Every time you sell that $1,000 worth of craftwork your profit is $100.

If it takes all year to sell that $1,000 worth of work, your investment will have returned $100. But suppose you can sell that $1,000 worth of work in one month, take your $100 profit, and invest the original $1,000 to make more craft objects, again producing $100 in profits. Do this every month and you'll have an annual profit of $1,200 over and above the original you invested. You have turned over your initial investment twelve times a year.

Ask any successful retailer and he'll tell you that he watches his turnover rate as closely as he watches his cash register. The smaller the per-unit profit, the larger the turnover has to be. Thus a big supermarket can make it on a profit margin of 1 to 2 percent because the goods on the shelves move in and out fast. Turning over $1,000 worth of inventory once a day at 1-percent profit ($10 a day or close to $300 a month) is three times as profitable as turning it over once a month at 10 percent ($100).

But the total turnover is not the only important consideration. Examine all the items in your line to see whether some turn over faster than others. If you find an item that stays in your inventory month after month, it may be putting a drain on your earnings by tying up the money you spent to make it. Perhaps it doesn't belong there at all, and it's time to get rid of it so that you can invest the money in making something more profitable.

There are exceptions, of course. The profit margin on a slow-moving piece may be so high that it is worth your while to continue making it even though it doesn't turn over fast. Another factor may be the prestige piece which helps to sell your other work. A large $500 batik wall hanging may not turn over rapidly, but displaying it at a craft show may help draw attention to the $40 and $50 batiks which sell fast. That makes the expensive piece an integral part of your total merchandising operation, and its absence might slow down sales of all your other work, and thus retard your total turnover.

There's a simple formula for determining the turnover rate. Divide sales by investment:

$$\frac{\text{Sales}}{\text{Investment}}$$

Thus, if your investment was $1,000 and your sales were $5,000, the formula would read:

$$\frac{\$5,000}{\$1,000} = 5$$

The turnover rate in this example, then, is five times.

If you apply this formula to the various craft objects you produce, you may find to your surprise that the most profitable turnover is not necessarily in the items which sell best.

Let's assume you are a potter who makes mugs and vases. In a given period you sell $1,000 worth of mugs and $900 worth of vases. The mugs cost you $500 to produce, and the vases $300. Now apply the formula and see where your better turnover is:

$$\text{Mugs:} \frac{\$1,000}{\$500} = 2 \text{ times}$$

$$\text{Vases:} \frac{\$900}{\$300} = 3 \text{ times}$$

Even though your total sales of vases brought in less than the total sales of mugs, your investment in making the vases was more profitable.

This doesn't mean you stop making mugs, but it reveals that finding new outlets for vases will bring a better return than finding new outlets for mugs.

Watch your turnover carefully, item by item. It is an important ingredient of your production and merchandising decisions. The real key is not simply how much you sell, but how much those sales bring back to you in earnings on the money you invest. And that depends on how quickly and how often you turn over your investment and your inventory.

(*See also: Inventory, Multiple Production, Production, Record Keeping, Systems*)

Unemployment Insurance

Unemployment insurance is a federal and state program to provide cash benefits to unemployed people who are seeking work but cannot find a job. Eligibility requirements and the size of weekly checks vary from state to state. Payments are made by employers in the form of a payroll tax. The weekly check received by the unemployed is based on the amount of money the individual earned during the qualification period.

Unemployment insurance is not relief or a handout. It is exactly what the name implies: insurance which provides benefits as a matter of right without regard to need, as long as the unemployed applicant meets the conditions of the law. A major benefit to society at large during recession periods is to stimulate consumption, production, and employment by introducing dollars and purchasing power into the economy.

The federal share of the unemployment insurance payroll tax is 3.2 percent. In New York, for example, the state tax averages around 2.7 percent, for a total of 5 percent. This share differs for different employers based on their experience rating, which means how much unemployment insurance was paid to their former employees and how much money remains in the particular employer's fund balance.

The specific rules and regulations which apply in the different states are available through each state's Department of Labor, in the state capital.

(*See also: Employees, Insurance, Workmen's Compensation*)

Unions

Labor unions are organizations of employees who work for wages. They gain their strength from two principles: 1) an individual employee is not able to negotiate wages, fringe benefits, hours, and working conditions as effectively alone as all the workers together, since the loss of one dissatisfied worker will not seriously hinder production; and 2) the ability to bargain collectively and, if necessary, withhold their labor (strike) to exert pressure on the employer to meet the workers' demands.

Few craftspeople are ever faced with a union situation in their shops or studios, since they usually work alone or with only a few employees. However, if a craft operation begins in a field where a union already exists (such as jewelry or woodworking), the likelihood increases that an effort will be made to organize the workers and negotiate a contract with the employer. This is especially true where the employees are not themselves skilled craft artists.

The success of such an organizing effort depends in large measure on the employees' satisfaction with their wages and working conditions, and their relationship with the employer. When a union can offer workers something they do not or cannot get from their employer, its chances of success are much greater. That's not always related to wages. Even if the pay scale is good, a union may be able to convince employees that benefits such as medical plans, pension programs, sick leave, job security, and holiday and vacation schedules can be obtained through negotiations and a union contract.

While a union contract does, of course, impose numerous conditions on the employer, it can also serve to stabilize labor-management relations, reduce the possibility of friction between individual employees and the employer, and provide the employer with a more predictable annual labor cost.

Many employers go into a state of shock when they first glimpse the union organizer outside their door. A more reasonable reaction might be to call your lawyer, find out what you may or may not do under the law (beware of illegal unfair labor practices), and approach the situation rationally. Be prepared for the fact that unions have become part of our way of life, and you may have to learn to live with them. Better to do that in peace and harmony than in rage and anger.

(*See also: Employees, Minimum Wage*)

United Parcel Service

No, Virginia, the post office is not the only way to ship parcels from one place to another. Private firms such as United Parcel Service have provided an alternative for many years (UPS since 1907), and with the steady deterioration of postal service accompanied by hefty increases in postal rates, these alternatives have become real competition. United Parcel Service makes delivery by truck to any place in the continental United States, and ships by air to major cities and Hawaii.

UPS provides a number of advantages over postal service:

1) Every parcel is automatically insured up to $100 (additional insurance at 25¢ per $100).

2) UPS's delivery charges are often less expensive than the post office's.

3) Delivery time is often faster than the post office's. It takes one day to deliver parcels locally via UPS. To send a package all the way across the country by truck takes five days, two days by air.

4) UPS claims a 98 percent perfect delivery record, with only 2 percent of its parcels damaged or lost.

5) UPS will accept parcels larger than those accepted by the post office. UPS parcels can measure up to 108 inches in length and girth combined. The post office maximum is 84 inches. (Girth is like waist: measured all around at the middle.)

6) UPS picks up as well as delivers. You don't have to drag the packages to the post office and wait on line there. Furthermore, UPS will make delivery attempts three days in a row if no one is available to receive the parcel on the first try. The post office leaves a slip in the mailbox on the first day to notify you of their attempt to deliver. Then you have to pick up the package yourself or call the post office to have it redelivered.

Rates

UPS shipping rates are, like the post office, based on weight, distance, and manner of shipment (ground or air). On that basis alone, UPS is usually less expensive than the post office. However, there is a minimum weekly pickup charge which varies in different parts of the country, ranging from $2 to $4. The weekly charge applies whether you make only one shipment or a thousand.

For only an occasional shipment, then, the post office is less expensive. However, if you ship 100 packages a week, and the minimum in your area is $4, then the cost of each shipment is increased by only 4¢, which still keeps it way below the post office rates.

For example, a ten-pound package from New York to Washington costs $1.35 via UPS, plus the $4 weekly pickup charge which applies in New York. That's a total of $5.35, compared to $1.61 for the same package via the post office. However, if you ship 100 such packages over that distance, the UPS charge is $1.35 x 100, or $135, plus the $4 weekly pickup charge, for a total of $139—as compared to $161 for the same 100 packages shipped via the post office. Plus, you don't have the bother or expense of bringing them to the post office, and minimum insurance is included.

Shipping by air brings economies even sooner. Again, if you ship only one or two packages per week, the post office is the better buy. A ten pound package from Los Angeles to Philadelphia via UPS costs $5.20 plus $4, a total of $9.20. The post office will handle that for $6.80. But when you ship three packages, the total UPS cost is $19.60 ($5.20 x 3 plus $4), compared to $20.40 at the post office. And if you had a hundred such packages to ship in a week, the difference between UPS ($524) and post office ($680) would be $156.

Regular Accounts

Businesses which ship many parcels on a regular basis can establish an account with UPS. Account holders are supplied with a record book stamped with an individual account number, cost charts, and special shipping labels. You fill out a daily slip that lists and describes all the parcels being sent out that day. The UPS truck comes by regularly every day to pick up all the packages, and the UPS driver signs for them.

Tracing

Since every package is signed for, from pick-up to delivery, it is simple enough to trace a parcel which may have gone undelivered. In such cases, UPS furnishes a Xerox copy of a signed receipt within three days, or handles the claim if a package was lost. Rates for the regular account service vary in different parts of the country, and billing is done once a week. The same weekly minimum pick-up charge applies to regular accounts as well, but amounts to almost nothing when the $2 or $4 charge is distributed over hundreds of packages.

Insurance

A package sent by ground may be insured up to $5,000, by air up to $1,000. Since UPS insurance is limited (the post office will insure for any amount), it is not advisable to send irreplaceable or unusually valuable objects, such as one-of-a-kind craftwork, via UPS.

Restrictions

UPS does not deliver to Canada or overseas. It makes no Saturday or Sunday pick-ups, although it makes Saturday deliveries in many areas. UPS does not handle packages weighing more than fifty pounds, and does not handle more than 100 pounds per day to any one addressee.

For craftspeople who ship a good many parcels, particularly for those who do a sizable mail-order business, United Parcel Service often provides a less costly and less bothersome alternative to the post office. For single pieces, or those that require considerable insurance coverage, the post office is the better way.

(See also: Post Office, Shipping, Transportation)

U.S. Department of Agriculture

(See: Government Activities)

U.S. Department of Commerce

(See: Government Activities)

U.S. Department of Health, Education and Welfare

(See: Government Activities)

U.S. Department of Labor

(See: Government Activities)

Utilities

(See: Overhead, Pricing)

Vendor

A vendor is, simply, one who sells. This term is commonly used by lawyers, which is why you often find it in sales contracts and on order forms. It is also used by purchasing agents as a generic reference to any source of supply.

When you sell your craftwork to a department store, you are the vendor. When you buy raw materials from your supply dealer, he is the vendor.

Wages

In the handsome catalogue of the Smithsonian's 1975–76 Craft Multiples exhibit, craftsman Joseph Mannino is quoted why he is a craftsman: "Freedom is why. . . . Freedom to play many roles: artist, chemist, laborer, salesman."

The very freedom Mr. Mannino describes can also cause some severe economic headaches if not carefully handled. Since most craftspeople work by themselves, they often confuse wages and profits. Since they get both, it doesn't seem important to make a distinction.

But it is important. All wages, including the craft producer's own, are part of the production costs which determine the price you will ultimately charge for your craftwork, and are as important as materials, equipment, overhead, shipping, and other costs. Profits are added afterwards, and represent your training, your investment, your management skills, even your creative talents. But the actual work you or others do must be calculated as wages. Since this is often the single largest ingredient in the cost of production, it must be handled with tender care.

The productive time you put into your craftwork covers the time you spend at the loom or the wheel or the workbench. But don't overlook the service time you spend repairing equipment, packing orders, taking them to the post office, doing the bookkeeping, designing a brochure, selling at shows, running to stores to make sales calls, and uncountable other functions.

How, then, can a crafts producer figure his or her own wages? It is impractical, in most cases, to keep a time sheet to record your time as a chemist at $15 an hour, a laborer at $4 an hour, a bookkeeper at $5 an hour, and so on. It is important, however, to keep a diary of labor time invested by yourself, family, friends, and employees in the production of various types of items. This helps not only to price objects properly, but to determine whether the various objects bring the proper return, and to project future pricing possibilities for similar objects.

The crafts producer, wearing many hats, must determine his or her hourly or weekly salary according to a few reasonable assumptions:

1) What would it (or does it) cost to hire someone to replace me in one or more of my functions?

2) What could I earn if I worked for someone else?

3) What do I need in terms of money, and will it fit into the price structure of the craftwork I produce?

There are a good many craftspeople who might find, on close examination, that they work for a dollar or two an hour. There's nothing wrong with that if you decide that's what you want to do, or if you have some other source of income, such as teaching. But if you work at that salary level simply because you've never figured out what you're actually earning, it may be wise to analyze the situation a bit more carefully.

If one item takes an hour to produce, and another item, selling for the same price, takes two hours, then you are obviously cutting your hourly pay in half every time you work on the second item.

You have three alternatives for solving that problem:

1) If you can find a more efficient production method, you may be able to produce more of the second item every hour than you did before, and thus give yourself a raise.

2) Perhaps you can increase the price of the second item to properly reflect the time you spend producing it.

3) You can cut back on producing Item #2 and concentrate on the more profitable items.

Your efficiency and experience are key elements in this situation. An obvious example: a potter can undoubtedly produce more finished pots per hour if he or she throws two dozen at a time, then glazes them all, then fires them all, instead of making one pot, glazing it, firing it, and starting all over again with another pot.

The specific procedure you develop depends on a variety of circumstances: the nature of the work, how much room you have to work in, how many people you have working with you, the capacity of the equipment, etc. There can be no readymade blueprint for this sort of thing. Everyone has different problems, different purposes, different work styles. In general, it helps if you can organize the various stages of producing multiples of an object by repeating each step ten or twenty times before going on to the next step.

But how do you figure out the time cost for each piece if you make a dozen or more at a time, especially if you work on a variety of items during the same period?

You'll simply have to keep a careful record of time spent on each type of item, and then divide the time into the total number of items produced. It doesn't matter whether the various steps occur consecutively or are carried out on different days. As long as you make a note on a time sheet or job ticket of all the time you spend on each group of items, it's a matter of simple addition.

Once you have the time elements down on paper, there are various ways to calculate the wages per piece that must be included in the final price. The simplest method works somewhat as follows:

Let us assume that you want to earn $5 per hour and work forty hours per week. That's a total of $200. You are working on a particular group of craft objects and find that you need a total of four hours to produce twenty pieces. That averages five pieces per hour. The value of your productive time is thus $1 on each piece.

But look how dramatically your production procedure can affect your wages. If instead of four hours you need five hours to make those same twenty pieces, your production is down to four pieces per hour. The difference may not seem world-shaking, but your production time per piece now costs $1.25 ($5 divided by four). That will mean an increase in the price of the finished object.

Suppose you don't bother to figure out such things and continue to include only $1 as labor cost. You have now cut your own pay to $4 an hour, and all for three little minutes of production efficiency on each piece.

This becomes even more critical if you are paying wages to someone else. If you pay an employee $5 per hour but get only $4 worth of production, you'll go broke in record time.

The other side of the coin is equally surprising. Suppose you find a way to average six pieces per hour instead of the five in the original example. Your cost of labor now goes down to about 83¢ per piece ($5 divided by six).

This gives you two options. You can either reduce the price, or you can stay at $1 and quick as a wink give yourself a raise from $5 to $6 per hour.

There is one other important wage factor to consider. The time you spend in bookkeeping, shipping, cleaning up, and so forth can be called service time. It is not productive in the sense that nothing is created in that time and it can therefore not be applied to any particular item or group of items. But you're entitled to be paid for it nonetheless. If you spend eight hours a week on service time and promptly forget about it, you've lost $40 at the rate of $5 an hour.

The amount of service time may vary from day to day and week to week. The most practical way to include this time in your total costs is to keep a careful record for several typical weeks. When you have arrived at an average you consider reliable, the dollar amount of this service time should be included in your overhead costs. That way it won't be forgotten when you calculate the total cost of producing a craft object.

None of this is intended to offer an iron-clad formula. There are many methods of cost accounting to help you calculate such things. But the key factor is to apply every expense item to a specific craft product so that the price accurately reflects the cost.

Raw materials and actual production time are fairly easy to apportion. Service time and other overhead have to be averaged. How to apply these averages is discussed under "Overhead."

Examine and reexamine your production methods and cost factors on a regular basis. It is the only way you can determine whether you are paying yourself a decent wage, or whether you get your money's worth for the wages you pay others.

(*See also: Cost Accounting, Employees, Income Tax, Job Ticket, Overhead, Pricing, Production, Social Security, Withholding Tax*)

Warranty

Buyers have a right to expect that the products they buy will perform more or less as expected under normal conditions. The legal basis for that right is known as a warranty. A warranty always involves a provable fact.

As both a buyer and a seller, a craftsperson needs to know precisely what rights and responsibilities that word imposes.

Warranties need not be in writing. They can be made orally. The written warranty is, of course, preferable because it is easier to document if trouble develops.

There are two kinds of warranties: express and implied. An express warranty is one which states a specific fact. If you sell a set of glasses and tell the customer they can be washed in the dishwasher without danger of breakage, you have given an express warranty, whether you put it in writing or not. If the glasses break in the dishwasher, you are liable not only to return the customer's money, but if the broken glass jams the dishwasher you may have to pay other damages as well.

An implied warranty means that the product is made with all proper care and that it will perform as similar products of its kind will perform under normal conditions. A customer need not, for example, inspect each glass to make sure that there are no unfinished edges; he or she can rely on the implied warranty.

As a buyer, you rely on both express and implied warranties every day. When you buy a drill you expect that it will work when you take it out of the box and plug it in. That's an implied warranty. If the manufacturer states that the drill will turn at 1800 rpm, that's an express warranty. When you buy a can of tomatoes you expect that they will not be contaminated. That's an implied warranty. If the label reads ten ounces, that's an express warranty.

Remember: the important ingredient of a warranty is the provable fact aspect. The glass either breaks or it doesn't; the drill turns or stands still; there are either ten ounces of tomatoes in the can or there are not.

Sales talk is quite another thing. If you tell your customer that yours are the most beautiful glasses ever made, or if the hardware salesman tells you the drill will make your life a lot easier, no warranties have either been implied or expressed. Those puff statements are not provable facts.

Warranties are also involved when you show a sample to a store buyer. If the store places an order, it expects that the items it eventually receives will be of the same quality and will perform the same way as the sample. That's your warranty: express or implied, written or oral. If you tell a store they'll sell a million of those, that's no warranty. That's just sales talk, and if they sell only half a million they have no legal recourse.

If you sell craft products you know to be defective in some way, be sure to mark them "seconds" or "as is." While this does not absolve you of all obligation, it does place on the customer some responsibility to either ask what the defect is, or inspect the product carefully.

(*See also: Guarantee*)

Wholesale Days

(*See: Shows and Fairs, Wholesaling*)

Wholesaling

There are three ways in which a crafts professional can sell his or her craftwork:

1) Sell directly to the ultimate customer (retailing);
2) Sell to a store or some other outlet which in turn sells your work to the ultimate customer (wholesaling);
3) Furnish your work to a store or gallery with the understanding that you are paid only if and when the work is sold to a customer (consignment).

The difference between the three involves both work and money. Let us assume that you have a craft object which is sold to the ultimate customer for $10.

If you retail it directly, you get the whole $10, but you also have the work and expense of retailing, such as operating a store or taking a booth at a craft show.

If you wholesale to a store which then resells the work, you generally get 50 percent of the retail price, $5 in this example. However, you have none of the work and problems of retailing, you can spend your time in producing more craftwork, and you can presumably sell a larger number of pieces.

In consignment selling, you generally receive between 60 and 70 percent of the retail price, approximately $6.50 in this example. However, you are investing your time and money in the store's inventory, and there are other dangers and problems associated with consignment selling.

Retailing and consignment are discussed in greater detail elsewhere in this book. Here we will concern ourselves only with the wholesaling operation, in which a store purchases your work outright and pays you for it, whether or not it then resells the work to its customers.

Some craftspeople do not understand, and even resent, the notion that a store doubles the price of craftwork it buys from them. Statistics show, however, that most of that markup is not profit, but spent for rent in expensive high traffic locations, for payroll, advertising, delivery, and all the other costs associated with running a store. Most stores consider a

5-percent profit on the retail price an acceptable ratio. In other words, their profit on that $10 craft item might be around 50¢. In food stores the profit ratio is much smaller, generally between 1 and 2 percent. The small per-unit profit, of course, can turn into a handsome annual profit if the store succeeds in selling a large quantity of merchandise.

So much for why a store doubles the price of the goods it buys for resale. If you have priced your work properly at the wholesale level, the wholesale price should bring you a satisfactory profit. What you lose (or think you lose) in retail markup is more than compensated by the fact that you can sell larger quantities of your craftwork through wholesale distribution.

What type of retail outlet you approach depends in large measure on how much you can produce. If your production is limited, stick to the smaller stores, boutiques, gift shops, and the like. Department stores and chain stores are very demanding, both in terms of price and in terms of delivery.

To meet the price demands of department stores which are in a very competitive situation, it is perfectly legitimate to have a schedule of wholesale prices which varies according to the quantity ordered. Ten pieces or fewer of a particular craft object, for example, may be priced at $5.50 each, between ten and 100 the price can be $5, and for more than 100 you might charge only $4.50. If you organize your production schedules and packing operations properly, you can probably save the difference in the price you charge for different quantities, and come out with the same profit margin in the end.

Wholesale buyers normally use their store's order form to buy from you. Read all the conditions on the form carefully. Are you prepared, for example, to allow a 2-percent discount if the bill is paid within ten days? Can you meet the delivery date? Do you understand the billing procedure? Does the order form include the store's sales tax exemption number so that you don't have to collect the sales tax?

Big stores, like big anything-elses, are bureaucracies. If the paperwork isn't done right, everything comes to a dead stop. On the other hand, having a big store customer who keeps you profitably busy all year can be worth the extra effort to meet the bureaucratic requirements.

How do you approach wholesale buyers? In a small shop it's fairly simple: the owner does the buying. Telephone first to make an appointment. Don't just drop in, especially at a time when the owner is busy with a customer.

With department stores the problem is a bit more complicated. Different departments have different buyers, and most buyers have a specific day each week when they see suppliers. Depending on how the store's buying operation is organized and what craft you are selling, you may have to see the gift buyer, the jewelry buyer, the home furnishings buyer, or whoever is responsible for buying the particular type of item you have to offer. A phone call to the merchandise manager's office will generally tell you whom you have to see and when. If possible, try to make an appointment.

Buyers are busy people. Be prepared to state your case clearly and succinctly. Bring samples, a price list, and any other information. Be prepared to leave all this material and information with the buyer if requested.

Try to acquaint yourself with the particular store's general merchandising approach and clientele, so that you can discuss your craft objects from the store's point of view, namely how it will sell in that store. If the store has no jewelry department, for example, it is hardly worth the effort for a silversmith to try selling earrings to that store.

The other major area of investigation concerns the store's pricing. Does the store you want to approach already sell your type of craftwork? At what prices? Are their price lines, in crafts or otherwise, compatible with yours? A quick trip through the store will reveal whether your work fits into the store's merchandising and pricing pattern.

This type of approach is all well and good for stores in your area, but how do you find stores elsewhere, assuming that your production capabilities are such that you can supply stores in various parts of the country?

The crafts field is one of the few in which agents or manufacturer's representatives are not too common—and for good reason. Most craftspeople, even if their production is extensive, cannot keep a sales organization busy enough, nor can they afford to pay the extra commission to salesmen or agents. However, there are a number of sales representatives in various parts of the country who handle noncompetitive craft lines. They have the contacts with the store buyers, and craftspeople who can meet the volume demands often find the extra commission worth the extra volume.

Finally, in the enthusiasm of making a sale, don't overlook one important question: How do they pay? What is their credit rating? There's no point in making a sale if you don't get paid for it. Ask around. Talk to some other people who have sold to the same store. If it's a big sale out of town, your bank may be helpful in getting a credit report.

You've convinced the store buyer that your craftwork will sell, the price is right, everything is set. You should be aware that there are still four important questions rummaging around in the back of the buyer's mind:

1) Can you maintain the quality of the work according to the sample?
2) Can you maintain the price?
3) Can you meet production needs?
4) Can you meet delivery schedules?

The initial orders from wholesale buyers, especially department stores, may be small until they are satisfied that you can meet all four of those requirements. Once you prove that you can perform, wholesaling can be a very profitable experience.

(*See also: Consignment, Credit Reference, Memo, Orders, Retailing, Salesmanship, Sales Representatives*)

Withholding Tax

Whether you're a million-dollar tycoon or a part-time cashier at the supermarket, some portion of your wages or salary is withheld whenever you get paid to pay your income taxes. The employer, in effect, acts as the collection agent for the Internal Revenue Service, or for state and local governments which impose income taxes.

If you are an employer, there are several specific procedures to follow:

1) You must obtain an Employer Identification Number by filing form SS-4 with the Internal Revenue Service.

2) The IRS then provides you with a number of copies of Form 501, a punch card which has to accompany the remittance of the tax money you withheld from your employees (including yourself if you are incorporated and draw a salary).

3) The employer deposits the tax money in his bank with Form 501 according to the following schedule:

a) if the total Social Security taxes (both employer and employee contributions) and federal withholding taxes is less than $200 at the end of a quarter (three months), you remit quarterly.

b) if at the end of a month it is between $200 and $2,000, you must make the deposit within fifteen days after the end of the month; if it is over $2,000, you deposit within three banking days.

c) if the total is more than $2,000 on the 7th, 14th, 21st, and 30th of any month, you must make the deposit within three banking days after each of those dates.

The bank gives you a receipt for the deposit, and in turn deposits all the money and all the Forms 501 with the Internal Revenue Service.

Every three months every employer is required to file Form 941 directly with the Internal Revenue Service. This form is a summary of all the withholding tax payments that were made on behalf of his or her employees during that quarter.

4) Between January 1 and January 31 of each year, every employer is required to furnish a W-2 form to all employees. This is a summary of all the wages paid during the previous year, and all income taxes and Social Security taxes withheld during the previous year. The W-2 form is needed by the employees to file with their income tax returns. The form

must be furnished to all employees who were on the payroll at any time during the previous year, even if they worked for only a day and even if they are no longer employed by you.

One important observation: when cash supply is short, some employers are tempted to use the tax money they withheld for other purposes, hoping to have the money available when it has to be deposited at the end of the week or month or quarter. That's a temptation which should be resisted. Failure to deposit the withholding taxes is a very serious federal crime.

(See also: Estimated Taxes, Income Taxes)

Wool Products Labeling Act

The Wool Products Labeling Act (WPLA) was passed by Congress in 1939 to protect everyone involved in some way with things made of wool: manufacturers, distributors, and consumers. Every product made in whole or in part of wool must conform to this law, except for upholstery and floor coverings (which are covered by the Textile Fiber Products Identification Act).

Although enforcement of the WPLA is concentrated among large manufacturers of wool products, the act's provisions apply to craftspeople as well. While it is hard to imagine a government agent going after a one-of-a-kind wall hanging at a craft fair, technically everyone creating items for sale that are made of wool or other fibers is expected to know the composition of the item and label it properly.

The act established three specific categories of wool which have to be identified according to the percentage (by weight) used in a particular product:

1) "Wool," "new wool," or "virgin wool" which has never been used. Certain special names for fibers that fall into this category are mohair, cashmere, camel hair, and alpaca.

2) "Reprocessed wool," which is wool fiber taken from wool already woven or felted, but never used or worn.

3) "Reused wool" is precisely that: wool that was knitted or woven to make items that were once worn or used and is later used again to make other things.

The Wool Products Labeling Act makes no requirements about the quality or amount of wool used in each category, only that it be properly identified.

The act requires that an identifying label accompany the wool item through each step of manufacture, from yarn to finished product. The label must state, in order of amount, the types of wool used in the item, along with the percentage (by weight) of each fiber used.

If nonwoolen fibers are used in a product made of wool, they must also be identified. However, all nonwoolen fibers which do not exceed 5 percent of the total may be lumped together as "other fibers." Thus a product made of 55 percent virgin wool, 33 percent reprocessed wool, and 4 percent each of rayon, linen, and cotton may be labeled:

> 55% virgin wool
> 33% reprocessed wool
> 12% other fibers

The same principle applies to ornamentation, such as buttons and handles. If the extra design features make up less than 5 percent of the total fiber weight of the item, the label must read "exclusive of ornamentation." If it is greater than 5 percent, it must be identified as part of the total fiber content.

Two other points to consider:

1) Get a complete fiber content breakdown before you buy wool supplies. The information should be printed on tags or labels attached to the yarn or bolts of fabric. If you can't find it, ask your supplier. You are ultimately responsible for the correct labeling of any wool item you make and sell.

2) It is helpful to your customers to include specific instructions on cleaning, where applicable. If you attach a label anyway, you might as well add "dry clean only" or "wash gently in lukewarm water" or some similar information.

(See also: Textile Fiber Products Identification Act)

Work Area

Since craftspeople spend so much time in their workshops or studios, the manner in which these work areas are designed can contribute greatly to the satisfaction of working in them, and to the efficiency in producing crafts for profit.

Here's a list of checkpoints that should be helpful:

1) If you work at home, make the work space serve your craft exclusively. First of all, it helps to justify the tax deduction which you can claim as a business expense. Secondly, it makes it so much easier to find things, to get down to work, and to protect the work you've produced. A rumpus room where children play is rarely a safe place for your equipment or finished work, or one that allows you the concentration to create beautiful things. And if you constantly have to set up and take down your tools and equipment, you'll spend more time getting ready to work than working.

2) Be comfortable. There's no reason why artists should suffer. Working in solitude and being creative can be difficult enough, although it has its exquisite rewards when your hands have produced an object of beauty. Is the table so low so that you have to bend over unnecessarily? Or is it so high so that your arms get tired too soon? Is the light good enough to avoid eye strain? Are your surroundings too hot, too cold, or too noisy to provide the proper attention to your creative work?

3) The physical layout of your work area is important for both safety and production. Electrical outlets should be readily available wherever you use electric tools or equipment. Extension cords running all over the place are a prime source of fire danger. Equipment and workbenches should be located in some logical relationship to each other so that you don't have to drag your work from one end of the place to the other and back during the various stages of production. It makes sense, for example, to have the table where you pack orders located next to the area where you store the finished work.

4) Plenty of shelving, peg boards, and other storage devices help to keep raw materials, supplies, tools, and finished craftwork easily accessible and in good condition. Small supplies can be kept in jars or cans, properly labeled. Dangerous tools should be protected, and hazardous substances such as flammable liquids should be properly stored. This is important not only when there are small children around, but for your own safety as well.

(*See also: Production*)

Workmen's Compensation

The law has always held an employer liable for injuries or death suffered by his employees if the condition arose from the employer's negligence in not providing safe working conditions.

Workmen's Compensation laws in every state now hold an employer liable for injuries or death suffered by employees while on the job, regardless of whose fault it was, unless it was self-inflicted or caused by intoxication. The laws vary from state to state, and so does the extent of the employer's liability. But in most states an employer is required to carry Workmen's Compensation insurance to protect his responsibility.

Premiums are generally based on a percentage of the payroll as related to two factors: the hazard of the job, and the accident record of the employer. Premiums can be reduced, therefore, by increasing safety precautions and reducing accidents.

Craftspeople need not carry Workmen's Compensation insurance if they work all alone. But the moment you hire an employee, even a part-timer, the Workmen's Compensation Law of your state may apply. Before you put anyone on the payroll, talk to your insurance broker or write to the state Labor Department in your state capital to find out what's required of you under your state's Workmen's Compensation Law.

(*See also: Employees, Unemployment Insurance*)

Workshops

(*See: Education*)

World Crafts Council

The World Crafts Council is a nongovernmental organization founded in 1964 which represents craftspeople in eighty countries. It is associated in an official consultative capacity with several United Nations agencies, including UNESCO, UNICEF, and ECOSOC. Membership is obtained through the WCC national committee (The American Crafts Council in the United States) or the WCC representative in the various countries.

The WCC publishes a bulletin periodically, and has also published *In Praise of Hands, Crafts of the Modern World,* and *World Crafts Directory;* several surveys are in preparation. The WCC is governed through a General Assembly which has met bicentenially in Switzerland, the United States, Peru, Ireland, Canada, and Mexico. It is active in the development of marketing and technical assistance programs through an office for Craft Development and an Office for Information and Research. The world headquarters of the World Crafts Council is at 29 West 53rd Street, New York, NY 10019.

Writing

Writing a letter, a press release, an article, a sales brochure, or any other form of written communication makes most people freeze. Perhaps our constant exposure to nonwritten communication such as television, radio, movies, and telephone has made writing a dying art. But there is hardly anything more basic and important than being able to express oneself in clear, concise terms, especially if trying to sell something via the written word.

One need not be a writer to write well. A few simple rules of communication will make it easier:

1) Before you sit down to write, even if it's a letter, make some notes of the major points you want to include and in what order you want to present them.

2) Make your most important points at the start, to be sure the reader

gets the basic information even if he or she doesn't read beyond the first paragraph or two.

3) Study some letters that have impressed you to see how they are constructed. Note how a newspaper story is written. Try to analyze what makes them interesting or attention-getting.

4) Use simple language. Many of us who know how to speak clearly get all fouled up in complicated words and complex sentence structures when we sit down to write.

5) Use short sentences and short paragraphs. They're easier to read, to understand, and to write.

6) Make a draft, especially if it's an important message. Read it carefully. Show it to someone else to see whether you've expressed yourself clearly.

7) Don't be afraid to rewrite if you think your thoughts should be reorganized or stated in some other fashion. Most of the words you read every day did not come out of their authors' typewriters right the first time.

(P.S. This section was rewritten three times.)

(*See also: Press Release*)

Zoning

Most cities and towns impose regulations on the use to which various areas under its jurisdiction can be put. Thus, some sections or streets may be zoned for residential use only, others for retailing or light manufacturing or heavy industry. Zoning regulations sometimes specify the number or size of buildings in relation to land area. This is done to preserve the character of a community and to protect residential areas, for example, from the noise of heavy industry. A grandfather clause in most zoning regulations permits activities which existed prior to the establishment of the regulations to continue. That's why you might find a gas station or a drug store on a street otherwise zoned for residential use only.

Zoning regulations can sometimes have an important impact on the conduct of a crafts business. If you have a loom in the basement, for example, and you don't have heavy customer or truck traffic coming to your door, it is unlikely that you would be found in violation of residential zoning regulations in most areas. If you install a large kiln, or run a blacksmith's forge, or open a retail outlet, you can almost count on having the authorities on your back, especially if the neighbors complain.

Most zoning regulations have provisions for granting a variance, or an exception. This normally happens after hearings are conducted in which you present your case and your neighbors or such agencies as health, building, or fire departments have an opportunity to state their objections. The fire department, for example, may consider an open-hearth forge at the end of a narrow dead-end residential street of frame houses an additional hazard. The neighbors may simply object to the noise.

Before you make major alterations in your workshop or building, be sure they conform with the zoning regulations. Violations can be an awfully expensive mistake to correct.

(*See also: Lease*)